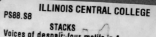

EDWARD STONE

 Ohio University Press

La vérité monte d'un coup d'aile
jusqu'au symbole.

ÉMILE ZOLA

Voices of Despair

■ **Four motifs in American literature**

Copyright © 1966 by Edward Stone
Library of Congress Catalog Card Number: 65–24646
Manufactured in the United States of America
by H. Wolff, New York
Designed by: Cynthia Muser

To Joseph Ingraham Stone

This book is an attempt to write a history of despair in the literature of the United States: of the conflict between optimism and pessimism, between the concepts of design and chaos.

Many valuable inquiries already have been made into one or more of these attitudes: transcendentalism, by Perry Miller; naturalism, by Lars Åhnebrink, Malcolm Cowley, Harry Hartwick, Alfred Kazin, V. L. Parrington, R. E. Spiller, and Charles C. Walcutt; and the "lost generation," by Malcolm Cowley and Frederick J. Hoffman. In addition, there is the work of James Baird, Charles Feidelson, Harry Levin, F. O. Mattheissen, and Edmund Wilson on the symbolic methods of many of the writers in question. My book uses the findings of all of these scholars as a foundation for a structure yet all my own. It is an historical account in four separate parts along thematic lines.

By their images ye shall know them, Professor Stanley E. Hyman notices about the successive ages of western culture in his The Tangled Bank:

The image of the great Chain of Life is ordered, hierarchic, and static, essentially medieval; the great Tree of Life is ordered, hierarchic, but dynamic and competitive, a Renaissance vision; but the great Tangled Bank of Life [of Darwin's Origin of Species] is disordered, democratic, and subtly interdependent as well as competitive, essentially a modern vision.

My book, considering as it does the imagery of a fairly large body of material (the entire range of American literature, more or less) finds it advisable to restrict itself to tracing the history of despair by the examination of single motifs. Each of the book's chapters studies a different motif of that history. Chapters One and Two are companion parts: they treat the entire range of American literature, the first chapter using a form of animal life as motif; the second, a color. Chapter Three concentrates on the post-Civil War generation; its motif is the story of the life and works of a representative American man of letters. Chapter Four, whose main emphasis is on the present century, has a phrase or its variation as its motif. The Appendix contains several collateral examples from English or continental literature or from painting that I could not justify working into my text (or even into its footnotes) but that I could not bring myself to discard.

My approach and scope lack the thoroughness of studies of the various writers as individual artists but make possible an understanding of the various periods under study. Moreover, I have hoped, after all, for the thoroughness of the book-

length studies that I have referred to above (and gratefully
made use of below). Readers more interested in individual
authors than in motifs will be able to circumvent my structures by consulting the index, which I have made as comprehensive as possible. This will be particularly useful in
forming a composite impression of certain authors (Hemingway, Melville, Poe, Twain, to cite the most important) who
are considered in more than one chapter.

A word about terms. By fatalism, determinism, and naturalism I mean concepts that premise in common the subordination of the individual will to other forces, but that differ
in ways that literary historians (such as Parrington, Hartwick,
Cargill, and Åhnebrink) have already defined: fatalism as the
subordination of the human will to the outside force of
chance; determinism as the subjection (whether optimistic or
not) of the human will to other forces, whether inner or
outer; and naturalism as a pessimistic form of determinism
which considers man with the lower types of animal life.

This book got its start in Professor Theodore Hornberger's
seminar at the University of Texas just before World War II.
It continued for a long time at a slow pace, then at an acceler-
ated one during the last few years. Small versions of three of
its chapters have appeared in periodicals (University of Texas
Studies in English, Emerson Society Quarterly) or books
(Essays on Determinism in American Literature), and some
of the primary materials cited or discussed in these three
chapters have been anthologized in What Was Naturalism?
Even so, the completion of the manuscript would not have
been possible if not for a leave of absence granted by the John
C. Baker Foundation, endowed by Mr. and Mrs. Edwin C.
Kennedy, who thus encourage scholarly pursuits at Ohio
University.

Edward Stone
Athens, Ohio

■

CONTENTS

VOICES OF DESPAIR

They considered the ant

The acres brought into cultivation, the cattle bred, the houses
built, proved no doubt that human beings, like ants . . . ,
could indefinitely multiply their numbers, and could lay up stores
of food; but these statistics offered no evidence that the human
being, any more than the ant . . . , was conscious of a
higher destiny, or was even mechanically developing into a more
efficient animal.

Henry Adams, *History of the United States*

■

Direct your gaze outward, Baudelaire tells us in one of the
classic passages of the last century, and it will find in the
world of nature over which it wanders whole forests of symbols which watch it in turn with a look of kinship. Emerson,
who had said it earlier, had taken his cue from Swedenborg;
long before them, of course, Plato saw everyday objects as

forms of universal essences. And after them, Tennyson, looking in his hand at the little flower plucked from the crannies of a wall, reflected that if he could understand its composition, he would know what God and man were.

The meaning could be inconstant, to be sure. Coleridge reminded Wordsworth in his Dejection poem that we bring back out of nature only what we ourselves took in, and Byron agreed.* "Nature always wears the colors of the spirit," Emerson admitted, and Montaigne noted that to the jaundiced, all things seem yellow. At the putrefaction of the flesh, Emerson marvelled ("The laws of disease, physicians say, are as beautiful as the laws of health"), while Baudelaire was as nauseated as Hamlet.

And in myth too earlier conceptualists than Baudelaire had perceived meaning: were not the demi-humans of legend deliberate configurations, rather than abstract grotesques? That half-man-half-horse tutor of antiquity, Chiron, we are reminded by Machiavelli, taught by his very construction the lesson of the duality of human beings; and Pico della Mirandola saw in Proteus an ever greater variegation and potentiality for his fellow inhabitants of the natural world.†

They might, these gazers, emerge from their contemplation with many different, even opposed, interpretations of what

* No more—no more—Oh! never more on me
   The freshness of the heart can fall like dew,
Which out of all the lovely things we see
   Extracts emotions beautiful and new;
Hived in our bosoms like the bag o' the bee.
   Think'st thou the honey with those objects grew?
Alas! 'twas not in them, but in thy power,
   To double even the sweetness of a flower. (Don Juan, Canto First)

† Five hundred years later: "It was in order to escape the necessity of prophesying that he changed his shape, from lion to serpent to panther to swine to running water to fire to leafy tree—a series of transformations that corresponds with the seasons of the sacred king in his passage from birth to death." Stanley Kunitz, "Roethke: Poet of Transformations," The New Republic, CLII, (January 23, 1965), 23.

they had seen; but meaning it had, all of it, they mused, like
Melville's Ishmael. Had they been aware of it, they would
all have rejected the thesis of their demonic contemporary
Kierkegaard that one could not come to any certain conclusions about God from nature itself, as well as Nietzsche's
scorn for regarding nature "as if she were a proof of the goodness and the fatherhood of a God." With or without his
trusting exuberance, they felt with Browning's Renaissance
painter that

> . . . . . *This world's no blot for us,*
> *Nor blank; it means intensely, and means good—*
> *To find its meaning is my meat and drink.*

To the believer in the ideality of the world about us, no correspondence was too insignificant for speculation. Had not
Solomon, for example, (in *Proverbs*) tried to rouse the Hebrew sluggard with the example of a mere ant:

> . . . . . *consider her ways, and be wise:*
> *Which having no guide, overseer, or ruler,*
> *Provideth her meat in the summer, and gathereth her food in*
> *   the harvest.*
> *How long wilt thou sleep, O sluggard?*

It happens that a number of later thinkers have proceeded
to just this consideration, but their conclusions have by no
means always agreed with Solomon's. Indeed, in the variety
of their reactions to the lowly ant we can trace the changing
attitude of the human mind and spirit to matter and nature
—the hopes and fears, the exhilaration and the dread with
which man has contemplated his place in creation and the
universe. In Poe's "The Masque of the Red Death," the fire
in the central corridor has a different effect on the castle's
seven chambers, depending on the color of the glass wall
that reflects it: the motivating object in each event remains

the same, for all that its effect varies from room to room. So with symbols, one object acquires differing meanings as its effect varies from century to century, from thinker to thinker.* Like Poe's medieval Italian fire, the insect ant is both itself and a symbol which has returned man's gaze with a look of kinship over the centuries and thereby written an important chapter in the history of western literary thought, even in the brief one of the United States.

■

In that vast bright morning that dawned on the America of the second quarter of the last century, before the shades of its prison house of industry, war, and science would close upon the growing land, the spirit was moving mightily in New England. "I count it a piece of good fortune, that I was a young man when these things were taking place, when great questions were discussed, and the public had not yet taken sides," Theodore Parker recalled toward the close of his, and its, not very long life. The Unitarians had conquered, could rightfully deny the Trinity, "the Achilles of dogmas"; the Universalists "had fought manfully against Eternal Damnation," and were preaching that "God's chief attribute is LOVE, which is extended to all men"; that great new star Emerson was leading "ingenuous young people . . . forward along new paths, and towards new hopes"; phrenology was unseating the old supernaturalism; Wordsworth was "drawing men to natural piety"; Coleridge was "helping to emancipate enthralled minds"; Victor Cousin, in review and translation, was doing much "to free the young mind from the gross sensationalism of the academic philosophy on one side, and

* In "The Transcendentalist" Emerson exulted that "Even the materialist Condillac, perhaps the most logical expounder of materialism, was constrained to say, 'Though we should soar into the heavens, though we should sink into the abyss, we never go out of ourselves; it is always our own thought that we perceive.' What more could an idealist say?"

the grosser supernaturalism of the ecclesiastic theology on the other"; and that "most formidable assailant of the ecclesiastical theology of Christendom, . . . young Mr. Strauss," was rigidly scrutinizing the genuineness of the Gospels with a scientific detachment and absence of reverence.* Looking back in the 1860's at "Emerson the Lecturer," James Russell Lowell said that "he brought us *life*. . . . Was it all transcendentalism? magic-lantern pictures on mist? As you will. Those, then, were just what we wanted." For all the wisdom and folly of the short-lived *Dial*, Parker recalled, "America has seen no such sight before; it is not less a blessed wonder now." [1] And when those times were fading away in the post-Civil War world, a witness of the next generation would —in a most unexpected place—insist about Brook Farm, one of the concretions of that spirit, that "there must have been in the enterprise a good deal of a certain credulity and faith in the perfectability of man, which it would have been easier to find in Boston in the year 1840, than in London five-and-thirty years later"; that the Farmers' ardor was "a moral ardour, and the lightest breath of scandal never rested upon them, or upon any phase of Transcendentalism." [2]

That noble credulity, "what are called *new views* here in New England," Emerson explained in 1842 ("The Transcendentalist"), were "not new, but the very oldest of thoughts. . . ." This is why transcendentalism, which had supplanted Unitarianism, which had supplanted Calvinism, displays the same tendency to glorify God which Scripture had advocated and the Puritans had taken as their mission in the new western wilderness; and why, accordingly, the transcendentalist found sermons in stones very much as the

* Parker did not forget, however, that entering into the lists against this multifarious new spirit, Henry Ware championed "the written Word"; other Unitarian preachers "protested against the union of philosophy and religion"; Norton upheld Scripture, denounced German philosophical thinkers, Cousin, and the critics of the Bible as atheists all, more or less.

Psalmist had done. When Emerson stated in *Nature* (1836), that new bible of the old thought, that "things are emblematic," and asked whether there was "no intent of an analogy between man's life and the seasons. And do the seasons gain no grandeur or pathos from that analogy?"—he could be sure that these questions would be received as rhetorical, that his readers—whatever their degree of orthodoxy—subscribed to his belief that analogies "are constant, and pervade nature." The mere seed of a plant could yield "affecting analogies." Had not Paul called the human corpse a seed? ("It is sown a natural body; it is raised a spiritual body.") In scriptural tradition, Emerson himself considered the ant:

The instincts of the ant are very unimportant considered as the ant's; but the moment a ray of relation is seen to extend from it to man, and the little drudge is seen to be a monitor, a little body with a mighty heart, then all its habits, even that said to be recently observed, that it never sleeps, become sublime.

Now the intellectually sophisticated Oliver Wendell Holmes could use the chambered nautilus as an example of growth and expansion and the orthodox Longfellow could find in the lowly seaweed an emblem of the poetic process from which he might profit; yet neither of these contemporaries of Emerson's was actually investing the object of his gaze with the transcendental significance with which, say, Wordsworth had invested the cataracts at Tintern Abbey. Essentially, although they all seemed to speak the same language and find a symbolical significance in nature as old as Solomon's in *Proverbs*, only Emerson is viewing his natural object in a truly ontological sense. This was because transcendentalism, the least confining of creeds, afforded the amplest of fields for viewing the wonders of God's creation.

To a great extent, it was to Germany that America owed
this first nineteenth-century invasion of thought, to the idealism of Immanuel Kant. James Freeman Clarke recalled that
something within him revolted against his father's favorite
thinker, against John Locke's "polemic . . . against innate
ideas," and his attempts "to explain soul out of sense"; and
that he turned eagerly to Coleridge, who showed him "from
Kant that though knowledge begins *with* experience it does
not come *from* experience." Alexander H. Everett confirms
this. The greatest influence of all on the transcendental philosophy was that of Kant, who "abandons the external world
to the skeptics, and founds the certainty of our knowledge
upon the supposed reality of the notions originally inherent
in our own understanding. . . ." [3]

To the transcendentalist, mind was "the only reality," and
"the procession of facts" which people call the world, he saw
as merely phenomenal, "as unsounded centre in himself,"
Emerson tells us in "The Transcendentalist." For the idealist-
transcendentalist, when speaking of events, "sees them as
spirits." When he looks at things, he sees each as "a sequel
or completion of a spiritual fact. . . ." * For him, "Nature's
dice are always loaded; . . . in her heaps and rubbish are
concealed sure and useful results." What is implicit or merely
aphoristic in *Proverbs* is stated dogmatically in *Nature*. "God
never jests with us," Emerson observes there, "and will not
compromise the end of nature by permitting any inconsequence in its procession." At the furthest remove from God,
down in the rubbish heap under our feet, the ant goes marvellously and unquestioningly about his business. Part of the

---

* Charles C. Walcutt describes transcendentalism as "a monistic philosophy which attempts to draw together the nature-spirit poles of orthodox dualism until they are touching, until, indeed, they are one. . . .
[S]pirit and nature, soul and body, are various expressions of one uni-
fied reality. There can be no basic separation of them, as there was in
the medieval view of the cosmos." (*American Literary Naturalism*, A
Divided Stream, Minneapolis, 1956, pp. 10–12.)

"Not Me" (whose other part is Emerson's own animal correspondence, his body), the ant yet may be embodying His creation, which is inherently good, and fulfilling its own potentiality for good by eternal industry. It would occur only to the scoffers Emerson opposed that there was anything contemptible under foot in the grass. With Plato, he took it as an article of faith that "a law determines all phenomena, which being known can be predicted," and there seems no substantial difference between his theory and the one the historian tentatively ascribes to St. Thomas Aquinas.* He, in turn, found rhapsodic paraphrases in the nineteenth century. As Parker explained, transcendentalism eliminates the distinction between the supernatural and the natural: in so considering everything in nature as natural and considering everything natural as an emanation of the divine, it invests the entire creation with some degree of divinity. To Parker the essence of this divinity was its infinity:

God with no limitations, infinite, absolute, looked at from sensation, infinite power; from thought, infinite intellect; from the moral sense, infinite conscience; from the emotional, infinite affection; from the religious, infinite soul; from all truth, the whole human nature names him Infinite Father!

This conception, the belief that "consciousness of the infinite is the condition of a consciousness of the finite," [4] is also Henry Thoreau's conception of nature. We shall dwell on the ants whose warfare he recorded unforgettably in *Walden*, and if we are a little surprised at the point of view,

* ". . . he seems to be understood as holding that every created individual—animal, vegetable, or mineral—was a special, divine act. Whatever has form is created, and whatever is created takes form directly from the will of God, which is also his act. . . . A crystal was as miraculous as Socrates. . . . The whole universe is . . . a simple emanation from God." (Henry Adams, *Mont Saint-Michel and Chartres*, Ch. XVI.)

it is at any rate one which underlies his "consciousness of the finite" in nature and can be found in a number of places in his writing. Professor Perry Miller speaks of his "Natural History of Massachusetts" (1842) as "an expert demonstration of the transcendental methodology for coping with the multifarious concreteness of nature," the method of seeing "the particular as a particular, and yet at the same time so to perceive it as to make it, of itself, yield up the general and the universal." [5] That general, that universal, to Thoreau, was the goodness, the perfection, that Emerson postulated, and like Emerson he saw its particulars as expressions of that ideality. His "Natural History" is a rhapsodical hymn to its perfection. He tells us that "the universe is not rough-hewn, but perfect in its details. Nature will bear the closest inspection; she invites us to lay our eye level with the smallest leaf, and take an insect view of its plain. . . . She has no interstices; every part is full of life." Characteristic of this perfection is its abundance, and characteristic of this abundance is joy:

Surely joy is the condition of life. Think of the young fry that leap in ponds, the myriads of insects ushered into being on a summer evening, . . . the nonchalance of the butterfly carrying accident and change painted in a thousand hues upon its wings, or the brook minnow stoutly stemming the current. . . .

And consonant with this joy is health: "In society you will not find health, but in nature. . . ." Serenity of nature, joyfulness, healthfulness—Thoreau's use of these terms is intended as a reproach to his contemporaries' feelings about nature (his insistence here, like Emerson's, is a reminder to us of the small extent to which they spoke for their generation, whose sensationalism-oriented thinking they were well aware of): "The doctrines of despair," he tells us, "were never taught by such as shared the serenity of nature. . . . The spruce, the hemlock, and the pine will not countenance despair." And we may be reminded of Whitman's reproach to man from contemplating the serenity of cows in pasture as Thoreau comments "how the trees grow up without forethought, regardless of the time and circumstances." Even in winter "The 'winter of *their* discontent' never comes. . . . They are our vegetable redeemers. . . . Who was the benignant goddess that bestowed them on mankind?"

Now this consciousness of nature's health, its joy uncontaminated with intellection (such joy as made Emerson view the squirrel with envy) is also a consciousness of the innocence of that immense and perfect act of creation. He had noted in his journal on August 1, 1841, a Sunday:

I never met a man who cast a free and healthy glance over life. . . . [T]he best live in a sort of Sabbath light, a Jewish gloom. The best thought is not only without sombreness, but even without morality. The universe lies outspread in floods of white light to it. The moral aspect of nature is a jaundice reflected from man. To the innocent there are no cherubim nor angels. Occasionally we rise above the necessity of virtue into an unchangeable morning light, in which we have not to choose in a dilemma between right and wrong, but simply to live right on and breathe the circumambient air. There is no name for this life unless it be the very vitality of *vita*. Silent is the preacher about this, and silent must ever be, for he who knows it will not preach.[6]

This submergence in *vita pura*, this intuitive, visceral concept of the amorality of nature and this almost shocking (even to Thoreau, apparently) proposal that man desist from factitious moral responsibility and return to an essentially non-cognitive, pre-lapsarian innocence—they underlie the masterpiece of reporting that is the fight between the red and black ants in the "Brute Neighbors" chapter in *Walden*.

The essential jocoseness of the long passage seems to convey to the reader a mock-heroic quality. Emerson considered his ants in an act of construction; Thoreau, in an act of self-destruction, one in which entire armies are locked in deadly conflict, with great loss of limb and life. His key words are *resoluteness, assiduousness, firmness, ferociousness.* The word *excitement* appears four times, and two of these appearances are in the places in which Thoreau makes this particular episode "yield up the general and universal":

I was myself excited somewhat even as if they had been men. The more you think of it, the less the difference.

. . . I felt for the rest of that day as if I had had my feelings excited and harrowed by witnessing the struggle, the ferocity and carnage, of a human battle before my door.

Thoreau has by no means patronized the ant: he has, far more seriously than jestingly, raised it to the level of man,* has dignified its struggle by likening it to the struggles of the Trojan War, the American Revolution, and the Napoleonic Wars. Both ant and man emerge as creatures endowed with boundless vitality, marvellously unconquerable will. The universal, then, that this ant-fight yields up is the "free and healthy" essence of life, the "vitality of *vita.*" The bloodshed excited him with its innocence. For all that this example of ant behavior differs from Emerson's, like his it is tran-

---

* He was capable of the reverse, it should be added. In the posthumous "Life Without Principle" (1863) he makes this observation: "What are nations? . . . Like insects, they swarm. The historian strives in vain to make them memorable. It is for want of a man that there are so many men." (At the very time this appeared, his countrymen, by swarms, were performing in a way to make them memorable to historians for at least a hundred years.)

For an equally contemptuous attitude toward men (as opposed to *man*) in Emerson, the worshipper of the poetry of the commonplace, see Chapter Three, below.

scendentally (that is, intuitively) derived—which is to say, mystically.* Thoreau had his eye close to the struggle of the ants (and later, to be in an even better position, his microscope); it was the eye of the secular religionist, the mystical philosopher. He is both on the level with and far above the carnage, and like Emerson, finds compensation in the proof of the *vitality* of creation which the carnage has provided. Collaterally, in the "Spring" chapter of *Walden*, he celebrates the "tonic of wildness," the sight of nature's "inexhaustible vigor," and—again and again—the *healthfulness* of it all. The vulture derives *health* from feeding on the carrion whose stench sickens us: the "assurance" the smell gave Thoreau "of the strong appetite and inviolable health of Nature" was his "compensation."

I love to see that Nature is so rife with life that myriads can be afforded to be sacrificed and suffered to prey on one another; that tender organizations can be so *serenely* squashed out of existence like pulp,—tadpoles which herons gobble up, and tortoises and toads run over in the road. . . . With the liability to accident, we must see how little account is to be made of it. The impression made on a wise man is that of universal *innocence*. Poison is not poisonous after all, nor are any wounds fatal. Compassion is a very untenable ground.† (My italics)

* What Basil Willey writes about the "Nature" of Wordsworth and Coleridge—that "in a sense . . . they return to 'whatever is, is right,' but it is on a higher level of insight—the level of Plotinus, Spinoza, and the mystics"—could be written with equal appropriateness about the Nature of Emerson and Thoreau. (See *The Eighteenth Century Background*, [1940], Boston, 1961, p. 256.)

† This very liability to accident would make the naturalist Theodore Dreiser see how very *much* account was to be made of it, and how essential compassion therefore was: "Let no one underestimate the need of pity. We live in a stony universe whose hard, brilliant forces rage fiercely. From the prowling hunger of the Hyrcan tiger to the concentric grip of Arcturus and Canopus there is the same ruthless, sightless disregard of the individual and the minor thing. . . . And in the midst

Professor Carl F. Hovde recently has found evidence of just this kind in Thoreau's *A Week on the Concord and Merrimack Rivers*. The quotations Thoreau interpolated into this book, he notes, avoid the topic of Christianity "most persistently,"—a truly striking silence in view of Thoreau's great levies on the metaphysical poets. From George Herbert's "The Elixer" he chose the only stanza which made no clear reference to God. But most extreme of all his treatment of other authors is his use of a quotation from Giles Fletcher's "Christ's Victory in Heaven." In Thoreau's hands "an image which . . . is part of an apocalyptic vision, written as an invocation of ultimate terror, becomes . . . part of an evocation of positive joy. . . . Imagery written to convey terror becomes part of the exultation." [7]

Thus uncompromisingly does Thoreau pursue idealism to its furthest reaches and divorce it from the "untenable" ground of the compassion in the romantic writers America was reading. (We remember Blake's "Each outcry of the hunted hare/A tissue from the brain doth tear.") And thus irreconcilably does his transcendentalism, his intuitive (visceral?) grasp, oppose itself to the observations of that other viewer of nature close up in Thoreau's lifetime, Arthur Schopenhauer. When the victim—not the hero—who is protagonist in a Hemingway novel of 1929 picks up *his* chip with its struggling ants and places it under *his* tumbler in order the better to see their agony—not their vitality, their heroism —he does it, we shall see, in a way that is much more in sympathy with the thought of that gloomy font of German philosophy.

"Oh, that some young genius would devise the 'novum organum' of humanity, determine the 'principia' thereof," Theodore Parker, rapturously in worship of human and ani-

---

of the rip of desperate things . . . there spring and blossom these small flowers of sentiment. Tenderness! Mercy! Affection! Sorrow!" (*The Financier*, New York, 1912, p. 409.)

mal life, cried around the middle of the century, and "write
out the formulas of the human universe, the celestial mechanics of mankind!" [8] Schopenhauer had slowly been doing
precisely this for years. He too had observed those ants (and
those tortoises), as well as the amorality of God's creation.
And his reactions were as opposed to Thoreau's as Thoreau's
red ants were to his black. Joined with the scientifically ar-
rived-at conclusions of the biologists of his day, they were
responsible for a latter-day conception of man's relationship
to lower animal forms and to the universe that was as much
anathema anathemata to the new heterodox thinkers of the
River Charles as it was to the thought, by and large, of the
civilizations of the Tigris and the Euphrates.

∎

A subtle chain of countless rings
The next unto the farthest brings;
The eye reads omens where it goes,
And speaks all languages the rose;
And, striving to be man, the worm
Mounts through all the spires of form.

I have been quoting the epigraph to a book of scripture for
a small and centrifugal group of New England writers during
the second quarter of the nineteenth century; but I have also,
in effect, been quoting Scripture. For there is nothing in
these words of Emerson's that is not implicit or stated
throughout the history of Judaeo-Christian thought. In the
opening chapters of *Genesis* we are told that only after the
worm did God create man; and that whereas God formed
man out of lowly dust, still He personally "breathed into his
nostrils the breath of life" and made of man "a living soul."
Originally conceived as both base matter and divine spirit,
man has come up through the centuries in this dualistic
image, his partial spiritual status characteristically serving as

an encouragement toward complete spirituality (divinity);
his base origin correspondingly as a reminder of "all the spires
of form" whose culmination he is. To the extent that God
has created all forms of matter, they partake of divinity. As
St. Augustine had written in *City of God*, "God . . . is so
great a creator in great things that He is not less great in
small." [9] This divinity could be consubstantial, even, in the
pantheistic philosophy, where, as in Whitman's *Leaves of
Grass*, the ant no less than the heavens declares His handiwork:

*I believe a leaf of grass is no less than the journeywork of
  the stars,
And the pismire is equally perfect. . . .**

Or, as in Wordsworth's Immortality Ode, where

*To me the meanest flower that blows can give
Thoughts that do often lie too deep for tears.*

But as a matter of course, whether Pope's rationalistic "great
chain" of being, with its "strong connections, nice depend-
encies," and "gradations," or Tennyson's pious "great world's
altar-stairs/That slope through darkness up to God"—the
concept is of an ascending order of divinity from microscopic
animal life through man to God. That is why, for all his
extravagant (and amused) analogy between struggling ant and
struggling man, despite his humble (and mystical) identification of himself as "partly leaves and vegetable mould,"

* In arguing against a heretic, Tertullian "maintains that Nature, in the
sense of 'all creation,' is permeated with the spirit of God and that one
looking at it could not fail to admire its Creator"; in his *Adversus
Marcionem* he writes: "Though you may laugh at the smaller animals,
. . . imitate, if you can, the hive of the bee, the hill of the ant, the web
of the spider, the thread of the silkworm." (Boas, *Essays on Primitivism*,
p. 89.)

Henry Thoreau characteristically effects a neat division of himself into flesh and spirit. This censorious passage in the "Higher Laws" chapter of *Walden* is characteristic of mid-century belief:

The wonder is how [we] can live this slimy, beastly life, eating and drinking. . . . He is blessed who is assured that the animal is dying out in him day by day, and the divine being established. Perhaps there is none but has cause for shame on account of the inferior and brutish nature to which he is allied.

So is the regret he expresses in "Life Without Principle" (1863) that "We quarter our gross bodies on our poor souls, till the former eat up all the latter's substance." Another mid-century antagonist of matter (Tennyson in *In Memoriam*) enjoins his generation to "Move upward, working out the beast,/And let the ape and tiger die." The sentiment was common to all ages, going back to oriental doctrines and to Saint Paul.

When Dante describes the lustful sinners in the *Purgatory* (XXVI, 31–36) as approaching and greeting each other briefly very much as ants do, he would not permit the implicit reproach were there not also implicit the high state from which man may fall (nor were he and his readers not also inclined to believe that any communication between such lowly creations also testified to the magic of God's ways). For the Dantean theory of the world rested on Holy Writ, which proclaimed the duality of creation. In *Proverbs*, 12:1, the distinction between the person who can learn and one who cannot is the distinction between human and "brutish" ways. In *Psalms*, 8, man is extolled as having dominion over all others of God's works—"All sheep and oxen, yea, and the beasts of the field"; and in *Daniel*: 5, the terrible punishment administered by God to Nebuchadnezzar for doubting God is to change his human heart into a beast's, to make him eat grass with the beasts of the field, to coat him with hair like an eagle's, and to turn his nails into the claws of birds. When Paul lectures the Galatians (5:16–17), it is to

Walk in the Spirit, and ye shall not fulfill the lust of the flesh.

For the flesh lusteth against the Spirit, and the Spirit against the flesh; and these are contrary the one to the other. . . .

And Jude speaks of humans acting in a state of nature as "brute beasts"; of "sensual" beings "having not the spirit." But most importantly, Paul tells the Corinthians (I, Ch. 15:39): "All flesh is not the same flesh; but there is one kind of flesh of men, another flesh of beasts, another of fishes, and another of birds."

Such a concept runs forward to Dante, who, like Aristotle, while not denying man's brutishness, reserves his severest condemnation for the evil that results from the abuse of that distinctively human trait—reason. To the Humanist Pico della Mirandola, whose God tells Adam

"The nature of all other things is limited and constrained within the bounds of laws prescribed by me: thou, coerced by no necessity, shalt ordain for thyself the limits of thy nature in accordance with thine own free will. . . . I have set thee at the world's center. . . . [T]hou mayest with . . . freedom of choice . . . fashion thyself. . . . Thou shalt have the power to degenerate into the lower forms of life, which are animal; thou shalt have the power . . . to be reborn into the higher forms of life, which are divine. . . . [W]e may become that which we will to be. . . . [I]t should never be said against us, that although born to a privileged position, we failed to recognize it and became like unto wild animals and senseless beasts of burden. . . ." [10]

We find it in the literature of the Renaissance, where man is praised in proportion to the degree by which he lives up

to his privileged status in the kingdom of nature and cen-
sured as he sinks toward the mechanistic, unthinking level
of all the other dwellers on its limitless plain. Marc Antony
accuses the throng assembled around Caesar's body:

"O judgment, thou art fled to brutish beasts,
And men have lost their reason!"

Hamlet's first words accuse his mother of forfeiting this di-
vinely bestowed gift: "O God, a beast that wants discourse
of reason/Would have mourned longer. . . ." He spares
himself as little when he suspects himself of animal-like
torpor:

. . . . . . What is a man
If his chief good and market of his time
Be but to sleep and feed? a beast, no more.
Sure he that made us with such large discourse
Looking before and after, gave us not
That capability and God-like reason
*To fust in us unused. . . .**

As he talks to Rosencrantz and Guildenstern soberly, his
praise of God takes the form of a self-conscious confession of
a malaise within him that makes it difficult for him to pay
tribute to His manifest glory. In the lines which follow, is he
not reproaching his own inability to see man as God created
him and the Psalmist celebrated him rather than reproaching
that creation itself?

"What a piece of work is a man! how noble in reason! how
infinite in faculty! in form and moving how express and admirable! in action how like an angel! in apprehension how

* Browning would make the same point in "Rabbi Ben Ezra": "Irks
care the crop-full bird? Frets doubt the maw-crammed beast?"

like a god! the beauty of the world! the paragon of animals!
And yet, to me, what is this quintessence of dust?"

Surely he goes to his death, trusting in God's infinite mercy,
confident that "there's a special providence in the fall of a
sparrow," that "There's a divinity that shapes our ends/Rough
hew them how we may."

Maddened by pain, Gloucester may speak of man as "a
worm" and complain that

"As flies to wanton boys are we to the gods,
They kill us for their sport,"

yet Edmund does not dispute him when Edgar renders this
quite different judgment on Gloucester's fate:

"The gods are just, and of our pleasant vices
Make instruments to plague us.
The dark and vicious place where thee he got
Cost him his eyes."

In fact, when Shakespeare's characters are not breaking into
puns or conceits, they seem to be quoting Scripture: whether
it is Hotspur explaining his annoyance at Glendower to
Mortimer by the terms of *Proverbs* or the Fool in *King Lear*
lecturing Kent by holding up to him the very model with
which this chapter began: " 'We'll set thee to school to an
ant, to teach thee there's no laboring i' the winter.' "

Yet from the start, the materialists had had a voice as well.
The Psalms bear witness, it happens, as well to man's despair
of, as his trust in, God's power and mercy. The Psalmist on
one occasion (Ps. 23) speaks of entrusting himself reverently
to the Lord as a sheep to his shepherd; but he can also
complain that "Thou has given us like sheep appointed for
meat; and has scattered us among the heathen." (Ps. 44)

And against Paul's sentences to the Corinthians (I, Ch. 15:29ff):

Else what shall they do which are baptized for the dead, if the dead rise not at all? why are they then baptized for the dead? . . .
If after the manner of men I have fought with beasts at Ephesus, what advantageth it me, if the dead rise not? let us eat and drink; for tomorrow we die—

we might set the sentences of *Ecclesiastes* which Paul's appear to challenge:

. . . the sons of men . . . might see that they themselves are beasts.
For that which befalleth the sons of men befalleth beasts; . . . as the one dieth, so dieth the other; yea, they have all one breath; so that a man hath no preeminence above a beast. . . .*
All go into one place; all are of the dust, and all turn into dust again.
Who knoweth the spirit of man that goeth upward, and the spirit of the beast that goeth downward to the earth? (3:18–21)

In Shakespeare too can be found metaphor for man as beast, as of-the-earth-earthy. Iago's sneer at sexual union among humans comes to mind ("making the beast with two backs") and Hamlet's enraged comparison of his mother's bed to a pigsty.

---

* Or, as in *Job*, Ch. 14:
". . . there is hope of a tree, if it be cut down, that it will sprout again. . . . But man dieth, and wasteth away. . . . As the waters fail from the sea, and the flood decayeth and drieth up: So man lieth down and riseth not. . . .
Also, see Lucretius, *De Rerum Natura*, Bk. III, Sec. 2.

The nature that Edmund invokes as *his* goddess in *King Lear*, to whose law his services are bound, is not Hamlet's goddess of justice at all but of license, chaos, and force; it is the same concept of amorality that Hamlet rails against in a bitter moment as "an unweeded garden,/That grows to seed; things rank and gross in nature/Possess it merely." *

The agnostic Montaigne in effect provides a commentary on Hamlet's wild and whirling words by pointing out that "this unruliness of thought . . . is an advantage that is sold [to man] very dear . . . for from it springs the principal source of the ills that oppress him: sin, disease, irresolution, confusion, despair." And wherefore the assumption, so dear to man, that what the beasts do by natural necessity, by instinct, man does by reason and choice? "We must infer

---

* A. C. Bradley considers "a very striking characteristic of *King Lear*" "the incessant references to the lower animals and man's likeness to them. These references are scattered broadcast through the whole play. . . . The dog, the horse, the cow, the sheep, the hog, the lion, the bear, the wolf, the fox, the monkey, the polecat, the civet-cat, the pelican, the owl, the crow, the chough, the wren, the fly, the butterfly, the rat, the mouse, the frog, the tadpole, the wall-newt, the water-newt, the worm . . . 'hog in sloth, fox in stealth, wolf in greediness, dog in madness, lion in prey.' 'The fitchew nor the soiled horse goes to't/With a more riotous appetite.' . . . Goneril is a kite: her ingratitude has a serpent's tooth . . . : her visage is wolvish: she has tied sharp-toothed unkindness like a vulture on her father's breast: for her husband she is a gilded serpent: to Gloster her cruelty seems to have the fangs of a boar. She and Regan are dog-hearted: they are tigers . . . : each is an adder to the other: the flesh of each is covered with the fell of a beast. Oswald is a mongrel, and the son and heir of a mongrel: ducking to everyone in power, he is a wag-tail: white with fear, he is a goose. Gloster, for Regan, is an ingrateful fox: Albany, for his wife, has a cowish spirit and is milk-liver'd: when Edgar as the Bedlam first appeared to Lear he made him think a man a worm. As we read, the souls of all the beasts in turn seem to us to have entered the bodies of these mortals; horrible in their venom, savagery, lust, deceitfulness, sloth, cruelty, filthiness; miserable in their feebleness, nakedness, defencelessness, blindness; and man, 'consider him well,' is even what they are." ("Lecture Seven" in *Shakespearean Tragedy*, Cleveland, 1955, pp. 214–215.)

from like results like faculties, and consequently confess that this same reason, this same method that we have for working, is also that of the animals." * Scorn the lower orders though he may, man is actually at their mercy: lice ended Scylla's dictatorship and the contemptible little worm sits down to breakfast on emperors (a reflection that Hamlet would echo in the graveyard). The ant, he pointed out, is as industrious as man in providing for winter. But let us not assume that Montaigne is merely quoting Solomon: his intention is not to inspire man but to level him, and his method is to ascribe to the ant not merely actions that man can write off as sheer instinct but the most sophisticated.† He does not stop short of religion. Quoting at length (in his *Apology for Raymond Sebond*) from the philosopher Cleanthes, Montaigne tells the fascinating story of *his* two groups of ants. One emerges from its hill bearing the corpse of a dead ant. It approaches

* "Is there any organization regulated with more order . . . than that of the bees? . . . Do the swallows . . . conduct their search [for a nesting place] without judgement? . . . Why does the spider thicken her web in one place and slacken it in another? . . . We may see well enough, in most of their works, how much the animals surpass us. . . . So that their brutish stupidity surpasses in all their contrivances everything we are able to do with our divine intelligence." (*Apology for Raymond Sebond*, Donald Frame transl.)

† This is the reverse of Emerson's argument in "The Transcendentalist," where he presents man's self-consciousness as a hindrance to (and the lower animals' sheer intuitiveness, as a condition of) the "purely spiritual life" that transcendentalism would have him aspire to: "Only in the instinct of the lower animals we find the suggestion of the methods of it, and something higher than our understanding. The squirrel hoards nuts and the bee gathers honey, without knowing what they do, and they are thus provided for without selfishness or disgrace." And whereas man admits "the dignity" of the involuntary actions of nature's animals about him, "he is balked when he tries to fling himself into this enchanted circle, where all is done without degradation. Yet genius and virtue predict in man the same absence of private ends and of condescension to circumstance, united with every trait and talent of beauty and power."

and parleys with a group from another colony. The latter group confers again and again with the other members of their colony. Only then do they emerge bearing a dead worm. An exchange being effected, the second group returns to its hill with the corpse, which evidently was that of one of their colony and which can now be given proper burial!

Now, in ancient times Saint Paul had related the purgation of his own pride: "And lest I should be exalted above measure through the abundance of the revelations, there was given to me a thorn in the flesh, the messenger of Satan to buffet me, lest I should be exalted above measure." (II *Corinthians*, 12:7.) And frequently thereafter man had suffered deliberate buffetings, not from the devil's emissary, but from his fellow-man, lest he succumb to overweening pride. Professor George Boas has given an account of theriophilism, of beast fables popular in Europe in ages gone by. Their purpose was to wound man's pride and to reduce his arrogance; their technique was to point out that the beasts are more prudent, temperate, and chaste than humans; their moral was "like that of most satirists and no more to be taken as founded on a serious zoology than Gulliver's Travels." * (In this tradition is Robert Frost's comic "Departmental." It is ants that are satirized for the rigidity of the division of their occupations —philosophizing, embalming—into departments, but there is also a *de tibi fabula* suggestion.) When these fables went beyond mere entertainment, they worried the gentle and devout Joseph Addison, whose own tendency was to find his analogies by looking above, rather than below: he deplored satire that "endeavours to shew by some superficial Strokes of Wit, that Brutes are the most excellent Creatures of the two" and reproves those (including La Rochefoucauld) who

---

* *The Happy Beast*, Baltimore, 1933, p. 56. In Herman Melville's *Mardi*, for example, Babbalanja demonstrates that plants are either as high as or higher than man in the scale of creation.

"endeavor to make no distinction between man and man, or between . . . men and . . . brutes." * But Montaigne's voice, in the mouth of posterity, would drown out this grieved devoutness. Addison's contemporary, Alexander Pope, was proclaiming in his *Essay on Man* that

All are but parts in one stupendous whole,
Whose body Nature is, and God the soul,

and sternly enjoining man in that dawn of the scientific day from drawing doubting judgments about the infinite: only our imperfect understanding keeps us from realizing that apparently careless "nature" is actually carefully designed "art"; that all "chance" is actually "direction"; all "discord" is really "harmony"; "partial evil, universal good"; and, finally and flatly, "WHAT EVER IS, IS RIGHT." † Another contemporary, the Earl of Shaftesbury, was finding in the data of nature support for an equally fervid optimism: they assured him that

to the existence of the spider that of the fly is absolutely necessary. . . . In the same manner are flies . . . necessary to the existence of other creatures. . . . And thus are other species or kinds subservient to one another, as being parts

---

* *Spectator*, No. 209; *Tatler*, No. 108.
". . . whether one traced descent from the shark or the wolf was immaterial even in morals. This matter had been discussed for ages without scientific result. La Fontaine and other fabulists maintained that the wolf, even in morals, stood higher than man. . . ." (Henry Adams, *The Education of Henry Adams*, Ch. XV.)

† ". . . what had science revealed? Everywhere design, order, and law, where hitherto there had been chaos. Whether one contemplated the infinitely great through the optic glass of the Tuscan artist, or the infinitely little through the microscope of Malpighi, one received at every turn new assurance that all was 'according to the Ordainer of order and mystical mathematicks of the city of heaven.'" (Basil Willey, *The Eighteenth Century Background*, p. 5.)

of a certain system. . . . If the ill of one private system be
the good of others (as when one creature lives by the destruction of another . . .), then is the ill of that private system no
real ill in itself. . . . So . . . [no] being . . . is wholly and
absolutely ill unless . . . what we call ill is nowhere good
besides, in any other system, or with respect to any other
order or economy whatsoever. (*Characteristics*)

Granting that pious dogmatism of this kind was made possible by the New Science itself; still, the mysteriousness of the
creation was growing in proportion as man's knowledge of it
increased, its increasing complexity serving to inspire doubt.
Pascal's is a more representative voice of the intelligent man
when it cries: If only nature's testimony to God were less
equivocal! * As it was, "Nature presents to me nothing which
is not matter of doubt and concern": ". . . seeing too much
to deny and too little to be sure, I am in a state to be pitied."
(*Pensées*, No. 229.) Alas, once question that God "maintains
Nature," and optimism may seem procrustean; and to question design and benevolence is to come to spiritual dismay or
even disaster; for then wherever man looks he may find only
the rationale of a will purposelessly working itself out, its
parts endlessly at war with each other. Seen in this light the
animals of Schopenhauer's world take on an appearance
much more like Montaigne's than Thoreau's.

There was a basic difference between man and beast,
Schopenhauer maintained (*i.e.*, man possessed reason, idea,
detachment); but basically beast and man alike were victims
of the immanent will of the universe, and "This universal
conflict becomes most distinctly visible in the animal kingdom . . . for each animal can only maintain its existence
by the constant destruction of some other. Thus the will to

* "As Pascal long ago saw, Nature proves God only to those who believe
in Him already on other grounds." (Basil Willey, *The Eighteenth Century Background*, p. 292.)

live everywhere preys upon itself . . ." * Like Thoreau,
Schopenhauer has his examples to cite. One, taken from an
1855 reprinting of an earlier report, is about the "bulldog-ant
of Australia," whose violent conduct seems like a senseless
parody of the ants which had seemed so heroic to Thoreau:

for if it is cut in two, a battle begins between the head and
the tail. The head seizes the tail with its teeth, and the tail
defends itself bravely by stinging the head: the battle may
last for half an hour, until they die or are dragged away by
other ants. This contest takes place every time the experiment
is tried.

Man, too, he tells us, exemplifies this purposeless and suicidal
quality: ". . . even the human race . . . reveals in itself
with most terrible distinctness this conflict, this variance
with itself of the will, and we find *homo homini lupus.*" Thus
whereas Thoreau had found exemplified in the ant-battle the
principle of heroism, of valor to match that of the human
battle at Concord bridge, Schopenhauer found in both proof
that "everywhere we see strife, conflict. . . . Every grade of
the objectification of will fights for the matter, the space, and
the time of the others. . . . This strife may be followed
through the whole of nature; indeed, nature exists only
through it. . . ." [11] This thing-in-itself, this will, has its
transcendental aspects in both man and animal: just as the
French father killed himself in order to exempt his son from
military service (and potential death), so

the love of the brute for its young has . . . a strength which
far surpasses that of the effort which merely concerns itself

* At the 1850 story of "a squirrel that was magically drawn by a serpent
into its very jaws," Schopenhauer winced as if in personal pain: Aristotle was right! Nature is demonic, not divine; the spectacle was "revolting and atrocious. What monstrous kind of nature is this to which
we belong!" (*The World as Will and Idea,* New York and London,
1883, III, pp. 112–113.)

as an individual. . . . [With] almost all species of animals
the mother encounters any danger for the protection of her
young. . . . An ant has been cut in two, and the fore half
been seen to bring the pupae to a place of safety.

But will it remains, and simply will: "Thus here, as also in
the sexual impulse, the will to live becomes to a certain extent transcendent, for its consciousness extends beyond the
individual, in which it is inherent, to the species." [12]

At this point—mid-century—we find ourselves confronted
with evidence of two major and opposing positions toward
man's place in nature and nature itself. To Thoreau, man is
the transcendent entity in the riot of nature. To Schopenhauer, he is the transcendent victim in a nature of riot.
These were the two standpoints possible to man: the particular (or self-conscious) and the universal (or unself-con-
scious):

Every individual, when he looks within, recognises in his nature, which is his will, the thing in itself, therefore that which
everywhere alone is real. Accordingly he conceives himself as
the kernel and centre of the world, and regards himself as of
infinite importance. If, on the other hand, he looks without,
then he is in the province of the idea the mere phenomenon,
where he sees himself as an individual among an infinite number of other individuals, accordingly as something very insignificant, nay, vanishing altogether. Consequently every individual, even the most insignificant, every I, when regarded
from within, is all in all; regarded from without, on the other
hand, he is nothing, or at least as good as nothing.*

* The World as Will and Idea, III, pp. 416–417.
    Thoreau's and Schopenhauer's exactly opposing and irreconcilable
interpretations are the more significant for being based on several identical note-takings: wherever these two philosophers looked, they found
still further evidence to confirm a judgment rendered by a spirit either
unshakably steadfast or irretrievably lost. Ants, or seeds. . . . The re-

port about an insect that emerged "strong and beautiful" from an egg
deposited in the leaf of a wood table sixty years earlier strengthened
Thoreau's faith in resurrection and immortality; yet the report of the
English scientist that he had raised wheat five feet tall from seeds deposited in a grave in Thebes three thousand years earlier yielded
Schopenhauer simply another example of the objectification of the immanent and purposeless will of nature. (And Melville, a Swiftian personal analogy. He wrote to Hawthorne in June, 1851: "I am like one of
those seeds taken out of the Egyptian Pyramids, which, after being
three thousand years a seed and nothing but a seed, being planted in
English soil, it developed itself, grew to greenness, and then fell to
mould.") Somewhere between these extremes, the representative thinking man of the century, Alfred Tennyson, found himself instinctively
trusting, like the transcendentalists but without their assurance, that
"somehow good/Will be the final goal of ill," and "That not a worm is
cloven in vain"; but also like Schopenhauer considering the evidence of
a discrepancy between God (love) and nature ("red in tooth and
claw/With rapine") and of the "evil dream" nature lends of man's
utter insignificance—

> So careful of the type she seems,
> So careless of the single life,
>
> That I considering everywhere
> Her secret meaning in her deeds,
> And finding that of fifty seeds
> She often brings but one to bear—

he feels helplessly baffled; and entertaining the terrible possibility that
"The spirit does but mean the breath," that man, nature's "last work,"
dies merely into the dust from which he came, that so far from caring
for the individual man, nature may not care even about the single type,
cries:

> No more? a monster, then, a dream,
> A discord. Dragons of the prime,
> That tare each other in their slime,
> Were mellow music matched with him.

The most innocent of wild birds. . . . We even have the two men's
speculations on the female woodcock's self-sacrificing conduct when its
young are threatened. In "Brute Neighbors" Thoreau relates the
mother's bravery: "spying me, she would leave her young and circle
round and round me, nearer and nearer till within four or five feet, pretending broken wings and legs, to attract my attention, and get off her
young. . . ." Shortly thereafter he concludes with "You only need sit
still long enough in some attractive spot in the woods that all its inhabitants may exhibit themselves to you by turns" a paragraph of

anecdotes of this sort that he had begun with the equally detached observation that "It is remarkable how many creatures live wild and free though secret in the woods, and still sustain themselves in the neighborhood of towns, suspected by hunters only." These are the reports of the pure naturalist, using that word only in its sense of scientific observer of outdoor life; if in context they yield any clue to Thoreau's personal reaction, it would be a feeling of wonder and admiration at the marvelousness of creation and the prodigality of the creator. But when Schopenhauer, in a similar list (III, p. 317) includes an identical example ("Mountain-cocks and woodcocks allow themselves to be taken upon the nest when brooding"), it is to demonstrate the prodigiousness of force in creation, the victimization of animal (and human) life by the sexual impulse (here evidenced in parental love): "At bottom it is the expression of the consciousness in the brute that its true being lies more immediately in the species than in the individual, and therefore, when necessary, it sacrifices its life that the species may be maintained in the young." (III, p. 316.)

Finally, and least forgettably, their turtles. . . . If so many "tender organizations" such as "tadpoles which herons gobble up, and tortoises and toads run over in the road"—if these "can be so serenely squashed out of existence like pulp," Thoreau concludes, "we must see how little account is to be made of it. The impression made on a wise man is that of universal innocence." But on Schopenhauer there was only an impression of horror when he thought about Yunghahn's story of the Java plain with its "skeletons of large turtles . . . which come . . . out of the sea in order to lay their eggs, and are then attacked by wild dogs . . . who . . . strip off . . . the small shell of the stomach, and so devour them alive. But often then a tiger pounces upon the dogs. Now all this misery repeats itself thousands and thousands of times. . . . For this, then, these turtles are born. . . . Wherefore the whole scene of horror? To this the only answer is: it is thus that the will to live objectifies itself."

These turtles reappear in the Galapagos Islands in Tennessee Williams' Nightmare for Seven Voices, Suddenly Last Summer (1959). Thither the late Sebastian Venable had taken his mother in his search for God. And this, she tells us, is what they found:

"We saw the great sea-turtles crawl up out of the sea for their annual egg-laying. . . . Once a year the female . . . crawls up out of the equatorial sea on to the blazing sand-beach of a volcanic island to dig a pit in the sand and deposit her eggs there. . . . She never sees her offspring, but we did. . . . And the sand all alive, all alive, as the hatched sea-turtles made their dash for the sea, while the birds hovered and swooped to attack and hovered and—swooped to attack! They were diving down on the hatched sea-turtles, turning them over to expose their soft undersides, tearing the undersides open and rending

As the century wore on, data such as Schopenhauer had assembled and brooded upon were being collected systematically by the biological scientists and will be seen to have had a far greater influence on literature than the transcendentally clear but distant music of the other nineteenth-century German invasion of western thought, its pessimism—as confirmed

and eating their flesh. Sebastian guessed that possibly only a hundredth of one percent of their number would escape to the sea. . . ." Mrs. Venable tells us that although it was Herman Melville's poetic description of the formation of these Encantadas (or Enchanted Isles, for an irony that Williams relishes) that originally impressed Sebastian, the horror that they found there was "something Melville *hadn't* written about." But never was an implication more amiss: no one would have been more appreciative a listener to Mrs. Venable's excruciating story than the Herman Melville who had watched those same vultures rend the butchered shark in *Moby-Dick*:

"The sea-vultures all in pious mourning, the air-sharks all punctiliously in black or speckled. In life but few of them would have helped the whale, I ween, if peradventure he had needed it; but upon the banquet of his funeral they most piously do pounce. Oh, horrible vultureism of earth! from which not the mightiest whale is free." ("The Funeral")

At about the time Melville uttered this wail, Charles Darwin himself was confronting this very vultureism. In an early (1844) version of the *Origin of Species* he had written:

"It is derogatory that the Creator of countless Universes should have made by individual acts of His will the myriads of creeping parasites and worms, which since the earliest dawn of life have swarmed over the land and in the depths of the ocean. We cease to be astonished that a group of animals should have been formed to lay their eggs in the bowels and flesh of other sensitive beings; that some animals should live by and even delight in cruelty; that animals should be led away by false instincts; that annually there should be an incalculable waste of the pollen, eggs and immature beings; for we see in all this the inevitable consequences of one great law, of the multiplication of organic beings not created immutable."

And in 1856 he had written in a letter: "What a book a devil's chaplain might write on the clumsy, wasteful, blundering, low, and horribly cruel works of nature!" But by the time the *Origin* appeared in 1859, he had deleted the passage about parasites, cruelty, and waste. (See Stanley Edgar Hyman, *The Tangled Bank*, New York, 1962, p. 38.) Yet the 1844 version had combined both Thoreau's admiring wonder and Schopenhauer's revulsion.

and documented by science—eventually devastating the
Kantian idealism.*

"Schopenhauer has analysed the pessimism that character-
ises modern thought," † Oscar Wilde stated in *The Decay of*

* Evidence of its influence abounds: in Hardy, Nietzsche, Mann—even
in cults, as Ernest Samuels has shown: "Schopenhauer found in the
Nirvana of Buddhism an appropriate symbol of the rejection of will
and he and his disciple Hartmann helped make the term one of the
cliches of educated circles. Sir Edwin Arnold's florid epic poem, *The
Light of Asia*, celebrating the life of Gautama Buddha, 'The Teacher
of Nirvana and the Law,' was now at the height of its immense vogue,
for the scientific study of mythology, as it diminished the authority of
Christianity, turned many minds to the exotic religions of the Far East.
Raphael Pumpelly . . . had been a pioneer orientalist and [John] La
Farge . . . had actively proselytized the cause in the early seventies."
(*Henry Adams: The Middle Years*, Cambridge, Mass., 1958, p. 246.)
    For an account of the retreat of Henry Adams's heroine (in *Democ-
racy*, 1880) to "Schopenhauer's non-human absolute Nirvana," see
Henry Adams: The Middle Years, pp. 74–85. In Henry James's "The
Point of View" (1882), the expatriate Mrs. Church, who has educated
her daughter abroad, discovers from her after their return to New York
that Schopenhauer is held lightly there: " 'In this country,' " she says,
" 'the gentlemen . . . care nothing for the results of modern research;
and it will not help a young person to be sought in marriage that she
can give an account of the last German theory of Pessimism.' " Yet in
recalling his first association with the James family, during the summer
of 1858, T. S. Perry said of himself and Henry and William James as
teen-agers that "We fished in various waters, and I well remember
when W. J. brought home a volume of Schopenhauer and showed us
with delight the ugly mug of the philosopher and read us amusing specimens of his delightful pessimism." (Percy Lubbock, ed., *The Letters of
Henry James*, New York, 1920, Vol. I, p. 7.) (Was it merely, then, that
"the gentlemen" preferred Schopenhauer for themselves?)
    Jack London's *The Sea-Wolf* (1904) begins with mention of Charley
Furuseth's summer cottage, which its owner "never occupied . . .
except when he loafed through the winter months and read Nietzsche
and Schopenhauer to rest his brain."
    When the essentially Schopenhauerian thesis of the supremacy of the
sexual instinct, as expounded by Sigmund Freud, reached the United
States early in the twentieth century, its influence was widespread,
as we shall see.

† But it was Hamlet who invented it, he adds: "The world has become
sad because a puppet was once melancholy." For the anecdote about

Lying; and Gamaliel Bradford, deploring those "shrieking fanatic[s], like Leopardi or Schopenhauer," yet began his survey of the spiritual climate of America in 1892 with the admission that "Pessimism is a philosophy greatly in repute just now. Schopenhauer and Hartmann are in the mouths of many people who have not read their works at all." [13]

Schopenhauer felt that he had gotten to the heart of the darkness: the predatory ways of nature were evil, were a universal horror. Thoreau, observing the same natural exhibits and even filtering them through the same oriental medium, arrived at diametrically opposed conclusions. He saw predatoriness as characteristic of nature, and therefore as a form of goodness, of innocence. Similarly, when Emerson expresses annoyance at men's tendency to point to the evil in the world, it is because he conceives of evil only as the absence of goodness and as that by which the immanent goodness of the universe can be recognized. Thus he writes that "the misery of man appears like childish petulance, when we explore the steady and prodigal provision that has been made for his support and delight on this green ball which floats him through the heavens." For him, evil is, Professor Chester E. Jorgenson has written, "not absolute, but fragmentary and privative." *

Now the pious clergyman-turned-ecologist, Malthus, could both concede nature's ruthlessness and yet contend that this evil in itself could work just such benefits; and the trail leads from him to the biological scientists whose thought towered over the second part of the nineteenth century, for better

---

Wilde's change of adjectives, see W. B. Yeats, *Autobiographies*, New York, 1927, p. 167.

* "Emerson's Paradise Under the Shadow of Swords," *Philological Quarterly*, XI (July, 1932), pp. 274–292.

For the ramifications of this venerable concept, see Ch. Two, below.

or for worse, as far as the writers of those years were concerned.

Actually, it was not completely for worse. Which is not the
same as saying that the post-Civil War American writer saw
eye to eye with the transcendentalists. Even from the retrospect of the Gilded Age, the transcendental yea-saying to
doubt, its rapt acceptance of God's plenty, seems merely a
brief, if intense, afterglow of an exotic sunset on the fresh
western land, rather than the rising of a sun. Idealism, which
had underwritten the Declaration of Independence, would
survive the triumph of materialism as it emerged in the twin
forms of science and industrialization, with the accompanying urbanification and competition—all, factors against which
the transcendental spirit was in revolt. But it would re-emerge
in a form altered by these new forms and expressed in terms
of their very exigencies. For the 1860's cancelled out far more
than merely the legality of slavery, notwithstanding the hopes
of the eloquent spokesmen of the transcendental gospel.

"Transcendentalism has a work to do," Theodore Parker
wrote in "Transcendentalism": it aimed to "revise the experience of mankind and try its teachings by the nature of mankind"; and to do something like that with a people "blinded
still by the sensational philosophy" of Bacon, Locke, and
Newton,"—a philosophy "which loves facts of experience, not
ideas of consciousness, and believes not in the First-Fair,
First-Perfect, First-Good," he added, in an understatement,
"is no light work." Would the human dream of the transcendental philosophy ever become a fact? If history said
no, at least Parker, trusting in human nature, could say
yes. Emerson, early in "The Transcendentalist," looking at
the movement with a historical sense and seeing a parallel
between it and the heresies of the past (Gnostic, Essenic,
and Manichean) was equally confident of its impact: although America's literature and spiritual history were, he

admitted, "in the optative mood," still, "whoso knows these seething brains . . . will believe that this heresy cannot pass away without leaving its mark."

After Emerson's death, Gamaliel Bradford, extolling him with a mighty pyramid of praise, felt that his and his fellows' enthusiasms had by no means vanished with them; and whereas he conceded that "Material prosperity has lured us all more or less from the things of the spirit," he could instance such results of the Concord thought as Christian Science, nationalism, "the followers of George and Bellamy," and the agitation for female emancipation.[14]

But, Ernest Samuels notes, "The spread of pessimism from the ark fountains of German thought had brought with it a side of oriental speculation largely ignored by Emerson and the Concord school." * And, by the 1890's, alas, a side completely obscuring the transcendental, Gamaliel Bradford complained:

The critical and destructive portion of Kant's work has become so widely known as the basis of German philosophy that an idealist is supposed to be one who believes the whole empirical world to be a delusion. . . . Could anything be more mistaken? Is there a philosophy more triumphant, more overflowing with faith . . . than true idealism? . . . Every-

---

* *Henry Adams; the Middle Years,* p. 246.

V. L. Parrington asks us to think of the thought of the Concord school as the victim of unforeseeable economic forces:

"Emerson was the apotheosis of two centuries of decentralization that destroyed the pessimism brought to the new world by refugees from the old, and found its inevitable expression in the exaltation of the individual, free and excellent, the child of a beneficent order; whereas Dreiser was the first spokesman of a later America once more falling within the shadow of the pessimism that springs from every centralized society shut up within the portals of a static economics; that dwarfs the individual and nullifies his will, reducing him from a child of God to a serf." (*Main Currents in American Thought,* New York, 1930, III, p. 319.)

thing shows . . . that Kant himself, in spite of his "world-overturning" speculations, was the profoundest of believers.[15]

Neither outspoken idealists like Carlyle and Ruskin nor gentler mystics like Emerson were in the main stream of western thought, which, Krutch observes, was flowing "swiftly and happily through Baconian channels." * Macaulay's complacency and Huxley's optimism "beckoning the scientist on to new triumphs . . . illustrate most typically the attitude of an age which had not yet either realized all that it was losing or taken the time to consider the meaning of the losses of which it was aware." [16] Emerson actually lived long enough to have to confront the massive evidence of the defeat of his 1842 hopes that the heresy of his idealism would persist,† to observe the increasing influence of the empirical method of science upon the thought of the century. During the earlier 1800's, Schopenhauer had relegated the relationship of the sexes of the human race with the sweeping fiat, "Male and female must neutralise each other like acid and alkali"; by the time the century was eighty years old (and so too, almost, was Emerson), men had been given to under-

* Thus, half a century after the "Annus Mirabilis" (1836) of the transcendental movement, the prediction of Convers Francis of that year was again coming true: "I have long seen that the Unitarians must break into two schools—the old one, or English School, belonging to the sensual and empiric philosophy, and the new one, or the German School (perhaps it may be called), belonging to the spiritual philosophy." (Quoted in Perry Miller, The Transcendentalists, p. 106.) But just as this oversimplified the complexity of the transcendental mind (item, Emerson's addiction to the findings of the empiricists), so did it that of the empiricists (item, Darwin's belief in man's moral sense).

† "For many an . . . overwrought intellectual in the nineteenth century, and for many a sufferer from the strange disease of modern life, looking up from amongst the dark Satanic mills of the industrial age, the authority of the Wordsworthian Nature-religion has seemed absolute. Nevertheless it was probably only relative to a certain passing phase of civilization: for an age, and not for all time." (Basil Willey, The Eighteenth Century Background, p. 291.)

stand by the French critic Taine that "Vice and virtue are products like vitriol," thus documenting Emerson's complaint that

In science the French *savant*, exact, pitiless, with barometer, crucible, chemic test and calculus in hand, travels into all nooks and islands, to weigh, to analyze and report. And chemistry, which is the analysis of matter, has taught us that we eat gas, drink gas, tread on gas, and are gas.*

So that Theodore Dreiser, his antipodes, would have shocked Emerson not at all had Emerson lived on to 1918 and had to hear a character in *The Hand of the Potter* borrow the *Rubáiyát's* metaphor of the Irresponsible Potter for scientific use: "Sometimes I think we're naht unlike those formulae they give ye in a chemical laboratory—if ye're made up right, ye work right; if ye're naht, ye don't, an' that's aal there is to it. . . ."

* "Historic Notes," in Perry Miller, *The Transcendentalists*, p. 496. With a seeming irony, Emerson himself remembered clearly that ". . . the paramount source of the religious revolution was Modern Science; beginning with Copernicus . . . showing mankind that the earth . . . was not the centre of the Universe . . . and thus fitted to be the platform on which the Drama of the Divine Judgment was played . . . but a little scrap of a planet. . . . Astronomy taught us our insignificance in Nature; showed that our sacred as [well as] our profane history had been written in gross ignorance of the laws, which were far grander than we knew; and compelled a certain extension and uplifting of our views of the Deity and his Providence. This correction of our superstitions was confirmed by the new science of Geology. . . . But we presently saw also that the religious nature in man was not affected by these errors in his understanding. The religious sentiment made nothing of bulk or size, or far or near; triumphed over time as well as space; and every lesson . . . which the old ignorant saints had taught him, was still forever true." (*Ibid.*, p. 499.)
    We in turn remember how he had cited science in his early writings himself. ("The microscope cannot find the animalcule which is less perfect for being little," he had written in "Compensation.")

But long before this, in between Emerson's hopes and their disappointment, the English savant had taught us that we were animals.

■

It was not by Charles Darwin alone that orthodox dogma was dethroned, and his victory was never complete. His was, for all that, the newest bible for mankind, and an essential departure from the King James version it was. Looking back in 1909, for the purpose of the semi-centennial anniversary of the publication of *The Origin of Species*, the philosopher John Dewey concisely defined the basic radicalness of its scientific conclusions: The classic notion of species, he pointed out, had carried with it a teleology, had assumed that nature does nothing that is not for an ulterior purpose. The events of nature contained a "spiritual causal force" invisibly spiritual but recognizable by reason. Matter and sense were subordinate to this spiritual principle, whose ultimate fulfillment was God's goal for nature and man:

The design argument thus operated in two directions. Purposefulness accounted for the intelligibility of nature and the possibility of science, while the absolute or cosmic character of this purposefulness gave sanction and worth to the moral and religious endeavors of man. Science was underpinned and morals authorized by one and the same principle, and their mutual agreement was eternally guaranteed. . . .

This was the philosophy that Darwin's principle of natural selection undermined.

If all organic adaptations are due simply to constant variation and the elimination of those variations which are harmful in the struggle for existence that is brought about by excessive reproduction, there is no call for a prior intelligent causal force to plan and preordain them.[17]

Now if the Darwinian principle caused some critics to accuse Darwin of substituting materialism for idealism and
chance for design, others were less hostile. The famous
preacher Henry Ward Beecher kept telling audiences in his
western tour of 1883: ". . . I hold that the foundations of
God stand sure, in the near future this very doctrine of evolution that alarms so many . . . will prove to be a soil down
into which the roots of Christian doctrine will go. . . ."
naturalists such as Herbert Spencer should be encouraged,
actually: "not because they bare the full truth, but because
they bring out the truth," he wrote a friend.[18]
    This piety is a reminder

of the way many moralists and theologians greeted Herbert
Spencer's recognition of an unknowable energy from which
welled up the phenomenal physical processes without and the
conscious operations within. Merely because Spencer labelled
his unknowable energy "God," this faded piece of metaphysical goods was greeted as an important and grateful con-
cession to the reality of the spiritual realm.[19]

    In any event, idealism was proving that it was not dead,
that it could ingest the foreign substance and even derive
nourishment from it. As B. J. Loewenberg has demonstrated:

Evolution underscored an earlier faith in reason, in progress,
and in man. A religious naturalism premised on the immanence of God followed as the philosophical consequent. . . .
Immanence became the core of later theological reconstruc-
tion. . . . The romantic idealists, loyal to Transcendental
metaphysics, interpreted evolutionism in terms of Plato, of
Kant, and of Emerson.*

* "Darwinism Comes to America, 1859–1900," *The Mississippi Valley
Historical Review*, XXVIII (1941), 354.
    Apropos the "secularizing or naturalizing of teleology" of the time of
Darwin's fame, Stanley Edgar Hyman writes that "it allowed those

As for supernaturalism, those "masses of men" that Thoreau had noted "lead lives of quiet desperation" continued to thrive on it, despite the defections of the clergy,* and its viability could never be doubted.†

---

like Gray who wanted teleology to claim that Darwin evidences it (all is designed to progress to perfection), and those like Huxley who wanted to believe that teleology 'had received its deathblow at Mr Darwin's hands,' as he wrote in 1864, to deny its presence (the Great Designer is out)." (*The Tangled Bank*, p. 40.)

* "If supernaturalism was losing ground among intellectuals, it was by no means, in the post-Civil War period, on the road to extinction among the masses." Church membership kept growing, volumes of dogmatic theology kept appearing (by Hickok, Hodge, and Shedd, for examples), the evangelist Dwight L. Moody commanded large middle-class audiences and the evangelical Salvation Army reached the down-and-out. "The popularity of certain books [also] revealed the appeal of supernaturalistic ideas and ethical values. When, in 1868, Elizabeth Stuart Phelps published *The Gates Ajar*, she tapped a vast reservoir of need; people still mourning for sons and husbands lost on the battlefields craved reassurance that life really is eternal, that Heaven really is just within reach. . . . At the same time the highly pious novels of E. P. Roe and J. G. Holland enjoyed immense popularity. But no book swept the land with such force as General Lew Wallace's *Ben Hur* (1880). This volume succeeded in dramatizing Christ as a hero without in the least lessening reverence for Him as a supernatural force." (Merle Curti, *The Growth of American Thought*, Third Edition, New York, 1964, pp. 519–521.)
    Curti goes on to cite the great postwar spread of spiritualism whose adherents ranged from quacks to William James, concluding: "The spiritualistic cult was . . . by no means smothered by the advance of naturalism." (pp. 521–522.) It was at least important enough for William Dean Howells to attack in *The Undiscovered Country* (1880). Another form that late nineteenth-century spirituality took, Christian Science, was attacked both by Mark Twain and Edward Eggleston. Neither it nor Annie Besant's "Theosophy" nor the sudden growth of Catholicism availed to "stem the rising tide of disbelief," Harry Hartwick writes: "The candles at the altar were smoking down. . . ." (*The Foreground of American Fiction*, New York, 1934, p. 14.)

† We are prepared to find Marcius Willson telling children and parents in 1860 that in his *Third Reader* (the Harper's Series of School and Family Readers) "We have not found it convenient, nor thought it advisable, to embrace *man* in [the] classification [of mammalia]" and

But there were attempts at reconciliation of Darwinism
and design that came from men trained in science, and these
were of course impressive. The eminent John Fiske argued
his case persuasively and popularly * in *The Destiny of Man*
(1884) as well as in other volumes. It is true, he concedes, that

those countless adaptations of means to ends in nature, which
since the time of Voltaire and Paley we have been accus-
tomed to cite as evidences of creative design, have received at
the hands of Mr. Darwin a very different interpretation. The
lobster's powerful claw, the butterfly's gorgeous tints, the
rose's delicious fragrance, the architectural instinct of the bee,
the astonishing structure of the orchid, are no longer explained as the results of contrivance. . . . The idea of beneficent purpose seems . . . excluded from nature, and a blind
process, known as Natural Selection, is the deity that slum-
bers not nor sleeps. Reckless of good and evil, it brings forth
at once the mother's tender love for her infant and the horrible teeth of the ravening shark, and to its creative indifference the one is as good as the other.

But despite "these appalling arguments," despite "the fact of
man's consanguinity with dumb beasts," we should beware of
their "fancied consequences." For the Darwinian theory does

---

citing Aristotle as well as various moderns in support of his stand. Yet
even he conceded that most biologists "classed *man* among *animals.*"
Whereas as late as 1925, in Dayton, Tennessee, the attorney (a former
member of the Cabinet of the United States) prosecuting a biology
teacher for teaching the doctrine of evolution in a public high school
spoke for a large body of citizens. And even in the middle 1960's,
hearings on high school textbook selections in Texas have revealed
strong opposition to the evolutionary theory.

* Quotations above are from John Fiske's *The Destiny of Man* in an
1899 printing (of 1000 copies) of an 1884 book, completing 25,000
copies, we read on the verso page. In the front matter of this printing
are cited the sales figures of Fiske's five other books on evolution:
105 printings, presumably of 1000 copies, of books ranging in price
from $1.00 to $6.00.

not degrade man but "shows us distinctly for the first time
how the creation and the perfecting of Man is the goal toward which Nature's work has all the while been tending."
Why? Because yet another revolution has followed the one
of Natural Selection, a "silent and unnoticed" one, a "wonderful moment" when "psychical changes began to be of
more use than physical changes to the brute ancestor of
Man. . . . Henceforth the life of the nascent soul came to be
of first importance, and the bodily life became subordinated
to it," we find him concluding just as Thoreau and Emerson
might have concluded half a century before. Now it is possible for us to take the "far higher view," to see "that in the
deadly struggle for existence which has raged throughout
. . . time, the whole creation has been groaning . . . in
order to bring forth that last consummate specimen of God's
handiwork, the Human Soul." [20] Would not Wordsworth
have accepted this, who had written in the *Prelude*:

Dust as we are, the immortal spirit grows
Like harmony in music; there is a dark
Inscrutable workmanship that reconciles
Discordant elements, makes them cling together
In one society. . . . Praise to the end! [21]

The scientist Asa Gray also attempted reconciliation. He held
that if

we conceive the "stream of variations" to be itself intended,
we may suppose that each successive variation was designed
from the first to be selected. In that case, variation, struggle,
and selection simply define the mechanism of "secondary
causes" through which the "first cause" acts; and the doctrine
of design is none the worse off because we know more of its
modus operandi.[22]

But, as Dewey has pointed out, Darwin's findings were
actually not amenable to such teleological interpretations:

granted that Darwin "asserts that it is 'impossible to conceive this immense and wonderful universe including man . . . as the result of blind chance or necessity,' " it is also true that Darwin

holds that since variations are in useless as well as useful directions, and since the latter are sifted out simply by the stress of the conditions of struggle for existence, the design argument as applied to living beings is unjustifiable; and its lack of support there deprives it of scientific value as applied to nature in general.[23]

Eventually, one had to face facts. Darwin had returned man to the world of nature, had "showed him to be as subject to universal laws as any other mammal." [24] It was more and more difficult to exalt him to John Stuart Mill's level of the reasoning man, the civilized, the morally free, the individual, for one by one these attributes had been stripped away from him.

He was not rational [and] his psychology could best be understood by studying that of animals or children. He was not civilized; . . . his social behavior was full of concealed survivals from barbarism. . . . He was not morally free . . . ; he was subject to his biological nature, to his physical environment, to his class loyalties, to a whole series of laws the existence of which had not even been suspected in the early nineteenth century. And finally he was not even an individual, . . . since his life as a human being was inseparable from his social life. Unless he belonged to a community, he was deprived of his human heritage, he was a beast among beasts.[25]

Accordingly, the practice of the 1830's and 1840's of equating man with lower—or even the lowest—animal life increasingly lost both the whimsicality of the theriophilist of old and the religiousness of the recent transcendental rhapsodists, not to mention the casual and innocent practice of the fiction writer of characterizing a creation in an animal metaphor. Balzac's describing Rastignac as finding the Maison Vauquer's eighteen boarders "in the act of feeding themselves, like so many cattle at a trough" is a striking but momentary metaphor. To describe Poiret as an eagle is innocuous enough; and Balzac's analogy of the title character of Old Goriot is humorously intended: ". . . the abuse of pleasures had converted him into a snail, into an anthropomorphical mollusk, to be classed among the casquettiferes, as a young man who was employed in the Museum . . . used to say." As was, basically, Thoreau's account of Concord as "a village of busy men, as curious to me as if they had been prairie-dogs, each sitting at the mouth of its burrow, or running over to a neighbor's to gossip. I went there frequently to observe their habits." [26]

This was by no means the same thing as (although it may have contributed to) "The 'universal drenching' of belles-lettres and journalism with natural selection" that amused an editor of *The Galaxy*, Professor Richard Hofstadter reports. "He noticed that a Washington reporter for the *Herald* had recently done a sketch of the Senate in which members were portrayed in Darwinian terms as bulls, lions, foxes, and rats." When Darwin's *The Descent of Man* came out in 1871, the clergy read into it an attack on human dignity: "Religious readers pointed with horror at Darwin's too vivid description of man's ancestor as 'a hairy quadruped, furnished with a tail and pointed ears, probably arboreal in habits.' " * If far

---

* *Social Darwinism in American Thought*, 1860–1915, Philadelphia, 1945, pp. 11, 12.

In our own century Robert Frost would theorize (in "The White-Tailed Hornet" of *A Further Range*) that

> . . . . As long on earth
> As our comparisons were stoutly upward
> With gods and angels, we were men at least,
> But little lower than the gods and angels.
> But once comparisons were yielded downward,

less shocking than so endlessly cited a genealogy, there were other passages eventually far more costly to man's sense of his own importance in *The Descent of Man* for all their (if not because of their) clinical objectivity. The question of monkeys aside, what was the percipient Victorian reader to infer from the information that "Man is liable to receive from the lower animals, and to communicate to them, certain diseases . . . and this fact proves the close similarity of their tissues and blood . . ." or that "Man is infested with internal parasites . . . and is plagued by external parasites, all of which belong to the same genera . . . as those infesting other mammals. . . ."? [27]

Journalism, the clergy—and what about imaginative literature, characteristically concerning itself, Professor H. S. Commager puts it, "not with the careful analyses and the nice distinctions of science, but with the dramatic and imaginative exploitation of its findings"? Men wrote early in the new century as they had done late in the old, when "the air . . . was . . . heavy with pessimism."

They shamelessly mixed Darwinian biology with Freudian psychology and blended in contributions from Spencer, Haeckel, Loeb,* Nietzsche, Einstein, Pavlov, and Jung to

---

    Once we began to see our images
    Reflected in the mud and even dust,
    'Twas disillusion upon disillusion.
    We were lost piecemeal to the animals.

Yvor Winters, who quotes this poem (in "Robert Frost: or, The Spiritual Drifter as Poet") complains that "We have seen Frost himself engaging in downward comparisons, and we shall see him doing it again."

* One of the earliest and strongest influences upon the novelist Theodore Dreiser was Jacques Loeb's *The Mechanistic Conception of Life.* "Loeb's explanation of human instincts and behavior in physiochemical terms seemed to Dreiser the next natural step after Spencer and Darwin and Haeckel, and his own descriptions of love in terms of 'chemisms' derive from this source. Yet Dreiser was never a consistent mechanist.

make what passed for a naturalistic brew. They were naturalists, they were determinists, they were behaviorists. They seldom paused to formulate their philosophy or even to defend their terms, and they rarely agreed in their use of these terms or these concepts. All was grist that came to their literary mill.[28]

Heretofore, whatever their religious orientation, writers had believed in the existence of human freedom of choice.

For the naturalists, however, men are "human insects" whose brief lives are completely determined by society or nature. The individual is crushed in a moment if he resists; and his struggle, instead of being tragic, is merely pitiful or ironic, as if we had seen a mountain stir itself to overwhelm a fly.[29]

If we merely confront the first writer of the seventeenth century in this country with the first of the twentieth, examine the metaphor by which they express their concept of the human being, we appear to be conducting an exercise in travesty. Both Edward Taylor and Theodore Dreiser, it is to the point, were writers who were scientifically oriented, but with what exactly opposed results! In "Upon a Wasp Chilled with Cold" Taylor watches the wasp sun itself, rub its limbs, finally recover from his numbing chill and fly off into the sun; this conduct elicits the reflection that the tiny insect, not without its spark of the divine down in its ignominious place at the bottom of creation, serves as an object lesson to the poet, at the height of that creation, also to celebrate God's divinity—in this case, with verse. In *Sister Carrie*, while Dreiser asserts that Herbert Spencer's "liberal analysis" of morals is insufficient to account for the complexity of the

---

". . . [H]e always became impatient with scientists who would not grant that 'mystery' was part of 'reality.' " (F. O. Matthiessen, *Theodore Dreiser*, New York, 1951, pp. 236–238.)

human personality,* yet he creates Caroline Meeber not as
someone to marvel at the moth's heliotropism but to embody
it: for, he tells us, "We are insects produced by heat, and
pass without it."†

* Yet Dreiser himself accounts for Hurstwood's eventual disintegration
as follows: "Now, it has been shown experimentally that a constantly
subdued frame of mind produces certain poisons in the blood, called
katastates, just as virtuous feelings of pleasure and delight produce help-
ful chemicals called anastates. The poisons generated by remorse inveigh
against the system, and eventually produce marked physical deteriora-
tion. To these Hurstwood was subject."

† "Mr. Dreiser drives home the great truth that man is essentially an animal, impelled by temperament, instinct, physics, chemistry. . . . His
heroes and heroines have 'cat-like eyes,' 'feline grace,' . . . One hero
and his mistress are said to 'have run together temperamentally like
two leopards.' . . . A pure-minded serving-maid, who is suddenly held
up in the hall by a 'hairy, axiomatic' guest and 'masterfully' kissed
upon the lips, may for an instant be 'horrified, stunned, *like a bird in
the grasp of a cat.*' . . . 'The psychology of the human animal, when
confronted by these tangles . . . ,' says the author of *The Titan*, 'has
little to do with so-called reason or logic.' No; as he informs us elsewhere in endless iteration, it is a question of chemistry." (Stuart P.
Sherman, "The Barbaric Naturalism of Theodore Dreiser," in *On Contemporary Literature*, New York, 1917, pp. 93–94.)
In Dreiser's philosophy "Men are chemical compounds, existing in
a world where they play about like water-flies, skipping restlessly and
unintelligently as their legs drive them, whom the universe in its vast
indifference suffers for a time." (Parrington, *op. cit.*, III, p. 355.)
Also, see William L. Phillips, "The Imagery of Dreiser's Novels,"
PMLA, LXXVII (Dec., 1963), pp. 572–585.
But it is also true (if not nearly so evident) that Dreiser's concept of
the animality of man changed late in life. (Perhaps it would be more
accurate to say that the refusal he voiced—quoted above—even in *Sister
Carrie*, to give in to the Spencerian concept eventually expanded.)
Although the record of his fiction was beyond altering by then, in
lesser writings of the 1930's he took various steps that have the effect
of disowning it. In "The Myth of Individuality" (1934) he speaks of
nature with a new reverence and quotes Emerson's "Brahma" by way
of illustration; and in 1939, in a long introductory essay he wrote to a
Thoreau anthology, he confessed to being moved by Thoreau's insistence that nature is "all mind" and to being impressed with the fact
that although Thoreau's observations on nature were scientifically
oriented, Thoreau did not stop with mechanical processes but believed

The distance between these two poles was bridged in large part by a latter-day devil whose notoriety eventually came to rival that of the one who had constructed the bridge between hell and the earthly paradise—the prolific, irrepressible Émile Zola. Daring beyond Wordsworth's daring stand of the 1800 Preface ("The remotest discoveries of the chemist, the botanist, or the mineralogist will be as proper objects of the poet's art as any upon which it can be employed"), he had now undertaken no less than a fusion of these two areas of intellectual activity.* George Moore remembered the excitement he felt at Zola's articles in the *Voltaire* (on *"Naturalisme, la vérité, la science"*) and at the first chapters of Zola's *L'Assommoir* as they appeared in periodical form:

The idea of a new art based upon science, in opposition to the art of the old world that was based on imagination, an art that should explain all things and embrace modern life in its entirety, in its endless ramifications, be, as it were, a new creed in a new civilisation, filled me with wonder, and I stood dumb before the vastness of the conception, and the towering height of the ambition.[30]

Scholarship has compiled a great deal of evidence of the impression Zola's work made on the American writers, who would have been more likely to acquire from him than from scientific sources the connection between man and animal. Maxwell Geismar's question, "Was the post-Darwinian view

in "a universal and apparently beneficent control . . . however dark and savage its results or expressions may seem to us at times." (F. O. Matthiessen, *Theodore Dreiser*, pp. 239–240.)

* As Oscar Cargill has reminded us, there were other tributaries to the Zola river than Darwin: "One cannot ignore the fact that Auguste Comte . . . must have had an influence upon Émile Zola. . . . And Taine, too, might well be considered a naturalist in literary history, before Zola became *the* naturalist in literature." (*Intellectual America*, New York, 1941, p. 48.)

of man based on the main functions of nutrition and reproduction, and life itself a blind expression of an infinite
fecundity?" [31] has already had this answer from Zola:

My work will be less social than scientific. Balzac . . . bases
his story on religion and royalty. . . . My own work will be
something different. . . . I . . . wish to paint . . . a whole
family, in showing the working out of race modified by
milieux. . . . What matters most to me is to be purely naturalistic, purely physiological.*

* What mattered most to Feodor Dostoevsky was the very opposite.
His *Notes from Underground* (1864) is a treatise on the irrationality of
human beings, and thus a thrust at the ambitions of science to measure
and explain them. Man loves, like the ant, to construct, the Underground Man tells us, but also to destroy; and when man builds, it may
be—unlike the ant—only for the purpose of leaving what he builds "for
the use of *les animaux domestiques*—such as the ants, the sheep, and
so on." This is fitting, for the ant is a model of "perseverance and
good sense," of respectability: "They have a marvellous edifice of that
pattern which endures forever—the ant heap." But man, he insists, is
distinguished by his unwillingness to yield only to common sense, to
reason, to method; and—unlike the ant or any other animal forms—
needs for his happiness suffering, not mere creature comfort.
    This reaction of Dostoevsky's is yet another departure from the
advice of *Proverbs*, one that can be found fairly frequently in the literature of the last hundred years: it is a reaction against the very qualities of the ant that Solomon celebrated, but now as a symbolic rejection
of the collectivistic trends (socialism, communism) or other pressures toward social conformity that characterize these years.
    Hawthorne also rejected the planned society, observing about some
anthills: "Here is a type of domestic industry, . . . perhaps, likewise,
. . . the very model of a [Fourieristic] community. . . . Possibly the
student of such philosophies should go to the ant, and find that nature
has given him his lesson there." (Julian Hawthorne, *Nathaniel Hawthorne and His Wife*, Boston, 1885, Vol. I, p. 504.)
    Professor Ernest Samuels, who quotes the famous passage about
men and ants in Henry Adams's *History of the United States* (see epigraph to this chapter), makes the comment that Adams "could not have
been truer to his Puritan heritage than by demanding a consciousness
of 'a higher destiny.' Life must be moral or it was not worth the history
that recorded it." (*Henry Adams: The Middle Years*, pp. 377–378.)
    Krutch wrote in 1929 of the sociology-minded man that "he may be

Instead of *principles* (royalty, Catholicism) such as Balzac used, he would have *laws* (heredity, atavism) like the scientist. "Balzac says that he wishes to paint men, women and things. I count men and women as the same, while admitting their natural differences, and submit men and women to things." [32]

This resolution utterly discards the premise of Emerson's "Ode" to Channing that

There are two laws discrete,
Not reconciled—
Law for man, and law for thing. . . .

And Zola lived up to the resolution. In that most impressive of exhibits, *La Terre* (1886) the individual characters are seen as things,—that is, as animals. Not even "the shadow of a thought" animates Delhomme's face, with its "big china-blue eyes staring into vacancy like those of a drowsy ox." His mother, Rose is "stupid," is "degraded in her home to the level of a docile, hardworking animal. . . ." Palmyre, worn out by toil, looks sixty at the age of thirty-five and "her last desperate struggles [are] those of a beast-of-burden on the edge of sinking down to die." When she screams it is "a long howling sigh, like the death-gasp of an animal having its

---

struck by the fact that the anthill represents something very close to that communistic Utopia generally evolved by the imagination which [pictures] an ideal society, and yet the contemplation of this . . . perfection strikes a chill to his heart, because it seems to have no meaning or value. . . . This perfected society is, that is to say, utterly devoid of human values. . . . The Spartan commonwealth . . . was not unlike a community of insects. It was marked by the discipline, the regularity, and the patriotism of the anthill. It subordinated the individual to the state. . . ." (*The Modern Temper*, pp. 33, 35.)

And it was precisely such a commonwealth that President Lyndon B. Johnson wanted his hearers to dissociate from the Great Society he envisioned when he said that this society was not "an ordered, changeless, and sterile procession of ants." (*Inaugural Address*, January 20, 1965.)

throat cut," moving a bystander to exclaim, " 'Sounds like a horse that's broken its legs!' " Tron, angered at the taunt about his mistress's lasciviousness, is "shaken with the rage of a dog whose bone is being snatched away." And we have yet to look at the main characters of the novel. As Fouan grows aged and feeble, "all that persisted was the human animal whose only instinct is to keep alive." Losing interest in life, "he was now in the last stages of decrepitude, an aged animal. . . ." The birth of Lise's baby is told in counterpoint to the birth of a calf. Her belly, like the cow's, is enlarged to an unusual size. She feels that, like the cow, "she was being stung by flies on the flanks." Her birth pangs alternate with the cow's and one of her cries causes the veterinarian to comment, " 'I thought it wasn't the cow making such a row.' " As the human birth begins, Lise's "blue-stocking legs drew up and opened again in unconscious movement like a diving frog." Buteau's face is so shaped that the lower part resembles that "of a carnivorous animal"; when he is trying to rape Francoise he treats her "just as if she were a beast he was trying to mount." Is it any wonder that at the end of the story Jean, looking back at the La Beauce farm people from his ten years' experience with them, thinks that "They were . . . rabid wolves let loose on the huge plain"?

These passages are from what is probably the most shameless work of the unspeakable literary prodigy who sheered off much of American literature in the 1890's and later from all that had gone before. It is in its light that we must examine the world, first, of Stephen Crane.

Not that the generally sullen or despondent colors of that world differ strikingly from those of the rest of Crane's contemporaries, victims as they were of the deterministic tinge of the times, Zola or no Zola. We detect this in the apparently casual remark about the four shipwrecked men afloat in the dinghy at the beginning of "The Open Boat": "None of them knew the color of the sky." It was almost dawn and "The process of the breaking day was unknown to them." Emerson, having "no hostility to nature, but a child's love to it," and wishing to "speak her fair," had no wish "to fling stones at my beautiful mother." To him the blue sky "with its eternal calm, and full of everlasting orbs, is the type of Reason." [33] We note that when night comes to Crane's correspondent, and he can know nothing else, the color turns out to be black: "A high cold star on a winter's night is the word he feels that she says to him. Thereafter he knows the pathos of his situation." And not stones but bricks would he throw at Emerson's "beautiful mother" *—but, alas there are "no bricks and no temples"! For him no temples had survived the third quarter of that century, so formative to his development.

By the time the second morning dawns, the shipwrecked men know that their fate is of no consequence to what they had thought to be God, that their impassioned cry of "I exist!" is incurring the cynical response of the universe in Crane's poem. At this point therefore the wind-tower takes the symbolic form of the destiny that presides over their fate: immense, inscrutable, and impersonal, the tower was "a giant, standing with its back to the plight of the ants"— neither cruel nor beneficent, neither treacherous nor wise, but "indifferent, flatly indifferent."

In earlier days, when troubled man lifted up his eyes, he could hope to see something dwelling in the heavens whence came his help:

* In Zola's La Terre, after a sudden and violent hailstorm has done great damage to the new fruit crop, the ancient woman La Grande rails against the force behind it: "Suddenly La Grande, mad with rage, collected some stones and threw them up to pierce the sky shrouded from sight. She screamed, 'Hey, you Goddamned swine! Can't you bloody well leave us in peace?'" (Earth, Ann Lindsay tr., New York, Grove Press, 1955, p. 98.)

Far and wide the clouds were touched,
And in their silent faces could he read
Unutterable love,

Wordsworth wrote.[34] But now, in the days of the *Rubáiyát,*
the fool kept saying in his heart that there simply was no
God up there worthy of the name:

And that inverted Bowl they call the Sky,
Whereunder crawling cooped we live and die,
Lift not your hands to It for help—for It
As impotently moves as you or I.

And in still later days Thomas Wolfe and William Faulkner
would both speak of "God's lidless stare"; and Robert Frost,
of Minerva as blind.* Things being so, God now being not
Reason but Indifference or even Impotence, did it not follow
that man must look to himself for help? And if so, in what
respect was he justified in thinking of himself as of diviner
stuff than the "lower" orders of creation?

Not at all, Zola—that eager intermediary between science
and literature—had insisted. And if the spirit of Crane's world
identifies it as of the grey melancholy of the 1890's, its metaphor is remarkably suggestive of Zola's, whatever Crane's
disclaimers.

---

* Professor Irving Howe has pointed out the "enigmatic statement indi-
cating an ultimate dissociation between the natural world and human
desire" in:

> And further still at an unearthly height,
> One luminary clock against the sky

> Proclaimed the time was neither wrong nor right.
> I have been one acquainted with the night.

("Robert Frost: A Momentary Stay," *The New Republic,* CXLVIII
[March 23, 1963], p. 27.)

A recent study of Crane's *Maggie* (1893) finds in it a Darwinism that "harps insistently upon the odious comparison implied by the specter of man's ancestor as 'a hairy quadruped, furnished with a tail and pointed ears, probably arboreal in habits' ": in *Maggie*, with its metaphors of humans as a tigress, a horse, a bug, a fly, etc., "Crane is not so much extending Darwin's notions of animal behavior to human society as he is reducing the conduct of human beings to the level of animal behavior." *

As we move from this patently sociological sketch covering the course of an entire family to Crane's masterpiece, which crowds far more, actually, into a few hours of the central character's consciousness, the animalism remains undiminished. What keeps the first part of *Gulliver's Travels* on a comic plane is the fact that the prostrate Gulliver need only rise up and exert his physical force to free himself from his insect-like adversaries; as protection against their massive volley of tiny arrows, he need simply cover his face with his left hand. But what if—in all seriousness, now—man is no more, essentially, than the ant? † Let us follow Henry Fleming in *The Red Badge of Courage*. Putting as much distance as he can between himself and the red war-god with its insatiable maw, he has finally reached a dense forest, wherein he hopes to bury himself, where "Nature had no ears." He penetrates to the distant heart of this distant thicket; so com-

---

* David Fitelson, "Stephen Crane's *Maggie* and Darwinism," *American Quarterly*, XVI (Summer, 1964), pp. 182–194. The Darwinism in question was non-historical: whereas Darwin and Huxley distinguished between baser animals and man (whose moral sense enabled him to transcend the terms of a mere struggle for existence), Crane does not. (*Ibid.*)

† Professor Harry Levin asks us to think of "the boundless distance between Robinson Crusoe's easy control over his environment and the crushed victims of Hardy's comic irony or Dreiser's chemical determinism." ("What Is Realism?" in *Contexts of Criticism*, [1957], New York, 1963, p. 73.)

pletely has he escaped that he thinks of his retreat, his
asylum, in religious terms: "the high, arching boughs made
a temple. He softly pushed the green doors aside and entered. Pine needles were a gentle brown carpet. There was a
religious half light." And there at once he comes to a horrified
stop. For so far from being the "fair field holding life," the
"religion of peace" that "would die if its timid eyes were
compelled to see blood," he has actually come face to face
with death, and for the first time has to look upon mortal
flesh as it suffers the ultimate indignity—so intolerable to the
human imagination—of reversion to carrion. The soldier's
corpse that Henry gazes on is a faded, decaying one. But it is
the face that evokes the horror. The inside of the mouth is
no longer red, but yellow. But worst of all, the ants have
taken the face for themselves: "Over the gray skin of the face
ran little ants. One was trundling some sort of a bundle along
the upper lip." Here truly is Man "at supper," as Hamlet told
Claudius: "Not where he eats, but where 'a is eaten. A certain convocation of politic worms are e'en at him." And
Crane tells us that when, immediately thereafter, Henry runs
frantically from the spot, "He was pursued by a sight of the
black ants swarming greedily upon the gray face and venturing
horribly near to the eyes." *Horribly,* because the eyes have
always been thought of as the incarnation of man's entity, his
spiritual essence, the windows to his soul (as in Poe's
"Haunted Palace"); and because, accordingly, in this last
affront the ant is giving the lie to man's belief in spirituality,
his hope of life evermore. Here is ant as the Conqueror
Worm of Poe's mad poem, but also as something that henceforth the sane observer will consider as more menacing than
industrious, as more revolting than diminutively divine! Symbolically speaking, how better could Crane have indicated the
lofty height from which man's concept of his dignity has
fallen in the 1890's than to liken him, as we shall see him do
in "The Blue Hotel," to the parasite on an animal's hide, or

as here, to make him yield a dinner to the lowliest of all in the animal creation, the ant? *

Stephen Crane's was not the only one of "the maiden fancies wallowing in the troughs of Zolaism," as the now aged monologuist of Tennyson's "Locksley Hall Sixty Years After" wearily phrased the fashion in 1886; and the anonymous reviewer of *The Red Badge* could also have been speaking for the fiction of others when he indicted Crane's novel for "animalism," a term used

to denote a species of realism which deals with man considered as an animal, capable of hunger, lust . . . , predacity, . . . and other passions and appetites that make him kin to the brutes, but which neglects, so far as possible, any higher qualities which distinguish him from his four-footed relatives, such as humor, thought, reason, aspiration, affection, morality, and religion.[35]

Certainly he could have been describing one of Zola's aptest American pupils, Benjamin Franklin Norris. His people too are often things of flesh and blood merely. They are, in *McTeague*, men in the mountains "like lice on mammoth's hides, fighting them stubbornly. . . ." They are, in *The Octopus*, "nothings, mere animalculae, mere ephemerides that fluttered and fell and were forgotten between dawn and dusk." † In *La Terre*, just about the time that Buteau and

* Like Zola's, Crane's writing about human beings can remind us of a walk through a zoo. Elsewhere in *The Red Badge* man is a cow, a sheep, a beast (Ch. 5), a rabbit, a chicken, a jaded horse (Ch. 6), a squirrel (Ch. 7). In the opening scene of *Maggie* the line of yellow convicts on the distant island is a worm. In "An Experiment in Misery" the men sleeping in the flophouse are described as "heaving like stabbed fish." In the poem "A Man Adrift on a Slim Spar," disaster results "Because The Hand beckons the mice."

† Also: "It was the human animal, hounded to its corner . . . , turning at last with bared teeth and upraised claws. . . ." And "It was the feeding of the People, elemental, gross. . . ." And the "droning, terrible note" of the people is "the growl of the awakened brute."

Jean are competing for her body, Francoise has a dream one night about "a scrimmage of dogs"; and the physical clash between Buteau and Jean is followed by the encounter of two flocks of geese and their respective gander leaders. In *The Octopus*, the scene in which the rabbits are hunted down and slaughtered, leads, we note, to the scene at the irrigating ditch where the men face the power of the Octopus, most of them too being slaughtered; and, as Parrington writes, "The flock of sheep destroyed by the train is only a symbol of the men and women of the valley, under the wheels of modern industrialism." [36] (The Psalmist had sung that "we are his people, And the sheep of his pasture!")

In *La Terre* we are given a vision of man and his relationship to the earth alternately through the author and through Jean (the other stranger to the La Beauce region). At first, it is a symbolic poetry, with man fertilizing woman (Buteau and Lise), bull fertilizing heifer, and man sowing seed in the ground (Jean and La Beauce), —a pageant of fertilizing, birth, growth, decay, and death viewed poetically, actually. But Jean's final vision is naturalistic: only nature counts. The last sentence of the book shows Jean "the endless plough-lands of La Beauce, filled with the unceasing gesture of sowing. Death and the sowing of seeds: and the life of bread growing up out of the earth." In view of the animal metaphor in which the farmers are described, their predatory, sensual nature, it is no wonder that Jean retreats from them in defeat and chooses possible death to bestialization. (He is on his way to volunteer for service in the Franco-Prussian War.)

At the close of *Germinal* (1885), Zola left his hero, Etienne Lantier, wondering: "Was Darwin right, then, and the world only a battlefield, where the strong ate the weak for the sake of the beauty and continuance of the race?" * In *La Terre*

---

* "In the bulk of his books Zola is interested in biological determinism; in *Germinal*, he is for once fairly absorbed by economic determinism." (Oscar Cargill, *Intellectual America*, p. 56.)

he gives an even more despairing answer: a battlefield, yes, but not for beauty of the race so much as for the mere endless repetition of the life process. Hourdequin, who is failing in large-scale farming only after modernizing his operation and who notes that all other farmers as well are failing largely from foreign competition, understandably sees it as "a crisis brought about by social causes outside the will of men." (pp. 391–392) But Zola sees his plight as only another aspect of nature's vast indifference to that race, heretofore deemed divine, which to her is reduced to the scale of the animal and more often than any other, of the ant.

In the first chapter we read that the men out in the fields in the spring "swarmed like black toiling ants brought up out of the earth by some huge task, throwing themselves into a mighty undertaking gigantic in comparison with their tininess." Theirs is an "insect stubbornness struggling with the immensity of the soil"; and although Zola goes on to describe this stubbornness as "ultimately victor over space and life," (p. 18) everything else in his novel belies this statement. Much later, at a midsummer moment when he is contemplating the "mighty harvest" soon to come, Zola asks: ". . . could man with his tiny insect form, a mere speck in the immensity, ever cope with the task?" (p. 192) Apparently, he could. So it seems, anyway; for as the harvest begins, "The slight creatures, dwarfed by the enormous labour, emerged from it victorious." And the vast farmland plateau known as La Beauce loses her cloak of grain "[s]trip by strip under the ant-like activity. . . ." (p. 194) And "The little black specks of the teams reappeared, swarming indefinitely on." (p. 198) But as Jean comes to think, after some years of experience with these people—these swarms—"If the earth was peaceful and gracious to those who loved her, yet the villages that clung to her like nests of vermin and the human insects preying on her flesh were enough to dishonour her and pollute all contact." (p. 358) This disillusionment

deepens as the novel ends and Jean sees that "The earth takes
no part in our maddened insect-struggles; she is the eternal
worker, ceaselessly toiling and taking no more notice of us
than a nest of ants." (p. 429)

In retrospect, *La Terre* seems an elaborate parody of
Wordsworth's idealistic statement, at the beginning of the
century, that in rural life "the passions of men are incorpo-
rated with the beautiful and permanent forms of nature." *

Zola follows this final melancholy reflection with a rhetorical gloss, an impassioned speculation about the insignificance
of human suffering to nature's inscrutable necessity, to
earth's own (and only!) immortality ("She uses even our
crimes and our miseries to make life and more life for her
hidden ends") that, Åhnebrink has noticed, Frank Norris
must have gone to school to, for he uses it as a model for the
final pages of his own *Octopus* (1901), his own American
"Epic of the Wheat." [37] Actually, if we go even further we
can find in the minute details of his metaphor the man-as-
insect (as well as other animal life) that Zola had taken over
from the pre-scientific writers. For to Norris too the vast proportions of nature's mystically inscrutable ends dwarf man
to the size of the ant.

As Annie Derrick sits "lost in all [the] limitless reaches of
space" that are the Los Muertos ranch, her terror rises, her
awareness of the essential uncongeniality of man and earth.

She recognized the colossal indifference of nature, not hostile,
even kindly and friendly, so long as the human ant-swarm
was submissive. . . . Let, however, the insect rebel, strive to

---

* *Lyrical Ballads*, Second Edition, 1800, Preface.

Similarly, in reply to—if not annihilation of—Wordsworth's theory
(Immortality Ode) of childhood as the blessed, innocent period of human life, Freud would formulate the concept of infantile sexuality; and
still later, possibly under Freud's influence (see *The Fox in the Attic*),
Richard Hughes would invest childhood with all of the vices of adult-
hood in *The Innocent Voyage*.

make head against the power of this nature, and at once it became a relentless . . . power, huge, terrible . . . knowing
no compunction, no forgiveness, no tolerance; crushing out
the human atom with soundless calm, the agony of destruction sending never a jar, never the faintest tremour through
all that prodigious mechanism of wheels and cogs. (Part I,
Ch. 5.)

If she is not the *raisoneur* of Norris's story, certainly Presley
is, and with him this impression is even more firmly fixed. As
he sees the battle between ranchers and railroad:

What were these heated, tiny squabbles, this feverish, small
bustle of mankind, this minute swarming of the human insect, to the great, majestic, silent ocean of the Wheat itself!
Indifferent, gigantic, resistless, it moved in its appointed
grooves. Men, Lilliputians, gnats in the sunshine, buzzed im-
pudently in their tiny battles, were born, lived through their
little day, died, and were forgotten; while the Wheat,
wrapped in Nirvanic calm, grew steadily under the night,
alone with the stars and with God. (Part II, Ch. 4.)

The sum total of destruction and bloodshed resulting from
the struggle between the octopus and the ants has been huge.
But Norris does not let Presley (his Etienne Lantier) rest
more than a moment with the possibility that there is no
hope, that evil has prevailed. "In that little, isolated group of
human insects, misery, death, and anguish spun like a wheel
of fire," to be sure,

But the WHEAT remained. Untouched, unassailable, unde-
filed, that mighty world-force, that nourisher of nations,
wrapped in Nirvanic calm, indifferent to the human
swarm, gigantic, resistless, moved onward in its appointed
grooves . . . ; the individual suffers, but the race goes on.
Annixter dies, but in a far distant corner of the world a
thousand lives are saved. The larger view always and through

all shams, all wickednesses, discovers the Truth that will, in the end, prevail, and all things, surely, inevitably, resistlessly work together for good. (End)*

For all the bombast, the factitious blend of Shaftesbury and Herbert Spencer, we perceive that the fond human dream that man's spirit will prevail, that his efforts toward self-purification are toward a benign Over-soul, is gone. As a matter of fact, the regnant deity in Norris's world is the financial titan Shelgrim, whose name, Norris tells us, "fell squarely in the midst of the conversation, abrupt, grave, sombre, big with suggestion, pregnant with huge associations": for the old gods of justice and love, Norris has substituted a "hated" and "dreaded" human god, "a giant figure" himself "symbolic of ungovernable forces."

Thoreau's playful analogy, by comparison, seems quite pristine, even quaint.† But then, had not Herbert Spencer

---

* Man apparently could victimize (rather than glorify) himself in building as well as in growing: a skyscraper or bridge could become symbolic of society's indifference toward the human ant, Åhnebrink notes. He cites this passage from a Hamlin Garland story ("Under the Wheel," 1890) in which a character looks down on New York from the Brooklyn Bridge:

"Over me soared and sung those stupendous cables, the marvel of man's skill, etched on the sky, delicate as a spider's web. I stood there looking down at the sea of grimy roofs . . . I saw men running to and fro like ants, lost in the tumult of life and death struggle. . . . And over me soared the bridge to testify to the inventive genius of man." (*Beginnings of Naturalism*, p. 219.)

† Quaint too now seems the symbol of universal goodness that Thoreau saw gazing back at him from the forest at Walden in the partridge's eyes: "The remarkable adult yet *innocent* expression of their open and *serene* eyes is very memorable. All intelligence seems reflected in them. They suggest not merely the *purity* of infancy, but a wisdom clarified by experience. Such an eye . . . is coeval with the sky it reflects. . . . The traveller does not often look into such a limpid well." ("Brute Neighbors." My italics.) These are not Stephen Crane's birds, the gulls that annoy the shipwrecked men in "The Open Boat": their "black bead-like eyes" are "uncanny and sinister in their unblinking scrutiny"; and

(who, he reminded his readers, had anticipated, not followed, Darwin's theory of evolution) already spoken glowingly of the advance of men's minds beyond polytheism, then monotheism; shown how "personal superintendence" of the universe yielded to "Universal immanence," and science had led to "the abandonment of such doctrines as those of 'platonic ideas,' 'pre-established harmonies' and the like . . ."? [38] Schopenhauer's ants have found a home in America, and to his anguished cry of *homo homini lupus,* the theorist of all the sciences could offer only the cold comfort that "the phenomena going on everywhere are parts of the general process of evolution, save where they are parts of the reverse process of dissolution," and that "all phenomena receive their complete interpretation only when recognized as parts of these processes." [39] And as for Spencer's secularly spiritual principle that "matter, motion and force are but symbols of the unknown reality," that spirit and matter are both "to be regarded as but a sign of the unknown reality which underlies both"—that possibly most ubiquitous phrase of the latter half of the century: could it hope to show Crane's ants in a different light or diminish one decibel Henry Fleming's shrieks as he perceived them venturing near those eyes? Tennyson's hopes "that not a worm is cloven in vain . . . or but subserves another's gain" have been crushed like the worm. Spencer, Darwin, Zola—mysterious force, inexorability—have claimed the literary American mind and metaphor.

Even so "unconscious" an artist as the humorist Mark Twain "swam during his whole career in the mainstream of

---

when one that seems to fix his eyes "wistfully" upon the captain's head is finally and only with difficulty dissuaded and the other three men "breathed easier because the bird struck their minds at this time [of danger to their lives] as being somehow gruesome and ominous," we may see in this situation more than an impromptu superstition: the complacent comfort of these birds in relationship to the dangerous situation of the men reminds us of the impudent ants and their gruesome, ominous antics in *The Red Badge of Courage.*

ideas that produced the naturalistic writers": Professor Sherwood Cummings at last has furnished the precise documentation for this general assumption. If in Twain's later years the "damned human race" suffered more and more by comparison with animals, we can now see, his reading probably accounts for it in part.* In that fierce indictment that would not appear until years after his death, an innocent boy is indoctrinated in nihilistic philosophy until he finds his corrupter's presence indispensable, so habituated has he become to this deadly infusion; and as *The Mysterious Stranger* (1916) ends, he tells us that

We flitted from place to place around the world as we had done before, Satan showing me a hundred wonders, most of them reflecting in some way the weakness and triviality of our race. He did this now every few days—not out of malice—I am sure of that—it only seemed to amuse and interest him, just as a naturalist might be amused and interested by a collection of ants."

There had actually been not one, but two such naturalists in Twain's reading, both intensely interested in ants and, if not amused, certainly fascinated by this particular insect. One was John Lubbock, whose work Darwin had cited respectfully, the author of *Ants, Bees, and Wasps* (1882).

* As early as 1856, when he was twenty, Twain had undergone an indoctrination in misanthropy in a Cincinnati roominghouse by a Scotchman named Macfarlane: "He said that man's heart was the only bad heart in the animal kingdom; that man was the only animal capable of feeling malice, envy, vindictiveness, revengefulness, hatred, selfishness, the only animal that loved drunkenness, almost the only animal that could endure personal uncleanliness and a filthy habitation, . . . in whom was fully developed the base instinct called *patriotism,* the sole animal that robs, persecutes, oppresses, and kills members of his own immediate tribe, . . . that steals and enslaves the members of *any* tribe . . . that man's intellect was a brutal addition to him and degraded him to a rank far below the plane of the other animals. . . ." (*Mark Twain's Autobiography,* New York, 1924, I, pp. 146–147.)

Twain owned two copies of this book, so that if its conclusion that ants "have a fair claim to rank next to man in the
scale of intelligence" seems to reappear in the statement in
Twain's *What Is Man?* (1898) that "evidences of formic intelligence abolish 'the intellectual frontier between man and
beast,'" the connection may be taken for granted. But greater
attention is owed to the other naturalist, for he was Charles
Darwin himself, and the book in question was *The Descent
of Man.* Twain had marked his copy to the extent that of the
109 pages of *What Is Man?*, Professor Cummings notes, no
fewer than fourteen are given to "the equating of man's intellectual machinery with that of the animals." [40] And if the
mysterious stranger of Twain's later book automatically
thinks of humans in ant terms, he could easily have had
Darwin to thank: Darwin cites a surprisingly large amount of
evidence about ants in a book ostensibly about man's descent,
and any inference that one may be inclined to draw from the
corresponding almost complete exclusion of such evidence
from his earlier book on animals themselves (*Origin*) is likely
to be strengthened not only by the volume of the ant data
that Darwin cites in *The Descent* * but by the use to which
Darwin puts it. Reviewing it today one wonders whether
Darwin actually expected his readers to agree that "The
moral sense perhaps affords the best and highest distinction
between man and the lower animals"; or even whether, on
the basis of the evidence he was submitting, he could consistently have believed it himself.† If by 1929 it could be

* All of it quoted from the Swiss naturalist Huber's *Les Moeurs des
Fourmis* (1800).

† "In the course of his life Darwin lost most or all of his Church of
England faith. In the *Autobiographical Sketch* he wrote in 1876, not
published until after his death, Darwin describes his views as having
gradually moved from theism to agnosticism after the publication of the
Origin, and in the years after 1876 he seems to have progressed to
atheism but kept quiet about it. . . ." (Stanley Edgar Hyman, *The
Tangled Bank*, p. 13.)

stated about the ant that "His industry and his foresight have
always been admired, but only patient observation has revealed how much more complex his virtues are," * surely it
was Darwin's observation that the present century had to
thank. He tells us that "the brain of an ant is one of the
marvelous atoms of matter in the world, perhaps more so
than the brain of a man," and provides an impressive display
of "the wonderfully diversified instincts, mental powers, and
affects" of the remarkable insects. That they are capable of
building structures, bridges, roads and tunnels, of gathering
food collectively, of storing seeds, of drying them when wet
in order to prevent germination, of enslaving other insects,
of emigrating by careful planning, etc., possibly was common
knowledge by 1871. But to have Darwin add that ants have
remarkable memories, recognizing their companions after a
separation of four months; that their antennae afford them
"considerable powers of intercommunication"; that they play
together—ants having been observed "chasing and pretending
to bite each other, like so many puppies"; and, finally and
most impressively, that they sympathize with each other
(". . . when two communities engage in a battle, the ants
on the same side sometimes attack each other in the general
confusion, but they soon perceive their mistake, and the one
ant soothes the other") and even sacrifice their lives "for the
common weal"—surely this was to require the reader to recon-
sider the prevailing conception of the basic differences in
spirituality between man and ant. If then, many years later,
the devil of doubt and despair appears in American literature
in the form of a mysterious stranger from outer (infernal)
space who can find no difference between concentrations of

* "Not only does he perform without question the part assigned him in
the division of labor, but he has even achieved a control over the
processes of reproduction which enables him to see to it that just the
right number of each type of citizen shall be born. . . . He is not
primitive or simple. . . ." (Joseph Wood Krutch, *The Modern Temper*,
p. 33.)

human beings and collections of ants, we do not have to
search long for an explanation.*

We shall see how the early Mark Twain seems to be bur-
lesquing the romanticism of Bret Harte's treatment of the
west in fiction; it is equally justifiable to see in his late *Mysterious Stranger* an attack now on the romanticism (albeit
philosophical) of Charles Darwin's unqualified agreement
with "the judgment of those writers who maintain that of
all the differences between man and the lower animals, the
moral sense or conscience is by far the most important." This
sense, Darwin would have it, redeems man from the mechanical and physiologically deterministic fate of the lower
orders of creation as he had traced that fate in his *Origin of
Species*. This same moral sense had been proposed † and
rejected ‡ before Darwin, but it is Darwin's term that Twain
selects for attack, thereby knocking out from underneath the
suggestible boy-narrator the foundations of his faith in the
human race. Philip Traum delights in mentioning it, always
with a sneer, and as a term that had a most familiar ring to

* Twain had also read *La Terre;* and after recovering from his shock at
its foulness he had confided from the grave that "there is hardly an
incident or a conversation in the book that has not repeated itself hundreds . . . of times in America. . . ." (Henry Nash Smith, ed., Mark
Twain, *Letters From the Earth*, New York, 1962, pp. 219–220.)

Tony Tanner notes that Henry Adams "continually chooses to compare himself to animals: and such animals—the small, the helpless, the
ones that crawl" (maggot, worm, horseshoe-crab) and quotes Adams's
remark to Tilden about Jefferson, Madison, and Monroe being "mere
grasshoppers kicking and gesticulating in the middle of the Mississippi
River. . . ." (See "The Lost America—The Despair of Adams and
Twain," in Henry Nash Smith [ed.], *Mark Twain: A Collection of
Essays*, New York, 1963.)

† In his *Inquiry Concerning Virtue or Merit* (1699), Shaftesbury had
predicated a natural faculty by which man could distinguish and prefer
what is right, a "moral sense." (See Willey, *The Eighteenth Century
Background*, p. 70.)

‡ In *Mardi*, wherein Herman Melville had advanced a curious pre-
Darwinian theory of the descent of man from the kangaroo, not the ape.

Twain's generation.* Man was an ant, a fly, a manure-pile, and God was a bad dream. True, it is now an old female bigot of the middle ages who is reciting the article of faith about providence and the sparrow, rather than a pious prince of Denmark, but Satan's cynical reply is meant to silence both: " 'But it falls, just the same. What good is seeing it fall?' "

If Twain was tired, discouraged by personal losses and defeats, progressively disenchanted with the wonders of the new religion (democracy) and the new way of life (industrialism),† what shall we look for in a later generation, whose flesh had not only inherited all of these ills but now had had added to them that of the senseless butchery of world war?

Joseph Wood Krutch was thinking in that seventieth year Anno Darwini that man "gradually . . . comes to suspect that rationality is an attribute of himself alone and that there is no reason to suppose that his own life has any more meaning than the life of the humblest insect that crawls from one annihilation to another." [41] In fact, if the question that Conrad Aiken asks in "Gehenna"—namely, "Is evolution only an evolution from the sublime to the ridiculous?"—is merely a rhetorical one, then there is really no difference between the madness (which is "the privilege and natural necessity of every consciousness, from the highest to the lowest") of man and ant:

* An American admirer wrote to Herbert Spencer in 1871, the year of the appearance of Darwin's book: "I have never known anything like it. Ten thousand *Descent of Man* have been printed, and I guess they are nearly all gone. The progress of liberal thought is remarkable. Everybody is asking for explanations. The clergy are in a flutter." (Richard Hofstadter, *Social Darwinism*, p. 14.)

† One of two voices in the room next to the one in which Sherwood Anderson tells us he is lying announces (in defense of machinery, for an irony): " 'It's a great age we live in. You can't down machinery. I read a book by Mark Twain. He knocked theories cold, I'll tell you what. He made out all life was just a great machine.' " (A *Story Teller's Story*, p. 189.)

Have we not been informed that an ant, afflicted with a
tumor of the brain, will walk in circles, bite his neighbors,
and in every sense behave abnormally? His internal order, or
habit, has been changed—and, *ipso facto*, the external order
has been destroyed. By that little speck of accidental matter,
unforeseeable, gods (perhaps) have been deposed. . . . The
fair page of the world, thus re-set, becomes a brilliant but
meaningless jumble of typographical errors.
And thus . . . it is with me.

John Steinbeck, in the story "The Leader of the People"
(1938), has an elderly man dejectedly tell his impressionable
young grandson that the migration he led westward to the
Pacific long years before essentially consisted of people who
all added up to "one big crawling beast" automatically fulfilling the westering instinct, that " 'We carried life out here
and set it down the way those ants carried eggs. And I was
the leader.' " It is Steinbeck's use of symbols of this kind that
led Edmund Wilson in 1940 to identify as the constant in
Steinbeck's eight volumes "his preoccupation with biology";
to indict him for the tendency "to present human life in animal terms"; not, "as Lawrence or Kipling does, of roman-
tically raising the animals to the stature of human beings, but
rather of assimilating the human beings to animals." *
A century after *Nature*, nature reappeared in William

* "The *paisanos* of *Tortilla Flat* are not really quite human beings: they
are cunning little living dolls that amuse us as we might be amused by
pet guinea-pigs, squirrels or rabbits." And about the conduct of the
Okies in *The Grapes of Wrath*: "It is as if human sentiments and
speeches had been assigned to a flock of lemmings on their way to
throw themselves into the sea." ("The Boys in the Back Room," reprinted in *A Literary Chronicle: 1920–1950*, New York, 1952.)
    But Alfred Kazin disagrees. Conceding Steinbeck's "close interest in
the biology of human affairs," he feels that "Steinbeck knew how to
distinguish, in works like *The Long Valley, In Dubious Battle*, and *The
Grapes of Wrath*, between animal life and social privation," that the
Joads' migration is invested "with a genuinely tragic quality. . . ." (*On
Native Grounds* [1942], New York, 1956, pp. 306, 307.)

Faulkner's *Wild Palms* as "the unmathematical, the over-
fecund, the prime disorderly and illogical and patternless
spendthrift"; God, as "the underlying All-Derisive"; and His
spacious land and firmament on high

were an empty globe, a vacuum, and what wind there was
was not enough to fill it but merely ran back and forth inside
it with no schedule, obeying no laws, unpredictable and coming from and going nowhere, like a drove of bridleless horses
in an empty plain.*

In that novel the tall convict is used only to the peacefulness of nature by the soil's orderly procession of the
seasons. While still in convict camp, he dimly perceives the
power of the river in flood from stories of "the antlike lines
of Negroes carrying sandbags, slipping and crawling up the
steep face of the revetment to hurl their futile ammunition
into the face of a flood. . . ." Finally, when he personally
confronts the violence that is innate in nature, the sound of
the flooding Mississippi leaves him speechless and shrivels
him:

he suddenly became aware that he had been hearing it all the
time, a sound so much beyond all his experience and his powers of assimilation that up to this point he had been as ob-
livious of it as an ant or a flea might be of the sound of the
avalanche on which it rides.

Later, when the alligator hunting has to end because the
levee is to be dynamited, he finds it hard to believe that with
all its "wealth of cosmic violence and disaster to draw from,"
the power (the river) whose victim he had been all these
weeks was lacking in imagination; "that this third time was
to be instigated not by the blind potency of volume and mo-

* Of the spotted horses from Texas in *The Hamlet*, Faulkner writes
that they "broke and rushed with purposeless violence. . . ."

tion but by human direction and hands: that now the cosmic joker,* foiled twice, had stooped in its vindictive concentration to the employing of dynamite." The convict reflects that he "would ever be no more than the water bug upon the surface of the pond, the plumbless and lurking depths of which he would never know. . . ." Even the ample steamboat which protects him and the other passengers, in its motion up the swollen river seems *"like an ant crossing a plate. . . ."*

Can this man possibly be related, however distantly, to the man of the older definition as someone who *mastered* nature? "Nature is thoroughly mediate. It is made to serve. It receives dominion of man as meekly as the ass on which the Saviour rode," Emerson had written in 1836; in this comedy of a century later, Faulkner would write an allegory of human impotence and outrage in the face of nature. Its convict seems to resemble—in his awareness of his microscopic insignificance compared with the "cosmic violence," the "blind potency" of nature—man as Voltaire referred to the race in his "Poem on the Disaster of Lisbon": "Tormented atoms on this pile of mud/Swallowed up by death, the mere playthings of Fate." As the convict looks out over the vast watery expanse in the grey dawn, he senses that peace is merely an interlude during periods of violence:

* In *The Sound and the Fury* (1929), man is spoken of as someone "who is conceived by accident and whose every breath is a fresh cast with dice already loaded against him" and who eventually realizes "that even the despair or remorse or bereavement is not particularly important to the dark diceman. . . ."

This fatalism can shift into determinism. In *The Wild Palms*, again, God becomes "the old primal faithless Manipulator of all the lust and folly and injustice." In *Light in August* (1932), Percy Grimm is no thinking being but an automaton moving with "blind obedience to whatever Player moved him on the Board," to "the Player who moved him for pawn"; as for the "unfailing certitude" that impels Grimm into the kitchen where he murders Joe Christmas, Faulkner tells us that "It was as though he had been merely waiting for the player to move him again. . . ."

it occurred to him that its present condition was no phenomenon of a decade, but that the intervening years during
which it consented to bear upon its placid and sleepy bosom
the frail mechanicals of man's clumsy contriving was the
phenomenon and this the norm and the River was now doing
what it liked to do, had waited patiently the ten years in
order to do, as a mule will work for you ten years for the
privilege of kicking you once.

This is precisely how William James's mind had reacted to
the fact of the San Francisco earthquake, which had shaken
his bedroom as a terrier would shake a rat:

It was to my mind absolutely an entity that had been
waiting all this time holding back its activity, but at last saying "Now *go* it," and it was impossible not to conceive it as
animated by a will, so vicious was the temper displayed.[42]

"Seems like when they get started they don't leave a guy
nothing," the boy narrator reflects at the end of Ernest
Hemingway's "My Old Man." This plural is, by extension,
the inscrutable deity borrowed from the Greeks, but now for
the purpose of presiding over no heroic struggles. At the end
of A *Farewell to Arms* Catherine's baby has been strangled
before birth, even; Catherine herself is being killed equally
capriciously. Her lover reflects: "That was what you did. You
died. You did not know what it was about. You never had
time to learn. They threw you in and told you the rules and
the first time they caught you off base they killed you. Or
they killed you gratuitously like Aymo." * Now this "they"

* This despair had come into Hemingway's fiction since *The Sun Also
Rises* of only three years before. There his hero is a hard-working man
who goes to church now and then and prays and whose faith, delicate
though it is, lifts him above the sordid or aimless ways of his companions. Jake Barnes thinks: "Perhaps as you went along you did learn
something. I did not care what it was all about. All I wanted to know
was how to live in it. Maybe if you found out how to live in it you

has changed markedly since Homer's day—when, for example, Menelaus had told Telemachus, explaining his long stay in Egypt, that "I had been anxious for some time to get home, but the gods kept me dawdling there, for I had omitted to make them the correct offerings, and they never allow one to forget the rules." In those days of giants in the earth there were also gods in the sky, and a reason for their actions. And even as late as the middle of the last century Henry Thoreau could voice his utter exasperation at the "world's raffle" that was the California gold rush. To make of life merely a matter of chance was nothing short of blasphemous: "Even Mahomet knew that God did not make this world in jest. . . . Did God direct us so to get our living, digging where we never planted—and He would, perchance, reward us with lumps of gold?" [43] But when there is no longer any design, there is only chance; if no logical cause and effect, then only cosmic irony. In the very next breath Frederic Henry treats us to a reminiscence of long ago and far away:

Once in camp I put a log on top of the fire and it was full of ants. As it commenced to burn, the ants swarmed out and went first toward the centre where the fire was; then turned back and ran toward the end. When there were enough on the end they fell off into the fire. Some got out, their bodies burnt and flattened, and went off not knowing where they were going. But most of them went toward the fire and then back toward the end and swarmed on the cool end and finally fell off into the fire. I remember thinking at the time that it was the end of the world and a splendid chance to be a mes-

---

learned from that what it was all about." (Ch. XIV.) And in the advice he gives to Brett at the bullfight about watching the bull and the picador rather than the goring of his horse lurks a philosophical idea equally existential, or at least stoic: "I . . . got her to watching . . . so that she saw what it was all about, so that it became more something that was going on with a definite end, and less of a spectacle with unexplained horrors." (Ch. XV.)

siah and lift the log off the fire and throw it out where the
ants could get off onto the ground. But I did not do anything
but throw a tin cup of water on the log, so that I would have
the cup empty to put whiskey in it before I added water to
it. I think the cup of water on the burning log only steamed
the ants.

The connection between this anecdote and what precedes
seems clear: for *I* substitute *the inscrutable powers that be*;
for *ants*, substitute *the human race.** *Walden* had closed
with its human observer musing at "the insect crawling amid
the pine needles on the forest floor, and endeavoring to conceal itself from my sight": "reminded of the greater Benefactor and Intelligence that stands over me the human insect," Henry Thoreau the transcendentalist wondered why
the insect persisted in hiding "from me, who might, perhaps,
be its benefactor, and impart to its race some cheering information. . . ." Ernest Hemingway the naturalist closes *A
Farewell to Arms* with the great Malefactor and Indifference
standing, in turn, over the human insect, and imparting to its
uncomprehending race only the dismal information that its
frenzied struggles are useless.†

* In Robert Frost's "Range-Finding" (*Mountain Interval*, 1916) a
bullet creates a miniature havoc in nature before it finds its human
target. Part of this harm it does is to a spider web, which it shakes
dry. The impact makes the spider come running, thinking he has a
fly; when he discovers that there is nothing there, he retreats sullenly.
Like Hemingway's ants, he has mistaken a by-blow of indifferent nature
for a boon.

† Malcolm Cowley has written some notes for a continuation of this relationship in his "Naturalism: No Teacup Tragedies." In Nelson Algren's
The Man With the Golden Arm, he writes, the roach that falls into
the slop bucket in Frankie and Sparrow's cell and that Frankie decides
to rescue only after he finds that it is drowned "is the familiar animal
symbol that is introduced at the beginning of so many naturalistic
novels; one remembers the land turtle in *The Grapes of Wrath*, crawling
obstinately to no destination, just as the Joad family would crawl westward on the highway; and one remembers the cornered rat that Bigger

EPILOGUE

Hemingway's Frederic Henry, who has told Count Greffi that he doesn't know about the soul, who is *croyant* only at night (when he can touch the object of his faith in bed?), is of a generation that has looked too wearily and knowingly at the forest to find benign correspondences there. The distinction between "Law for Man and law for thing" that Emerson had insisted on is meaning much less by 1929: only *things* are "lovely" now: a kind of wine, of gunstock. . . . He wasn't made to think, Frederic tells us; and lest we infer from this the transcendentalist Thoreau's correlative, "I wish I was as wise as I was the day I was born," or Emerson's "We are wiser than we know," Frederic quickly explains that what he *was* made for was to "[e]at and drink and sleep with Catherine." (Ch. 32.)

And so after all the centuries we are back armed only with "the fine hammered steel of woe" that, Herman Melville told Hawthorne, Solomon's *Ecclesiastes* was for him.

I was always embarrassed by the words sacred, glorious, and sacrifice and the expression in vain. We had heard them . . . and had read them . . . now for a long time, and I had seen nothing sacred, and the things that were glorious had no glory and the sacrifices were like the stockyards at Chicago if nothing was done with the meat except to bury it. (Ch. 27.)*

Thomas killed in the first chapter of *Native Son*, as Bigger himself would be killed at the end of the story. This time, however, the symbol is a mixture of the grotesque and the absurd, with a hint that the author feels a wry affection for his characters and even for the roach." (*The Literary Situation*, New York [1954], 1958, p. 89.)

* "Died some, pro patria,
    non 'dulce' not 'et decor' . . .
came home . . . to many deceits
home to old lies and new infamy. . . ." (Ezra Pound, "Hugh Selwyn
    Mauberley")

This is Hemingway's modern wording of the Preacher's "Who knoweth the spirit of man that goeth upward, and the spirit of the beast that goeth downward to the earth?" And the denial by them both of Christ's affirmation: "That which is born of the flesh is flesh; and that which is born of the spirit is spirit." (*John* 3:6) And for his weary promenade of broken, mutilated, and sodden wistfuls in his earlier novel Hemingway had borrowed a title from the Preacher himself: if the sun also rises, it is only to set in order to rise again. What did this leave to man?

Go thy way, eat thy bread with joy, and drink thy wine with a merry heart; for God now accepteth thy works. . . .
    Fear God, and keep his commandments; for this is the whole duty of man.

But what if even Solomon, in whom Melville could "read . . . every time deeper and deeper and unspeakable meaning," who was "the truest man who ever spoke"—if even *he* "a little *managed* the truth with a view to popular conservatism . . . ," then what unspeakable woe could he have been withholding from his generation? That if *this* was God, His Commandments were not worth the keeping? If so, what *then* was left to man-beast?
    There was only one answer that modern man could live with, even if a variety of ways of phrasing it. Charles Darwin's, in 1871, for one. In "The Moral Sense" section of *The Descent of Man* he had predicted that

as love, sympathy and self-command become strengthened by habit, . . . so that man can value justly the judgments of his fellows, he will feel himself impelled, apart from any transitory pleasure or pain, to certain lines of conduct. He might then declare . . . I am the supreme judge of my own conduct, and in the words of Kant, I will not in my own person violate the dignity of humanity.

And as though by way of confirmation, we have the belief that Bertrand Russell voiced in "A Free Man's Worship" (1903):

When, without the bitterness of impotent rebellion, we have learnt both to resign ourselves to the outward rule of Fate and to recognise that the non-human world is unworthy of our worship, it becomes possible at last so to transform and refashion the unconscious universe, so to transmute it in the crucible of imagination, that a new image of shining gold replaces the old idol of clay.

The last is American, for all that it is an English flower blossoming in a mud puddle in Madrid. In a godless universe, Lady Brett Ashley, Ernest Hemingway's wanton dipsomaniac, tells the mutilated Jake Barnes in 1926, it might please *man*, at least, to maintain a distinction between himself and the beast: " 'It's sort of what we have instead of God.' "

This " 'deciding not to be a bitch,' " this defiance of the modern deterministic assumption that "Men were simply insects of the most insignificant sort being driven by a tyrannical power along paths which had nothing to do with their own wills," that nature did not care whether humans "were faithful and monogamous or unfaithful and as promiscuous as guinea pigs" *—this was true renunciation, throwing off of the tyranny of the will as Schopenhauer had advocated, was it not? And if far short of a reaffirmation of "the bond of

*Quoted from a 1930 Louis Bromfield novel, to describe the beliefs of Haeckel and other scientists who "based the mysteries of thought on chemistry and physical components of the body." (Harry Hartwick, *The Foreground of American Fiction*, p. 8.)

love which Nature makes" of Dante's medieval creed, still it was a display of the modern ant's mighty heart and resoluteness sufficient to have won the endorsement of those transcendental ancestors of ours, Ralph Waldo Emerson and Henry David Thoreau, after all.

The devil is white

I discerned . . . beyond the picture
Through the picture, a something white, uncertain,
Something more of the depths—and then I lost it.
. . . . What was that whiteness?
Truth? A pebble of quartz?

Robert Frost, "For Once, Then, Something"

■

Just as there has always been a symbolism of flowers in literature (a brief discourse on which we get from the mad
Ophelia), so there has been one of colors themselves. While
certain color associations are persistent and predictable,
others are surprising; and if most often they are both, it may
be because, like lovers, colors seem to speak in two voices at
the same time.

Green, for example, as far back as the fourteenth century, symbolized not only coolness and verdure (and hope) [1] but also the devil in disguise, as a mimicry, for that oldest of all hunters in green forests.[2] And although Goethe found in green only "a distinctly grateful impression" ("The beholder has neither the wish nor the power to imagine a state beyond it") and categorically divides colors into those on the "plus" side (in that "the feelings they excite are quick, lively, aspiring") and those on the "minus" side (in that they produce "a restless, susceptible, anxious expression")—still, he conceded the possibility of qualified or even opposing reaction. By only a "slight and scarcely perceptible change," Goethe found, the effect on the spirit of yellow, that "colour of honour and joy" is "reversed to that of ignominy and aversion"; conversely, although in its darker hues the color red "conveys an impression of gravity and dignity," in its lighter tints its impression is one "of grace and attractiveness": "and thus the dignity of age and the amiableness of youth may adorn itself with degrees of the same hue." [3]

Now this same enigmatic ability of yet another color to evoke two conflicting feelings had been noted early and in a facetious context by Rabelais. He invests Gargantua with the colors of blue and white, the white expressing "joy, pleasure, delight, and rejoicing"; then he extends his discourse on "this symbolic use of colors" into the next chapter, finding data in pagan and Biblical times, yet introducing—even if only to refute it—the ancient argument that white also has a mysteriously terrifying effect as well: ". . . 'why does a lion, whose roar terrifies all animals, fear and respect only the white rooster?' " (Book One, Chs. 9, 10.)

Succeeding ages have not found an answer to this "insoluble" problem as jubilantly satisfying as Rabelais'. Indeed, in the past century there has been a gradual yielding in importance of the symbolic meaning of white to the rare meaning that had puzzled that forgotten contemporary of Marcus

Aurelius': increasingly white appears in the literature of
western man as the color of terror (at God's creation) and
despair (of His providence). In the Old Testament, "the
Ancient of days did sit, whose garment was white as snow,
and the hair of his head like the pure wool . . ." (*Daniel,*
Ch. 7); and that numberless multitude "clothed with white
robes, and palms in their hands," St. John tells one of the
elders, "are they which came out of great tribulation, and
have washed their robes, and made them white in the blood
of the Lamb" (*Revelation,* Ch. 7). But in the modern literary
testament, this purity and omnipotence have been trans-
ferred to the vision of His ancient foe. Indeed, in recent
years it would seem that despite our intellectual sophistica-
tion, the devil has not so much disappeared as he has merely
changed color. This trend has apparently also been one from
faith to a fatalistic or deterministic view of the universe.

It has not been a universal movement, to be sure—one that
the literary historian's eye can see wherever it turns; nor an
undeviating one even where it can be seen. One of our most
convincing exhibits will be a pursuit into the heart of Whiteness that is essentially a pursuit of Nothingness (*Moby-Dick*),
yet another exhibit as inadmissible as it is convincing would
be the pursuit of Nothingness that takes us into a *Heart of
Darkness.* In Wordsworth's boyhood moonlight boatride, the
huge, grim mountain peak that seemed to pursue him menac-
ingly, that oppressed him for many days afterwards, as he
tells us in Book One of *The Prelude,* "with a dim and undetermined sense/Of unknown modes of being" was a black
one; yet the phantom is white that follows Bigger Thomas so
frighteningly along the snow-covered rooftops as he flees
across them at the close of *Native Son.* It would be possible
to dwell both on an entire chapter ("Snow") in Thomas
Mann's *The Magic Mountain* that is a philosophical rhap-
sody-meditation about the impersonal deadliness, the
"deathly silence of the snows," and on a long passage about

the coffin-like quality of the black gondola in the same author's "Death in Venice." *

In truth, no matter where in literature we look, we can find authors clothing the kindred spirits of death, of the devil, of despair at evil in the universe and in man, with their traditional color—black. We may remember the early example of Chaucer's lovelorn Dorigen despairing of her dear Arveragus's safe return by sea, bitterly contemplating the grim black rocks of the Brittany coast as the handiwork, not of God, but of the devil, seeming as they do to her "rather a foul confusion/Of werk, than any fair creacioun." Or Shakespeare, savagely calling the faithless love of his sonnets "as black as hell, as dark as night." Or possibly even the depositions of the Salem villagers, in this country in the dreadful summer of 1692, as to the various appearances of The Black Man and his book.[4] But we would also find Herman Melville, only a generation before Conrad, singling out Shakespeare's "power of blackness" and insisting that "no writer has ever wielded this terrific thought with greater terror" than Hawthorne.[5] Very shortly Melville would embody this very power in the Babo of "Benito Cereno" (1855). On the simple mind of Captain Delano, a man "not liable . . . to indulge in personal alarms, any way involving the imputation of malign evil in man," the totality of the Negro's sinisterness never really registers; Delano sees "the benign aspect of Nature" up to the moment Babo's deviltry forces itself on his persistently disbelieving geniality, and he makes no understanding comment on Don Benito's final confession. But

---

* It is even possible to find both in the same piece. In Tennessee Williams's *Suddenly Last Summer* (1959) there is a precise matching of black and white as the colors of the two fatal factors in Sebastian's death. There is the blackness of the ravening humans ("black plucked little birds," "featherless little black sparrows") and the merciless whiteness of the day: "It looked as if . . . a huge white bone had caught on fire in the sky and blazed so bright it was white and turned the sky and everything under the sky white with it!"

Don Benito is so overwhelmed by "the negro" that he faints
when forced to look on Babo at the trial. As the story ends,
although Babo is executed for his crimes, his head, "that
hive of subtlety," fixed on a pole in the public square, confronts the tombs of his two white victims "unabashed." As
late as the turn of this century the writer in America could
color the deterministic silence black: as Laura Jadwin, "as-
sailed" at the end of Frank Norris's *The Pit* by "vague dark
perplexities, questionings as to the elemental forces," drives
by the Board of Trade Building—that "monstrous sphinx
with blind eyes"—at night, it rears "a black and formidable
facade against the blur of the sky behind it." And even the
modern poet Robert Frost uses what Melville calls "this
mystical blackness" to describe a variety of aspects of evil,
whether aboriginal mental void (as in "Mending Wall") or
extinction (as in "Stopping By Woods") or even horror (as
in "Design").*

Moreover, although it will shortly be seen that these last
three writers have contributed notably to the decline of the
traditional identification of white with purity (thus as black's
exact opposite, as the celestial radiance of the immortality
that ages of belief knew to follow death), still this concept
has always functioned in American literature. In *A Discourse
on Witchcraft* we find Cotton Mather writing that "There
is mention of creatures that they call *White witches*, who
do only Good Turns for their Neighbors," then rejecting the
phrase as a contradiction in terms: "I suspect that there are
none of that sort. . . ." To him white would without question always be the color of faith. Thus it had been with
Dante's *Purgatorio* (Canto 29) or the *Paradiso*, where the
holy church itself is a white rose (Canto 31). Or in Schiller's
Jungfrau von Orleans, where Joan of Arc had spoken:

* And the novelist Sinclair Lewis, attacking "the new Humanism" in his
1930 Nobel Prize Address, called it "a doctrine of the blackest reaction . . . , [a] doctrine of death. . . ."

Der Himmel ist für Frankreich. Seine Engel
Du siehst sie nicht, sie fechten für die König,
Sie alle sind mit Lilien geschmückt,
Lichtweis wie diese Fahn ist unsre Sache,
Die reine Jungfrau ist ihr keusches Sinnbild. (II, x, 1767–1771.)

[Heaven is for France. Her angels you do not see, but they
are fighting for the King; they are all adorned with lilies; radiant with light, like this banner of ours, is our cause; the pure
Maid is its symbol of virginal purity.] [6]

Or in Jonathan Edwards. Of his *Images, or Shadows of Divine Things*, Professor Harry Levin has written that "Since
holiness comprehends all the other virtues, it is typified by
white, which is also the type of purity because it signifies
mothers' milk and childish innocence." [7] Or in "Adonais,"
where Shelley had written that "Life, like a dome of many-
colored glass,/Stains the white radiance of Eternity."

Yet white has symbolized these things even to the writers
of the Lost Generation. In William Faulkner's "A Rose for
Emily" (1931), Emily Grierson as a maiden is "a slender
figure in white," but in her sinister aspect (of middle and old
age), "a small, fat woman in black." In *The Great Gatsby*,
Daisy and Jordan Baker wear white to signify an unconscious
desire to dissociate themselves from the sordidness of their
careless, mean lives; Daisy alludes to her beautiful white girl-
hood; and Gatsby himself (he who lives in the halcyon, the
uncontaminated of five years ago) courts her in a cream-
colored car. Moreover, even Fitzgerald's more famous contemporary, Ernest Hemingway, as deterministic a writer as
Fitzgerald is not, tends to associate white with pleasant or
even inspiring thoughts.* In *A Farewell to Arms*, Frederic
Henry tells why he had wanted to go to Abruzzi: "I had
gone to no place where the roads were frozen and hard as

* And death, or despair, with black. See discussion of "A Clean, Well-
Lighted Place" in Chapter Four, below.

iron, where it was clear cold and dry and the snow was dry and powdery and hare-tracks in the snow . . . and there was good hunting" (Ch. 3); and throughout Book Five of the novel it is the exhilarating effect of the snow that intermittently provides the only spiritual warmth as the final mortal griefs loom.* In "The Snows of Kilimanjaro" the title surely refers to God, to purity, and to vitality. This last emerges from the delirious revery of a man whose body is atrophying in quite an opposite atmosphere (the African plains): the times he recalls with most satisfaction often are winter times. In fact, there is a long snow-oriented revery in which snow appears only incidentally as the color of death (in the sense of exposure), but several times as generating a series of recollections, all invigorating. Harry remembers "the snow as smooth to see as cake frosting and as light as powder and . . . the noiseless rush the speed made as you dropped down like a bird . . . [A]nd then he remembered . . . the fast-slipping rush of running powder-snow on crust, singing 'Hi! Ho! said Rolly!' as you ran down the last stretch to the steep drop . . ." †

These feelings almost match Thomas Wolfe's in *Of Time and the River* (1935). For him one of the most invigorating of the "thousand lights and weathers" of this nation is winter's whiteness. America is

* Like Hemingway, a mid-westerner, Fitzgerald identified snow with health and cheer. In "Babylon Revisited," in one of the finest metaphors of our literature, he recalls the reckless, prodigal Twenties, "—The men who locked their wives out in the snow, because the snow of twenty-nine wasn't *real* snow. If you didn't want it to be snow, you just paid some money." What *real* snow was, he had had Nick Carraway recall at the end of *The Great Gatsby:* "When we pulled out into the winter night and the real snow, our snow, began to stretch out beside us and twinkle against the windows, and the dim lights of small Wisconsin stations moved by, a sharp wild brace came suddenly into the air."

† Hemingway considerably expands his recollection of this invigorating Austrian experience in the posthumous autobiographical fragment *A Moveable Feast*, New York, 1964.

the place of the wild and exultant winter's morning and the
wind, with the powdery snow . . . the branches of the spruce
and hemlock piled with snow; it is the place where the Fall
River boats are tethered to the wharf, and the wild gray snow
of furious, secret, and storm-whited morning whips across
them . . . the place . . . of lone hunters in the frosty
thickets. . . .

Other examples of the use of whiteness as a symbol for
idealistic thinking mark our literature at every step between
these dates. We are not surprised to find it characterizing
the writers of New England. We have seen that when for his
Journal notation that "the best thought" that man is capable
of is not sombre or gloomy, Henry Thoreau needed a metaphor for the purity and serenity of that thought, he wrote
"The universe lies outspread in floods of white light to it."
The Thoreau who can speak (in the "Solitude" chapter of
Walden) of the "indescribable innocence and beneficence of
Nature—of sun and wind and rain, of summer and winter,"
predictably finds that

It is a surprising and memorable, as well as valuable experience, to be lost in the woods any time. Often in a snow-storm,
even by day, one will come out upon a well-known road and
yet find it impossible to tell which way leads to the village.
Though he knows that he has travelled it a thousand times,
he cannot recognize a feature of it, but it is as strange to him
as if it were a road in Siberia . . . Every man has to learn
the points of compass again as often as he awakes, whether
from sleep or any abstraction. Not till we are lost, in other
words not till we have lost the world, do we begin to find
ourselves, and realize where we are and the infinite extent of
our relations.

If the phrasing of that last sentence borrows a rhetorical
effect from its variation on Holy Writ, it is not at all by
chance, for elsewhere Thoreau gives testimony to the holiness

of nature which he sees mutely manifested in its great whiteness. "Is there no religion for the temperate and frigid
zones?" he asks in "A Winter Walk": "We know of no
Scripture which records the pure benignity of the gods on a
New England winter night. Their praises have never been
sung, only their wrath deprecated."

Similarly, the Emerson of "The American Scholar" who
believed that "Nature is the opposite of the soul, answering
it part for part. . . . Its beauty is the beauty of his own
mind. Its laws are the laws of his own mind"—this Emerson
looks upon the snow as an equally blessed phenomenon. In
"The Snow-Storm" he calls the snow a "fierce artificer"; it
may be myriad-handed, wild, fanciful, savage, and mocking,
yet more than all else it is an artist whose natural effects are
striking enough to make human art gape in admiration. And
this, again, is essentially the snow of Whittier's "Snow-
Bound"—a phenomenon of "starry flake and pellicle" creating a "glistening wonder," "marvellous shapes," and fur-
nishing a whiteness that though violent is one that man
easily (and cozily) protects himself against by the effort of his
own hands; for "Snow-Bound" is consistently the testament
of an unquestioning faith in a God who watches the fall of
every sparrow. In Emily Dickinson, as we shall see, white
calls forth more than a single response. Certainly she could
think, in looking at children's graves, of "Sparrows unnoticed
by the Father/Lambs for whom time had not a fold"; yet
in most instances with her white is the white of purity and
heavenliness.* Her world is administered by God, and He
is in His heaven, firmly located in her mind's geography "as if
the chart were given." It contains angels, and when she
visualizes them in "To Fight Aloud Is Very Brave" it is as
"with even feet/And uniforms of snow."

Even with Hawthorne, no great variation is observed from

* When she considers it at all. In her color poem "Nature rarer uses
yellow," we note, she cites yellow, blue, and red only.

this way of thinking of white. It is true that the view (in Ch. V of *The Blithedale Romance*) of the surrounding countryside that the feverish Coverdale has from his cold bedroom window during his first night at Blithedale is a chilling one ("the moon was shining on the snowy landscape, which looked like a lifeless copy of the world in marble"), but we remember his physical condition. And in any event, the vision quickly is forgotten, steadfast as Hawthorne's faith was. In *The House of the Seven Gables* he pauses to reflect that

Life is made up of marble and mud. And, without all the deeper trust in a comprehensive sympathy above us, we might hence be led to suspect the insult of a sneer, as well as an immitigable frown, on the iron countenance of fate. What is called poetic insight is the gift of discerning, in this sphere of strangely mingled elements, the beauty and the majesty which are compelled to assume a garb so sordid.*

This beauty and majesty are exemplified in the story itself. It is the white roses with which Phoebe Pyncheon decorates her gloomy, history-crammed bedroom that by subtle suggestion transform it into a maiden's bedroom again—that is, purify it, associate it with virginity. And, of course, there is the excessive symbolic employment of white in *The Marble Faun*, where Hilda's white doves are meant to represent her

---

* Chapter II. In *The Blithedale Romance* he again entertains the idea of the indifference of a deterministic universe only to reject it. Even if nature is as "well pleased" with the "ranker vegetation" that grew from Zenobia's corpse as it was with "all the beauty" of Zenobia alive, this in no way weakens his "deeper trust" in God's providence: "It is because the spirit is inestimable that the lifeless body is so little valued." (Ch. XXVIII.)

Similarly, "Snow-Flakes" exactly transposes each minor note into a major. The snowy gloom outside is conducive to inner warmth, and what is an occasional icy corpse to the "unyielding strength of character" that snow nourishes in the rest of us?

purity and at the close of which Kenyon speaks of her "white wisdom . . . as a celestial garment."

Numerous other examples can be cited. In Longfellow's "Cross of Snow" the cross is a whiteness of immortality and of the beloved dead wife of whom the poet says "soul more white never through martyrdom of fire was led to its repose." In Bret Harte's story of 1869, the outcasts of Poker Flat voice no complaint against the snow that finally reaches twenty feet in depth; and although it causes their deaths, it emerges as a benevolent agent of the universe: "Feathery drifts of snow . . . settled about them as they slept. . . . [A]ll human stain, all trace of earthly travail, was hidden beneath the spotless mantle mercifully flung from above." The snow in James R. Lowell's "The First Snow-Fall" covers not the sinner but the innocent, yet it too glorifies God: in this melodic, nostalgic, and reverent pastoral, the falling flakes cloak evergreen in ermine and empearl the scrawny elm twig, gently blanketing the grave where the poet's daughter lies, "healing and hiding" it. To her questioning sister, Lowell replies that the snow is the work of "the good All-father," as inevitable and inscrutable, we infer, as the death of the child whose burial it recalls.

And for all the naturalistic symbolism of his fiction, in his poetry Stephen Crane uses white like a traditionalist. In "Walking in the Sky," the "radiant form" is presumably God (and the man in strange black garb, accordingly, the devil). In "Upon the Road of My Life" the "many fair creatures, /Clothed all in white, and radiant" are good deeds (even if Crane introduces them to unmask them). Then there is his love poetry. "Should the Wide World Roll Away," Crane declares, he would need only his beloved and her "white arms" for support. And, looking back at that love in "I Wonder if Sometimes in the Dusk," he sees it as "A supernal dream,/White, white, white with many suns."

Yet during the middle of the century this faith was weakening, eroding. " 'Our Wilderness is the wide World in an Atheistic Century,' " Teufelsdroeckh lamented. For these were the years of the century's Everlasting No, and Carlyle looking at his Professor is looking at himself and a great number of his contemporaries: "We behold him, through those dim years, in a state of crisis, of transition," in "mad Pilgrimings," in "aimless Discontinuity," and in "mad Fermentation." We are furnished the very words of the Professor's deterministic confession:

To me the Universe was all void of life, of Purpose, of Volition, even of Hostility: it was one huge, dead, immeasurable Steam-engine, rolling on, in its dead indifference, to grind me limb from limb. . . . Why was the Living banished thither companionless, conscious? Why, if there is no Devil; nay, unless the Devil is your God? [8]

That, at any rate, was the direction in which the mid-1800's were travelling, to judge from the literary record. Certainly, we can now detect a mixture of both faith and doubt in the same writer. The snow of Longfellow's "Snow-Flakes" for once is not raging or violent, yet is the more upsetting for its calm. Here whiteness expresses actual despair, whether in the white face of the human "troubled heart" or the "secret of despair"

Long in its cloudy bosom hoarded,
  Now whispered and revealed
  To wood and field.

Of Emily Dickinson's metaphor, "Death is the other way—/ It is the White Exploit," Professor Charles Anderson is moved to comment: "She never found a better image for its

ambiguity than this, man's bold adventure into blankness.
Death or immortality?" [9] But the ambiguity that charac-
terizes Dickinson's image of death vanishes and the whiteness
at least once emerges as basically nothing less than the color
of a deterministic universe. For she had looked at evil bare,*
had risen early enough to catch nature without her diadem:

Apparently with no surprise
To any happy flower,
The frost beheads it at its play
In accidental power.

The blond assassin passes on,
The sun proceeds unmoved
To measure off another day
For an approving God.

Carlyle might, like Dante long before him, emerge from
that *selva oscura*, might like his admirer Emerson fling back
his Everlasting Yea and exult that " 'The Universe is not
dead and demoniacal, a charnel-house with spectres; but
godlike and my Father's!' " Increasingly, however, it begins
to seem that our God may no longer be a mighty fortress
against his infernal antagonist. How pronounced becomes
the wavering of faith, the tendency to associate whiteness
with an anti-religious concept of the universe; and, whether
by statement or implication, with man as a helpless creature
in a fierce world whose events are determined by forces beyond his control, and possibly without direction.

* Although she knew and dealt cordially with "several of nature's
people," she tells us in "The Snake," this was one that caused "a
tighter breathing/And zero at the bone." And there are times when she
is incapable of the faith in God that we have quoted earlier:

> Faith is a fine invention
> For gentlemen who see;
> But microscopes are prudent
> In an emergency!

This tendency, which has never been absent from our literature, would seem to go back at least as far as Edgar Allan Poe. Modern criticism of the "horrific" with which *The Narrative of Arthur Gordon Pym* ends has called attention to the significance of this section from a metaphysical point of view. For example, Professor Edward Davidson calls *Pym* "a study of emerging consciousness," the "growth of the knowing and thinking self"; it demonstrates, he believes, that men "are maddened . . . because the invisible spheres themselves are formed in madness and insanity," and that its "chartless voyage" is *away* from "an assumption that man lives by law and design," and "toward simplicity and opaqueness"—to a white "terror [that] is the way to a knowledge of the world's primal unity." [10] And Professor Charles O'Donnell goes into an analysis of the use in *Pym* of white (Poe's "omni-color") as "the perfect condition" of the universe: "Whiteness or light is therefore associated in the novel with death,* with the . . . submitting to . . . the terrifying change to a bodiless condition of unity with the larger design." [11] But we need not limit ourselves to *Pym*. With Poe whiteness conveys terror, whether aesthetically or metaphysically. Commenting on Roderick Usher's paintings, the narrator cites as "one of the phantasmagoric conceptions" a picture of a long white tunnel with no outlets which Usher had bathed with "a flood of intense rays . . . in a ghastly and inappropriate splendour." Similarly, in the first paragraph of "The Pit and the Pendulum" the seven white candles on the

---

* Professor Levin disagrees: ". . . the milky water is more redolent of birth than of death; and the opening in the earth may seem to be a regression wombward." As for the gigantic protector, "clad all in white," Professor Levin reminds us that "Poe deliberately leaves the sexless image blank, and reverts to the problem of reading the earthwork inscriptions. The result is a *non sequitur*, as evaluated by Henry James in his preface to *The Altar of the Dead*. . . . The snowy apparition, whatever it betokens, performs the function of balking further inquiry. . . ." (*The Power of Blackness*, pp. 123, 125.)

table of the Inquisition tribunal appall and almost nauseate
the condemned narrator.* But the most telling is the evidence of "Berenice." It will be recalled that it is the whiteness of Berenice's teeth (as his mind separates them from
the spiritual being of which they are a part) on which the attention of the monomaniacal narrator fastens. . . . Now
Thoreau had been capable of recognizing "the animal in us,"
too. Indeed, he tells us (in "Higher Laws"), apropos his
finding "the lower jaw of a hog, with white and sound teeth
and tusks, which suggested that there was an animal health
and vigor distinct from the spiritual," that just as the hog
"succeeded by other means than temperance and purity," so
the animal in us "may enjoy a certain health of its own"; that
is, that "we may be well yet not pure," just as even in health
we have worms in our bodies. But Poe's morbid narrator is
capable of no such idealistic detachment. Musing too long on
"the alteration" in Berenice's teeth, he confesses that "I
shuddered as I assigned to them in imagination a sensitive
and sentient power, and even when unassisted by the lips, a
capability of moral expression." Thus does he divest God of
any identity other than as a creator of force.†

But, as Professor Levin has written, "the demonstration
that blackness and whiteness are not antithetical but com-
plementary—that is another story, not Poe's but Melville's." ‡

* On the other hand, there is a deliberate employment of black to convey the customary terror associated with darkness: "The blackness of
eternal night encompassed" the narrator; when the candles went out,
nothing but the "blackness of darkness supervened"; and as he went
groping around the dungeon, "all was blackness and vacancy."

† Poe's musing echoes Blake's question (in "The Tyger"), "Did he who
made the lamb make thee?" just as it anticipates Melville's own musing
on the shark. Yet Poe wrote no counterpart to Blake's pious "Mock On,
Mock on."

‡ *The Power of Blackness*, p. 123. "The coloration of Poe's tales is pre-
determined by the eidolon named Night who reigns supreme over his
poetry. Statistical investigation has shown what the common reader

What may we predict about a man who, in a palpable hit at
the first article of belief in the Nicene Creed (and St.
Augustine) insists that "Though in many of its aspects this
visible world seems formed in love, the invisible spheres were
formed in fright"? Who speaks of life as "a vast practical
joke"; says of the Pequod's crew that "we . . . blindly
plunged like fate into the lone Atlantic"; and from a contemplation of Pip's fate concludes that "man's insanity is
heaven's sense; and wandering from all mortal reason, man
comes at last to that celestial thought, which, to reason, is
absurd and frantic; and weal or woe, feels then uncompro-
mised, indifferent as his God"? The answer is in the "Whiteness of the Whale" chapter of *Moby-Dick*, the book baptized,
it will be recalled, *in nomine d-----*. Here (in a passage borrowed largely from Rabelais, as it happens) he speaks of a
"dumb blankness, full of meaning, in a wide landscape of
snows—a colorless all-color of atheism from which we
shrink." Shakespeare, whose recent rediscovery by Melville
had excited him (particularly his "blackness," his "occasional
flashings-forth of the intuitive Truth . . . ; those short, quick
probings at the very axis of reality," his crafty way of insinu-
ating "the things which we feel to be so terrifically true that
it were all but madness . . . to utter, or even hint of
them"),[12] had permitted the basically pious Hamlet a memorable probing of this kind in the graveyard:

"Now get you to my lady's chamber, and tell her, let her
paint an inch thick, to this favour she must come; make her

---

might expect: that blackness predominates, equalled—and slightly
eclipsed—by whiteness, when the latter is taken together with gray-
ness." (*Loc. cit.*, p. 120.) Certainly the narrator in "Ms. Found in a
Bottle" is as terrified by the blackness of the southern waters in the
eternal night ("the swelling of the black stupendous seas became more
dismally appalling") as he is by the "stupendous ramparts of ice, towering away into the desolate sky, and looking like the walls of the universe" that eventually engulf the ship.

laugh at that. Prithee, Horatio, . . . Dost thou think Alexander looked o' this fashion i' the earth? . . . And smelt so? pah!"

Now Melville gives Ishmael these very lines:

. . . the butterfly cheeks of young girls . . . are but subtile deceits, not actually inherent in substances, but only laid on from without; so that all deified Nature absolutely paints like the harlot, whose allurements cover nothing but the charnel-house within. . . .*

Melville follows Ahab's atheistic speech in "The Symphony" chapter with the comment that "blanched to a corpse's hue with despair, the Mate had stolen away." We remember Ishmael's inability to decide why white "appeals with such power to the soul; and more strange and far more portentous —why . . . it is at once the most meaning symbol of spiritual things, nay, the very veil of the Christian's Deity; and yet should be as it is, the intensifying agent in things the most appalling to mankind." [13] We should remember too that other great shock to Ishmael's soul, the giant white squid:

A vast pulpy mass, furlongs in length and breadth, of a glancing cream-color, lay floating on the water, innumerable long

---

* "The import of this controversial and disturbing image is fully revealed . . . in . . . The Piazza. . . . 'I could not bear to look upon a Chinese creeper of my adoption, and which, to my delight, climbing a post of the piazza, had burst out in starry bloom, but now, if you removed the leaves a little, showed millions of strange, cankerous worms, which feeding upon those blossoms, so shared their blessed hue, as to make them unblessed evermore.' This Chinese creeper . . . stands for this same deified, painted Nature visibly beautiful, invisibly repulsive." (James R. Baird, *Ishmael*, Baltimore, 1956, p. 259.)

Compare Hawthorne's characteristic notes of August 13, 1842: of the white water lilies he gathers, some were "partially worm-eaten or blighted . . . others as fair as Nature's own idea. . . .'"

arms radiating from its centre, and curling and twisting like a
nest of anacondas, as if blindly to clutch at any hapless object
within reach. No perceptible face or front did it have; no conceivable token of either sensation or instinct; but undulated
there on the billows, an unearthly, formless, chance-like apparition of life.*

Then there is the carcass of the slaughtered whale dumped
astern in "The Funeral" chapter. Its "peeled white body . . .
flashes like a marble sepulchre. . . . The vast white headless
phantom floats further and further from the ship. . . . For
hours and hours . . . that hideous sight is seen," and sharply
outlined against the cloudless blue of the sky, "that great
mass of death floats on and on. . . ."

Living too soon for the spread of the scientific conclusions
that would corrode the revelations of Scripture,† and completing almost his lifetime before coming upon the gloomy
verdict on Creation of that kindred spirit, Schopenhauer,
Melville must and can stand for the Christian man of any age
who ventures forth into the seas of experience in the vessel of
that faith and finds himself unaccountably on the reefs,

* Ch. 59. See Charles Feidelson, *Symbolism and American Literature*,
Chicago, 1953, p. 243, for comment on this frightening passage. There
is a discussion of the symbolic whiteness of *Mardi* in both Feidelson
(pp. 170, 322) and James Baird, *Ishmael*, pp. 267ff.

† And yet anticipating them, as Stanley Edgar Hyman has demonstrated
in his examination of *The Origin of Species*. That book's "archetypal
image," he finds, "is the war of nature." "The important thing now was
tearing off the pacific mask that life wears, and Darwin writes of the
illusion concealing the tragic reality like a Melville narrator:

'We behold the face of nature bright with gladness, we often see super-
abundance of food; we do not see or we forget, that the birds which are
idly singing round us mostly live on insects or seeds, and are thus constantly destroying life; or we forget how largely these songsters, or their
eggs, or their nestlings, are destroyed by birds and beasts of prey. . . .'"

(*The Tangled Bank*, p. 29.)

bruised and bewildered.* But, then, when had wise
men ever explained evil satisfactorily? The doctrine of
original good and of our loss of it through man's
first disobedience had been fashioned into a gigantic
splendor in the seventeenth century, but *Paradise Lost*
increasingly would seem to later centuries more of a
baroque monument to a dead myth than a dramatization of
a living theodicy: by the nineteenth, certainly, Housman
would scoff that "malt does more than Milton can/To justify God's ways to man." St. Paul, we have seen, had
defined man as basically dualistic: was this not an invitation
to interpret the world according to the same dualism—for
flesh and *spirit* to read *evil* and *good*? This was what the
Manichees had done, in fact. But while they thus had explained the existence of evil, they also had decreased to that
extent God's power and removed Him from the every-day
world. How to escape heresy? By interpreting the evil of
nature as fulfilling a perfect design of God. This concept
St. Augustine had set forth. He both offered to prove the

* In the "Mat-Maker" chapter of *Moby-Dick* he attempts a synthesis
of fatalism and determinism with freedom of the will, but with these
results:

". . . chance, free will, and necessity . . . all interweavingly working
together. The straight warp of necessity, not to be swerved from its
ultimate course . . . ; free will still free to play her shuttle between
given threads; and chance, though restrained in its play within the right
lines of necessity, and sideways in its motions directed by free will,
though thus prescribed to by both, chance by turns rules either, and has
the last featuring blow at events."

". . . [we] cannot, I think, justifiably call him a scholar or a philosopher. Melville's symbolism proceeds from feeling. Its elements are
emotive and intuitive rather than reasoned (or better, intellectualized)."

"This is the theology of feeling, quite apart from the traditional
theologies of intellection and dogmatism; and Ishmael, in making this
theology, selects from feeling what, in the light of his experience, seems
to him a just description of the nature of God." (Baird, *Ishmael*, pp.
xvii, 259.)

non-existence of evil and to establish its causal efficacy if its non-existence was disputed. In support of the latter position he had set forth that ". . . in no wise is anything in nature bad and this name is that of nought but a lack of goodness. But from heaven to earth, from the visible to the invisible, some things are good, others better than others. In this they are unequal, so that all kinds of things might be." [14] But, as Henry Adams pointed out in his chapter on St. Thomas Aquinas, St. Augustine

certainly tempted Satan when he fastened the Church to this doctrine that evil is only the privation of good, an *amissio boni*; and that good alone exists. The point was infinitely troublesome. Good was order, law, unity. Evil was disorder, anarchy, multiplicity. Which was truth? The Church had committed itself to the dogma that order and unity were the ultimate truth, and that the anarchist should be burned. She could do nothing else, . . . yet the Church . . . knew that evil might be an excess of good as well as absence of it; that good leads to evil, evil to good. . . . Thomas conceded that God Himself, with the best intentions, might in the end work benefits. He could offer no proof of it, but he could assume as probable a plan of good which became the more perfect for the very reason that it allowed great liberty in detail. [15]

For example, as Thomas had put it: "Boethius introduces a philosopher who asks: 'If there be a God, whence comes evil?' He should have argued: 'If there is evil, there is God.' For there would be no evil if the order of good were removed, the privation of which is evil; and there would be no such order, if there were no God." *

* Ralph L. Woods (ed.), A *Treasury of Catholic Thinking* [1953], New York, 1963, p. 19.
   This Thomist doctrine was not original, nor even originally Christian. The Platonic solution to the problem of the origin of evil, for example, was essentially that which Emerson espoused (see Chapter One, above): evil was not a positive essence but "simply a lack of *being* in those who

But with "the problem of the universe revolving" in him, Ishmael had warned of all lean-browed and hollow-eyed young watch-standers on whaling voyages: a "sunken-eyed young Platonist will tow you ten wakes around the world, and never make you one pint of sperm the richer." (Ch. 35.) He recalled the death of a man in Ohio who leaned over too far in the honey-tree, was sucked in, and died embalmed in the honey: "How many, think ye, have likewise fallen into Plato's honey head, and sweetly perished there?" (Ch. 78.) As for Thomas's dialectical demonstration in the name of the idealist's God, the passages from Melville's works already cited provide a thundering "No!" from experience. He was making fun of Wordsworth's "Resolution and Independence" as early as 1853 (in "Cock-a-Doodle-Doo!"), and we are told that in the reading matter of his later, buried years, Melville would jot caustic comments in the margins of his copy of the inveterately idealistic Emerson, who had also defined evil as the absence of good,* as that which was contrary to nature, and would find his final philosophical consolation in the works of Schopenhauer, whom Emerson found "odious." † In the unfinished *Billy Budd*, Melville was

---

are at the foot of the ladder which rises up toward perfect being, God." (Harold H. Watts, *The Modern Reader's Guide to the Bible*, rev. ed., New York, 1958, pp. 420–421.)

* ". . . the poetry of Emerson and Walt Whitman, writers who have begun to seem superficial and precisely because they lack the Vision of Evil. . . ." (W. B. Yeats, *Autobiographies*, p. 303.)

† So, earlier (1850), with great excitement Melville had discovered Nathaniel Hawthorne, Emerson's one-time neighbor and all-time antipodes. "Hawthorne's vision was all for the evil and sin of the world; a side of life as to which Emerson's eyes were thickly bandaged. . . . [H]e had no great sense of wrong—a strangely limited one, indeed, for a moralist —no sense of the dark, the foul, the base." (Henry James, review of Cabot's *Memoir*, 1887; reprinted in Leon Edel [ed.], *The American Essays of Henry James*, New York, 1956.)

In 1891, the year of his death, Melville was borrowing, buying, and reading Schopenhauer voraciously. He scored this passage in *The World*

still pondering the mystery of evil in human nature and citing
(as an item in a list attributed to Plato): "Natural Depravity:
a depravity according to nature." Against the Emerson who
preferred Plotinus, with his minimizing of evil, there was the
Melville who kept going back to that weariest of all Scriptures, *Ecclesiastes.* (The Hebrew prophets lighted up more
dark spiritual places than Coke or Blackstone do, he confided to himself in *Billy Budd.*) Alongside the opinion (in
"Prudence") of the sedentary Emerson that "The sailor
buffets it all day, and his health renews itself at as vigorous
a pulse under the sleet, as under the sun of June," the Melville who had set down in *White-Jacket* the hardships and
dangers of life on the high seas scribbled in his copy, "To one
who has weathered Cape Horn as a common sailor what stuff
all this is." * Another Emerson remark inspired the annotation that Emerson's "gross and astonishing errors and illusions spring from a self-conceit so intensely intellectual and
calm that at first one hesitates to call it by its right name." [16]
Would not Melville, this latter-day Job—unlike the first one,
unsubmissive to the end—have assented to Aldous Huxley's
pronouncement (in *Music at Night*) that "Our universe is
the universe of Behemoth and Leviathan, not of Helvetius
and Godwin"?

The fierceness of the artifice of God's whiteness that had

---

as Will and Idea: ". . . the insight to which [Voltaire] attained in
three respects, and which prove the greater depth of his thinking: (1)
the recognition of the preponderating magnitude of the evil and misery
of existence with which he is deeply penetrated; (2) that of the strict
necessity of the acts of will; (3) that of the truth of Locke's principle,
that what thinks may also be material. . . ." (Jay Leyda, *The Melville
Log,* New York, 1951, II, pp. 831–832.)

* So, on the "cosmic Toryism" of Soame Jenyns, Samuel Johnson, "who
knew that slow rises worth by poverty depressed," had commented:
"This author and Pope perhaps never saw the miseries which they
imagine thus easily to be borne." (Quoted by Basil Willey, *The
Eighteenth Century Background,* p. 50.)

inspired Emerson's admiration is just the quality that evokes
a spiritual shudder from Melville, who sees in the stark
shapes of arctic regions the charnel-house at last without its
deceiving allurement of color. In *Moby-Dick,* the cold and
desolate sailor gazing at the antarctic landscape "views what
seems a boundless church-yard grinning upon him with its
lean ice monuments and splintered crosses." (Ch. 42.) Melville says that this effect is created by "some infernal trick of
legerdemain in the powers of frost and air"—that is, the
mind of the imaginative man will find an apparitional quality
in it all. Interestingly, the same play of the imagination over
the same landscape is created in Melville's poem "The
Berg" by the technique of the dream. In it a formidable
man-of-war madly charging against an iceberg sinks instantly,
and not only without a trace but without disturbing even the
most fragile of nature's artistry, "the spurs of ridges pale," or
the "lace of traceries fine," or the "jackstraw needle-ice"; and
yet, it occurs to the dreamer, this cold and vast and hard
berg itself "With moral damps self-overcast," is "Adrift dis-
solving, bound for death"! So unreconcilable were the points
of view espoused by men who were almost exact contemporaries. Emerson had shared the yea-saying of Carlyle's Professor; Melville, his earlier despair; * yet Emerson's was the
far older of the two Americans in spirit, and it was in Melville's symbolic visioning of nature that the historian can
now see an anticipation of the American literature that was
to come.† By the end of the century, as we have noted,
Gamaliel Bradford had conceded the triumph of German
pessimism. He defined the "modern" pessimist as

* Carlyle's phrase, the "dead indifference" of the universe, reappears in
Melville's poem "The Berg." For other evidence of the Carlyle influence
on Melville, see the notes to the Mansfield-Vincent edition of *Moby-
Dick,* New York, 1952.

† And of others, as well. See Appendix. Curiously, in *Billy Budd* (1888–
1891), Melville restored to whiteness its old connotations.

a man who has embarked on the wide sea of intellectual discovery, and has found that for him it is a barren sea, blank,
desolate,—a sea shoreless, where the traveller voyages on aim-
lessly forever in a misty void . . . for whom the fevered, pas-
sionate whirl of life . . . is but a disordered dream . . . to
whom faith and hope are shadows. . . . [H]e has lost all
faith, if he ever had any. He has long ago recognized that the
intellect is a will-o'-the-wisp;

even if he would "shut up the cavern of his mind and strew
it over with the roses and the charm of life," yet he cannot
because "he is haunted with the consciousness of the drear
abyss beneath." [17] Yet it is a definition of Herman Melville
as well.

■

This "iconology of whiteness, pondered over by Melville,"
Professor Harry Levin writes, "has furnished one of the
farthest ranging chapters in our literature." [18] We follow it
now, as the nineteenth century wears to a close, buffeted by
winds of progress and troubled by the ebbing of faith, and as
the naturalists make their appearance in that literature.
"Stephen Crane and Frank Norris and Theodore Dreiser
were the intellectual children of the nineties, and their art
was a reflection of that sober period of American disillusion," Parrington writes in "The Darkening Skies of Letters."
From the Nineties on, "the realistic novel took a new course
from the shifting winds of scientific doctrine. The [new]
generation . . . came too late to maturity to share [Gar-
land's] faith in the benevolent universe of Herbert Spencer.
. . . It was the conception of determinism that after a long
denial was at last coming to wide acceptance—a conception
that underlay the thinking of such diverse men as Comte and
Spencer and Marx. . . ." [19]
But it is also true that the scientific doctrine of the century

had consistently tended toward conclusions that gave the
layman grounds for both dismay and inspiration. In an important way, this conflict of response was a repetition, if not
actually a continuation, of the controversy that that earlier
scientist, Isaac Newton, had provoked almost two centuries
before. The non-technical, the religious, and the poetic mind
concerned itself with the theodicy stated or implied in his
theories; and whereas all agreed that the continual activity
—not the mere laws—of a supreme being was necessary for
the governance of the universe, questions remained about the
importance of this personal factor. The laymen of the day, of
course, would not be expected to read Newton,

but their imagination would be touched by the conclusion of
the *Opticks*, with its speculative suggestion that the loss of
motion in the universe must be recruited by active principles,
and they would read or at least hear of the famous Scholium
added to the second edition of the *Principia* asserting that
God is the Soul of the world, not Eternity, Infinity, or Perfection but a spiritual being who holds domination. . . .
Following the doctrine of Henry More, the Platonist, Newton somehow brings together matter and spirit in space in
opposition to the absolute sundering of matter and spirit in
the philosophy of Descartes. . . .
Eventually gravitation came to be regarded as a purely
mechanistic principle, and the world view developed from
Newtonian physics excluded human values. But for much
popular thought of the 18th century, even when deterministic
or mechanistic aspects of the system are noted or stressed,
they do not terrify, for they point to an active and omnipresent intelligence.[20]

Herbert Spencer's influential books now created this kind
of division among educated men, even within the same man.
Which Spencer would one have? There was the Spencer who
inspired Hamlin Garland; he had anticipated and was popu-
larizing Darwin's theory about species. In his *Principles of*

Sociology he identified man and his ways with those of animals, postulating that with one as with the other there was a struggle for existence leading to the survival of the fittest species, and thus serving a benign end. In his *Social Statics* one could find the assurance that "The ultimate development of the ideal man is logically certain. . . . Progress is not an accident, but a necessity. . . . [C]ivilization . . . is a part of nature; all of a piece with the development of the embryo or the unfolding of a flower." But there was also the Spencer of *First Principles*, with its famous concluding passage about the utter inscrutability of the supreme power. When the philosopher William Hocking read this as a boy, he both disobeyed his father's orders and undermined his own faith.[21] And Theodore Dreiser recalled that his discovery of *First Principles* at the age of twenty-three "quite blew me, intellectually, to bits." *

Nor did the differences of opinion end here. The sociologist Lester Ward, for an eminent example, rejecting both Malthus-Ricardo-Darwin pessimism and Spencer optimism, was insisting in *The Psychic Factors of Civilization* that

man and society are not, except in a very limited sense, under the influence of the great dynamic laws that control the rest of the animal world. . . . The fundamental principle of biology is natural selection, that of sociology is artificial selection . . . If nature progresses through the destruction of the weak, man progresses through the protection of the weak.

And by the time of Kropotkin's *Mutual Aid* (1902) Americans would also be asked to believe that "Happily enough, competition is not the rule *either* in the animal world or in mankind. . . . Better conditions are created by the *elimina-*

* *A Book About Myself*, New York, 1922, p. 457. Van Wyck Brooks records the influence of Spencer on the minor writers Lafcadio Hearn and Ernest Fenollosa, as well as on the writers discussed here and further on, in *The Confident Years*.

tion of competition by means of mutual aid and mutual support."

Keeping these ramifications in mind,* we must still concede that the doctrines of science were directing much of the stream of literature into this channel of pessimistic determinism.†

But again it should be said that a great part of the important (and probably almost all of the unimportant) American fiction of the last quarter of the nineteenth century was going its own steadfast way, secure from the naturalistic con-

---

* For an exposition on which the above summary has been based, see Richard Hofstadter, *Social Darwinism in American Thought, 1860–1915*.

† England, where the poets had fled to nature for philosophical romance at the century's birth, was at its close retreating from her in disillusion; and to find Thomas Hardy looking back in anger at his idealistic poetic forbears is to read a page in the history of the imaginative mind of that pivotal century. In *Tess of the D'Urbervilles* (1891) he alternates references to the writings of Leopardi, Schopenhauer, the *Dictionnaire Philosophique*, and Huxley with sneers at Wordsworth. At the beginning of this lugubrious novel Hardy gazes down at the haphazardness of the fate of the Durbeyfield children ("six helpless creatures, who had never been asked if they wished for life on any terms, much less [on those] of the shiftless house of Durbeyfield"), and with unmistakable reference to Wordsworth's "Lines Written in Early Spring" comments that "Some people would like to know whence the poet whose philosophy is in these days deemed as profound and trustworthy as his song is breezy and pure gets his authority for speaking of 'Nature's holy plan.'" (Ch. 3.) Toward the novel's close, Tess laments her loss of faith in Providence, resolving "in default of faith" to be the children's Providence herself, "for to Tess, as to not a few millions of others, there was ghastly satire in the [lines from Wordsworth's Immortality Ode] 'Not in utter nakedness/But trailing clouds of glory do we come.' To her and her like, birth itself was an ordeal of degrading personal compulsion, whose gratuitousness nothing in the result seemed to justify, and at best could only palliate." (Ch. 51.)

So much, too, for Browning's optimism. Here is Hardy's projection of Angel Clare's state of mind as he sends Tess away: "Thus he beheld her recede, and in the anguish of his heart quoted a line from a poet, with peculiar emendations of his own—'God's *not* in his heaven: all's *wrong* with the world!'" (Ch. 37.)

tagion.* This was true of the established writers—of Henry
James and William Dean Howells. Consider in this regard
James's relationship to the work with which this study of the
new symbolical use of whiteness begins; for we have his
appropriation of the final section of Poe's *Pym* in a fiction of
his own and even his own commentary on that section. There
is a long passage in the first chapter of *The Golden Bowl*
in which the Prince senses the mysteriousness of his future
—now that he is married to an American girl—in terms of
Poe's novel, whose hero "found at a given moment before
him a thickness of white air that was like a dazzling curtain
of light, concealing as darkness conceals, yet of the color of
milk or of snow." Matthiessen finds it doubly interesting that
"James, as an American, should have felt the impenetrable
mystery of whiteness"; but he adds that "whereas Melville's
symbols take his reader ever farther into the multitudinous
seas of speculation, James's are more essentially those of a
novelist, and are designed, like every other detail in his book,
to illustrate character." He is referring to James's statement
that in *Pym* "There *are* no connexions; not only . . . in the
sense of further statement, but of our own further relation to
the elements, which hang in the void; whereby we see the
effect lost, the imaginative effort wasted." † Matthiessen is

* ". . . by the nineties, when realism had won its first victory, it was
being submerged by historical romanticism and Stevensonian gush. . . .
[W]ith the exception of Frank Norris, the younger men were not even
interested in the *theory* of naturalism, in the scientific jargon out of
Claude Bernard, Darwin, and Taine with which Zola and his school
bedecked *le roman expérimental*. . . . [A]s realism in America . . .
passed into naturalism, its very foundations . . . were overrun by . . .
Graustark fiction, . . . decorative trivialities . . . , and the growing
complacency of the American middle class in the epoch of imperialism."
(Alfred Kazin, *On Native Grounds*, pp. 7, 10.)

† *The Novels and Tales of Henry James*, New York Edition, XVII,
Preface. ("James felt that the climax . . . was a failure because there
the horrific was without connections," R. P. Blackmur later rephrased
this.)

thus justified in finding that James "has not caught the horror of its unrelieved light, which had been the main intention
of Poe's climax." * More important, as T. S. Eliot was quick
to note, James was "a critic who preyed not upon ideas but
upon living beings." †

No more was Howells (that amiable sponsor of naturalists)
attuned to the spiritual discomfort, not to speak of dread,
engendered by vast areas of whiteness. For a moment—in the
fifth chapter of A Modern Instance (1882)—he presents a
winter scene fertile in just such possibilities, but not actually
utilized. In fact, Howells has something quite different in
mind: his scene is the work of a realist purely, and it serves
no discernible purpose (unless possibly to suggest, not despair
and death, but—by contrast—their opposites of hope and
life). In Howells's scene Bartley and Marcia are taking the
"Long Drive" out from the village early one winter afternoon:

In the country, the winter which held the village in such close
siege was an occupation under which Nature seemed to cower
helpless, and men made a desperate and ineffectual struggle.
The houses, banked up with snow almost to the sills of the
windows that looked out, blind with frost, upon the lifeless
world, were dwarfed in the drifts, and seemed to founder in a

* The American Renaissance, New York, 1941, pp. 301–305.
    And the "great . . . surface" that "had remained impenetrable and
inscrutable" to Maggie Verver (The Golden Bowl, Ch. 25), so far from
that of a potentially universal symbol, is of the "outlandish pagoda" of
the marital parallelogram of the story, as she has so bizarrely conceived it.

† And his critical genius is best evidenced "in his mastery over, his
baffling escape from, Ideas. . . . He had a mind so fine that no idea
could violate it. . . . James in his novels is like the best French critics
in maintaining a point of view, a viewpoint untouched by the parasite
idea." ("Henry James. In Memory," Little Review, August, 1918. Reprinted in Edmund Wilson [ed.], The Shock of Recognition, New
York [1943], 1955; II, pp. 856–857.)

white sea blotched with strange bluish shadows under the
slanting sun. Where they fronted close upon the road, it was
evident that the fight with the snow was kept up unrelentingly;
spaces were shovelled out . . . ; but where they were somewhat removed, there was no visible trace of the conflict, and
no sign of life except the faint, wreathed lines of smoke
waving upward from the chimneys.

But no—the faint impressionism of that passage is almost
completely wasted,* for we read that although this is "all
wild and lonesome," the very solitude is "sweet" to Marcia,
who is alone with the man she loves. The wind is now rising
threateningly and Bartley stops "before striking out over one
of the naked stretches of the plain,—a white waste swept by
the blasts that sucked down through a gorge of the mountain,
and flattened the snow-drifts as the tornado flattens the
waves." But again we go on to note that the fury and deso-
lateness of the scene heighten the excitement for the young
couple: "They felt the thrill of the go as if they were in some
light boat leaping over a swift current." Hearts are young and
hopes are high: we are many years in advance of the New
England ride for two lovers that Edith Wharton would plan
one winter night in *Ethan Frome*. The "good feeling" and
"brotherly sympathy" that Howells ascribes to Americans
elsewhere in *A Modern Instance* shine through his winter
scene here. For Howells was practicing his own natural "concern . . . with the more smiling aspects of life" in America
that he would preach to his fellow-novelists in *Criticism and
Fiction*, wherein he would look back condescendingly at the
past as "a smaller and cruder and emptier world than we now
live in. . . ." When, with Whitmanesque fervor, a man as
literary critic insists that "nothing God has made is con-

* Professor Gordon Haight writes of Howells' *The Rise of Silas Lapham*
that "In contrast with *A Modern Instance*, the setting, masterfully rendered, is completely fused with the action." ("Realism Defined," *The
Literary History of the United States*, Ch. 54.)

temptible," when such a man, as novelist "held his ear close
to Nature's lips and caught her very accent," he would hear
a message in no way troubling.*

Howells's friend, Mark Twain, is, however, a bridge between
the earlier American literature and the new, even if only to
a limited degree. He could distinguish the actual from the
imagined, and he set great store by the difference.† Some of
his most successful comic effects come about when he ex-
plodes the romantics' manipulation of nature. But since his
mind had a limited receptivity to nature in an abstract sense,
it also had an immunity to the philosophical melancholy and
aesthetic dread that scenes of whiteness could create in the
naturalists.

Revulsion there is, and in abundance, in the brief description of Pap Finn's face in Chapter Five of *Huckleberry Finn:*
"There warn't no color in his face, where his face showed; it
was white; not like another man's white, but a white to make
a body sick, a white to make a body's flesh crawl—a tree-toad
white, a fish-belly white." But the viewer here is a boy, vig-

---

* There is an instructive contrast between Howells' realistic (pictorial)
introduction of whiteness in *A Modern Instance* and Hardy's naturalistic
(philosophical) use of it in Chapter Eleven of *Far From the Madding
Crowd* (1874). When at the low point of her spirit Fanny Robin seeks
out Sergeant Troy on foot, and gets in response to her pleas for marriage only his insincere evasions (overheard and laughed at by his
barracks-mates), Hardy sets the scene on a dreary, gloomy evening in the
season (winter) whose final touch is a heavy snowfall described as an
"obliteration of snow,"—a smothering of human hopes with its extinction of that source of hope, the sky: "The vast arch of cloud above
was strangely low, and formed as it were the roof of a large dark cavern,
gradually sinking in upon its floor; for the instinctive thought was that
the snow lining the heavens and that encrusting the earth would soon
unite into one mass without any intervening stratum of air at all."

† Even in the matter of speech. For example, he confided to posterity
about his old acquaintance, Bret Harte, that he "learned how to fasci-
nate Europe and America with the quaint dialect of the miner—a
dialect which no man in heaven or earth had ever used until Harte invented it." (*Mark Twain in Eruption*, New York, 1940, p. 263.)

orous and resourceful, and proud of his imperviousness to
that pallor (". . . after the first jolt . . . I warn't scared of
him worth bothering about.")* As for the sequence (Chs. 31–
33) in *Roughing It* (1872) that Professor Walter Blair has fittingly anthologized as "Lost in the Snow," it probably should
be looked upon as evidence of Twain's penchant for taking
"greater liberties with fact for art's sake"—as Dixon Wechter
has said—for the very purpose of satirizing earlier literary
libertarians. It may have been the truth or it may have been
a "stretcher" that Twain, Ollendorf, and Mr. Ballou "went
into camp in a snow-drift in a desert, at midnight, in a storm,
forlorn and hopeless," only fifteen steps away from a stage-
coach station. Certainly in their unsuccessful efforts to build
a fire Twain was making fun of the resourcefulness of earlier
travellers (they had "long ago accepted and believed *that
other* common book-fraud about Indians and lost hunters
making a fire by rubbing two dry sticks together") but elsewhere in this droll sequence he invites the modern reader
to wonder whether a more consistent object of his satire is
not his acquaintance and fellow-exploiter of life in the west,
Bret Harte: in particular, the sentimental and pious haze
Harte had thrown over his rugged scenes. In fact, in "Lost in
the Snow" he plays havoc with the "Outcasts of Poker Flat"
(so wildly popular at the time) in ways that are as revealing of
his repudiation of Harte's sentimentality as his explicit posthumous comments (in *Mark Twain in Eruption*). In fact,

* When this particular whiteness reappears in modern literature in
O'Neill, it is as a symbolic costume. Mildred in *The Hairy Ape* (1922) is
dressed all in white and O'Neill describes her as practically a disembodi-
ment of the "life energy" of her muscular ancestors. She represents
anemia, devitalization. Yank is as repelled by her whiteness as she is by
his hairiness, and his abhorrence of her is reminiscent of Huck's: "Yuh
skinny tart! Yuh whitefaced bum, yuh! . . . I was scared . . . I
tought she was a ghost, see? She was all in white like dey wrap around
stiffs. . . . Did yuh pipe her hands? White and skinny. Yuh could
see de bones through 'em. And her mush, dat was dead white,
too. . . ."

"The Outcasts" barely survives his mockery. To counter
Harte's strongest-weakest, card-sharping, hymn-singing Mr.
Oakhurst who kills himself in order that his fellow-outcasts
may have his rations, Twain offers a young Swede who

landed from the canoe and took his pedestrian way Carson-
wards, singing his same tiresome song about his "sister and
his brother" and "the childe in the grave with its mother,"
and in a short minute faded and disappeared in the white
oblivion. He was never heard of again. He no doubt got bewildered and lost, and Fatigue delivered him over to Sleep,
and Sleep betrayed him to Death.

How to do battle with Harte's "pathetics, imitated from
Dickens," that, Twain snickered from the grave, "used to be
a godsend to the farmers of two hemispheres on account of
the freshet of tears they compelled"? [22] At the close of
Harte's story, the snow finally invades the hut in which the
whore ("the Duchess") and the young innocent Piney huddle
together. Since the fire is dying out, they prepare for death:

The Duchess . . . putting her head upon Piney's shoulder,
spoke no more. And so reclining, the younger and purer pil-
lowing the head of her soiled sister upon her virgin breast,
they fell asleep.
    The wind lulled as if it feared to waken them. Feathery
drifts of snow, shaken from the long pine-boughs, flew like
white-winged birds about them as they slept. . . .
    They slept all that day and the next, nor did they waken
when voices and footsteps broke the silence of the camp. And
when pitying fingers brushed the snow from their wan faces,
you could scarcely have told from the equal peace that dwelt
upon them, which was she that had sinned.

It is this passage, I am confident, that reappears in a dras-
tically altered form at the close of Twain's story:

We put our arms about each other's necks and awaited the warning drowsiness that precedes death by freezing.

It came stealing over us presently, and then we bade each other a last farewell. A delicious dreaminess wrought its web about my yielding senses, while the snowflakes wove a winding-sheet about my conquered body. Oblivion came. The battle of life was done.

I do not know how long I was in a state of forgetfulness, . . . I shuddered. The thought flitted through my brain, "This is death—this is the hereafter."

Then came a white upheaval at my side, and a voice said with bitterness:

"Will some gentleman be so good as to kick me behind?"

Somewhere between his own farcical and Harte's sentimentalized distortion of it,* Twain is maintaining in effect, lay the *real* snow and *real* travellers beset by it; but although to have made this point was a great deal for American literary criticism—Twain's satire is just that—as early as 1872, at this point Twain's interest ceases. For, brooding and bitter though we know him to have become with the years, it was not until late in life that his writing would give this tendency symbolic utterance. Disenchantment bordering on despair —this he would confess, and early; but characteristically, it disappears in a twinkling, like a balloon of literary pretentiousness that Twain's own sense of humor pricks as exuberantly as it did Harte's (or, in a more celebrated context, James Fenimore Cooper's).† Consider his reaction to the forbidding alkali desert west of Salt Lake (in *Roughing It,* Ch. 18). The party is crossing it during an August day, and

* For the use to which James Joyce would put Bret Harte's snow in the next century, see Appendix.

† Interestingly enough, Bret Harte himself had already subjected the romantic writers of America to ridicule: James Fenimore Cooper (in *Condensed Novels*) and Longfellow's "Skeleton In Armor" (in "To the Pliocene Skull").

for a brief time the reader is impressed with Twain's dismay. "Imagine," he asks of us in a passage reminiscent of both Poe and Melville,

a vast, waveless ocean stricken dead and turned to ashes; imagine this solemn waste tufted with ash-dusted sage-bushes; imagine the lifeless silence and solitude that belong to such a place . . . ; imagine team, driver, coach and passengers so deeply coated with ashes that they are all one colorless color . . . and eyebrows like snow accumulations on boughs and bushes.

But immediately self-mockery cancels this effect: "It was so trying to give one's watch a good long undisturbed spell and then take it out and find that it had been fooling away the time and not trying to get ahead any!" It turns out that Twain has worked up to his fine effect more for the entertainment provided by exposing his own "romantic" anticipation of such a trip than for impressing the reader with his own spiritual discomfort. *Reality* was "harsh," it was "hateful," he keeps insisting to his eastern readers, and "the romance all faded" that August day.

For a phrase or two, to be sure, we wonder whether it is the rambunctious Sam Clemens viewing that "one colorless color" or the sardonic Ishmael:

The sun beats down with dead, blistering, relentless malignity . . . ; there is not a merciful shred of cloud in all the brilliant firmament; there is not a living creature visible in any direction whither one searches the blank level that stretches its monotonous miles on every hand; . . . not even a sob from the lost souls that doubtless people that dead air.

Then laughter breaks in and we are back to the mules and the "violent swearing" of the driver. Back from that brink steps our Missouri traveller, for we are on what was "a rare holiday frolic."

A more properly transitional figure is Hamlin Garland, grouped by Åhnebrink with Crane and Norris as a pioneer of naturalistic writing in this country. In 1884–1885, Garland, living in Boston (to which he had fled from the rigors of pioneer life on his claim in South Dakota), read wildly, including books of science:

Herbert Spencer remained my philosopher and master. With eager haste I sought to compass the "Synthetic Philosophy." The universe took on order and harmony as . . . I went directly to the consideration of Spencer's theory of the evolution of music or painting or sculpture. It was thrilling, it was joyful to perceive that everything moved from the simple to the complex. . . . I became an evolutionist in the fullest sense, accepting Spencer as the greatest living thinker.[23]

And in truth the influence of Spencer's theory of progress can be seen in Garland's early novel of prairie life, *Ol' Pap's Flaxen*. At its start we think that we are in the world of the prairie blizzard such as Crane or London would create for the purpose of underscoring man's puniness:

And all night long the blasting wind, sweeping the sea of icy sands, hissed and howled round the little sod cabin like surf beating on a half-sunken rock. The wind and the snow and the darkness possessed the plain; and Cold (whose other name is Death) was king of the horrible carnival. It seemed as though morning and sunlight could not come again, so absolute was the sway of night and death.

The next morning in —30° weather

. . . Gearheart crunched away over the spotless snow, which burned under his feet—a land mocking, glorious, pitiless. [Except for two or three hearth fires] the plain was level and lifeless as the polar ocean, appallingly silent, no cry or stir in the whole expanse. . . . There was perfect silence without and within, no trace of feet or hands anywhere. All was as peaceful and unbroken as a sepulcher.

For two weeks they are marooned in this weather: "Day after day the restless snow sifted or leaped across the waste of glittering crust; day after day the sun shone in dazzling splendor, but so white and cold that the thermometer still kept down among the thirties [below zero]." And yet Garland's overall picture is not of a malevolent, or indifferent, universe at all. It is of a varied one, a universe as capable of unbearable loveliness as of misery. We get a hint of this during the winter when the two pioneers take their young charge into the settlement to Captain Burdon's home. Mrs. Burdon, who welcomes them into her dwelling, is described as "a big, slatternly Missourian, with all the kindliness of a universal mother in her swarthy face and flaccid bosom. . . ." Later, when spring finally breaks through, Garland rises to rapture:

. . . and then came a day when a strange warm wind blew from the northwest. Soft and sweet and sensuous it was, as the breeze sweeping some tropic bay filled with a thousand isles—a wind like a vast warm breath blown upon the land. Under its touch the snow did not melt; it vanished.

With spring come hordes of land-seekers, men, women, children, cattle, and machinery. Houses spring up, railroad surveyors come through, locating towns, etc. And the first half of the novel ends on a note of excitement and hope and perceptibly Spencerian optimism:

With the coming of spring began the fiercest toil of the pioneers—breaking the sod, building, harvesting, plowing; then the winter again, though not so hard to bear; then the same round of work again. So the land was settled, the sod was turned over; sod shanties gave way to little frame-houses; the tide of land-seekers passed on, and the real workers, like

Wood and Gearheart, went patiently, steadily on, founding
a great State.[24]

Winter, it turns out, was a necessary tribulation, a terrible
hardship against which men would prevail, presumably, by
numbers, by society, by group effort. Gushing spring is the
sweeter for the horror of winter; and solitary confinement by
its whiteness is crowned by the victory of civilization, in the
form of the settlers who arrive in the spring.*

Garland, then, has faith that enables him to transcend his
feelings of helplessness and despair: faith in the symmetry
of nature's design. He is therefore in this novel no more last-
ingly infected with the virus of his age than was Thoreau
when, in his "Natural History of Massachusetts" (1842), he
paused to comment on leaves coated with hoar-frost in the
bitter cold of the December of 1837:

It struck me that these ghost leaves, and the green ones whose
forms they assume, were the creatures of but one law; that in
obedience to the same law the vegetable juices well gradually
into the perfect leaf on the one hand, and the crystalline
particles troop to their standard in the same order, on the
other. As if the material were indifferent, but the law one
and invariable, and every plant in the spring but pushed up
into and filled a permanent and eternal mould, which, summer and winter forever, is waiting to be filled.

Both were essentially voicing a belief in the over-all goodness
of creation, of the celestial artistry that Tertullian had voiced
in De Carnis Resurrectione:

* Ole Rolvaag's Giants in the Earth (1927) presents an even longer
and worse siege of prairie snow during the winter of 1880–1881. Although it completely paralyzes human existence and the final section in
which it is presented is captioned "The Great Plain Drinks the Blood
of Christian Men and Is Satisfied," still Rolvaag's emphasis is on the
indomitability of the prairie dweller's spirit.

Winters and summers come and go, springs and autumns
with their powers and laws and fruits. . . . What a marvelous rational order! . . . to take away in order to return;
. . . to lessen in order to increase! In fact, the restitution has
been richer and more beautiful than the destruction, in truth
a profitable destruction. . . . God . . . has sent forth Nature to you as a teacher. . . . And so, if all things rise again
for man, for whom they were prepared, and not merely for
man but also for his flesh, why should that perish entirely
for which and because of which nothing perishes? [25]

There is something of both Thoreau and the post-Spen-
cerian philosopher of nature Hamlin Garland for a brief
moment in that most naturalistic novel ever written by the
most naturalistic of novelists—Émile Zola's *La Terre*. Here is
Zola's Jean, the stranger from town, as he looks out on the
farmland of La Beauce after the first snow:

. . . La Beauce stretched away into infinity, all white, flat
and motionless as a sea of ice. . . . The utter stillness of extreme cold reigned all around. . . . His heavy boots went
on ringing against the ground . . . and as Jean turned into
the cross-pathway he remembered the field as he had sown
here a few days before. He looked to his left and recognised
the place beneath its shroud of snow.

But in his poetic vision of the wonders of nature, Jean immediately complements this chilling view with a pleasurable one
to follow: "How deep the seeds must be sleeping! How profoundly at rest within those icy flanks until that warm morning when the spring sun would reawaken them to life." *
    Zola had no comforting thoughts to solace Jean at the end,

* Just as in autumn, with manuring, "death would once more breed
life," and its "strong stink," Zola reminds his readers, "nourished what
would one day be the bread of men." (Citations of *La Terre* are from
the Ann Lindsay translation, pp. 74, 75, 331.)

as we have seen. And if not to Garland, yet certainly to others the message he gave was of despair. To Frank Norris, for example.

In his preface to an early novel (*Thérèse Raquin*) Zola had explained that for his lovers he had chosen "individuals wholly dominated by their nerves and their blood, without free will. . . . In short, I had but one wish: given a strong man and an unsatisfied woman, to find the animal in them, indeed to see nothing except the animal. . . ." He would try always to apply natural history to human beings, to render them victims of forces greater than their own, whether inner forces or outer or both. Thus, in his classic *L'Assommoir*, Gervaise's downfall results from her tendency to drift (which includes her animal susceptibility to maleness) and to the impersonal enmity of the elements when she is slipping down. The complete fusion of the two forces comes in a late chapter (Twelve), on the Saturday when Gervaise sinks to street walking, accosts and is befriended by her admirer Goujet. It is a chapter for which the title "Death" would be suitable. It begins with the starving woman's middle-of-the-night reflection on the desperateness of her situation, goes on to the horrible daylight details of Lalie's dying (the heroic fellow tenement dweller), and ends with Gervaise's hysterical entreaty in the early hours of the next morning to the grave-digger Bazouge to take her too to the cemetery. It is also a chapter to be entitled "Snow." The depressed Gervaise thinks of snow during the night (it has been in the sky for three days) as a threat; it finally comes down furiously as she slowly makes her way down the deserted streets that night, throwing its "soft white pall of silence" over the few stragglers, inviting her to make her last bed in it, and affording her her last appalled glimpse as she finally gets back to her tenement building. Thus does Zola ask us to depart from the literal level of observation, to conceive of the whiteness as having a transcendent meaning, and justifying his analysis of his art some years later to Henry Céard: "*La vérité monte d'un coup d'aile jusqu'au symbole.*" *

There is a resemblance between Zola's man and wife and Frank Norris's in *McTeague*, who are viewed as much like animals in their habitat as like humans with souls; but our concern here is to describe McTeague's final venture into death; for, like Gervaise's, it is a venture into whiteness.

An echo of what McTeague had found in Death Valley is contained in an early passage in *The Octopus*. Here the mystic Vanamee is recalling for Presley his wanderings during recent years in the western states, and he muses as he talks, "seeing again in the eye of his mind the reach of desert and red hill, the purple mountain, the level stretch of alkali, leper white, all the savage, gorgeous desolation of the Long Trail." But rather than an enriching experience, McTeague finds the alkali desert his nemesis and a murderer like himself. Norris's panoramic sweep of the Death Valley reads a great deal like Twain's:

Before him and upon either side . . . stretched primordial desolation. League upon league the infinite reaches of dazzling white alkali laid themselves out like an immeasurable scroll unrolled from horizon to horizon; not a bush, not a twig relieved that horrible monotony. . . . It was abominable, this hideous sink of alkali, this bed of some primeval lake lying so far below the level of the ocean. The great mountains of Placer County had been merely indifferent to man; but this awful sink of alkali was openly and unreservedly iniquitous and malignant.

His trail, Marcus tells the sheriff, would be "as distinct in the white alkali as in snow," but the sheriff refuses to go across

* Professor Philip Walker, who quotes this letter at greater length, observes that Zola's "symbolic treatment of color . . . suggests affinities with the symbolists, who were rising to a certain prominence in Paris in 1884, the year *Germinal* was written." ("Zola's Use of Color Imagery in *Germinal*," PMLA, LXXVII [Sept., 1962], pp. 442–449.)

the "alkali sink," leaving Marcus to pursue alone and to find himself eventually the victim of that whiteness, along with McTeague. That closing scene finds McTeague manacled to the dead Marcus and gazing helplessly out at the whiteness that is their doom. Here Norris continues beyond Twain.

Chaotic desolation stretched from them on either hand, flaming and glaring with the afternoon heat. There was the brazen sky and the leagues upon leagues of alkali, leper white. There was nothing more. . . . All about him, vast, interminable, stretched the measureless leagues of Death Valley.

No comedy breaks in as relief. This final effect is left unmarred and unmistakable.

Now Frank Norris early detected Zola at work in Stephen Crane. Crane was familiar with *Nana* and *La Débâcle*, Beer tells us, and it was *L'Assommoir* that Norris thought Crane had used as "the plan" of his *Maggie*.[26] If so, it should be no surprise to find echoes of *L'Assommoir* elsewhere in Crane— of symbolic projection as well as of philosophy. For this we must return to the late chapter in Zola's novel referred to above. It is the narrative of the terrible Saturday night of Gervaise's final degradation. The descent to streetwalking has the accompanying atmospheric medium of the descent of the long-dreaded snow. When, at the end of the chapter, Gervaise takes a last look at the exterior of her tenement home, it suggests the death that she fears awaits her:

In the courtyard everything was silent as a cemetery, and the snow had filled the square with its white pallor. The high walls rose up in livid grey, not a single light showing, looking like deserted ruins. Not a breath was stirring. It was like a whole village stiffened into death by cold and hunger and entombed beneath the snow.[27]

This is precisely * what Crane's snow looks like and symbolizes in "The Blue Hotel": first, as the men leave the hotel
to go out for the fight ("No snow was falling, but great
whirls and clouds of flakes, swept up from the ground by
the frantic winds, were streaming southward. . . . The
covered land was blue with the sheen of an unearthly
satin. . . ."), but more particularly when the death-
haunted and drunken Swede emerges from the blue hotel
into the whiteness:

He might have been in a deserted village. We picture the
world as thick with conquering and elate humanity, but here,
with the bugles of the tempest pealing, it was hard to imagine
a peopled earth. One viewed the existence of man then as a
marvel, and conceded a glamor of wonder to these lice which
were caused to cling to a whirling, fire-smitten, ice-locked,
disease-stricken, space-lost bulb.† The conceit of man was
explained by this storm to be the very engine of life. One was
a coxcomb not to die in it.

---

* *L'Assommoir* circulated widely in this country from around 1880 on, in
various expurgated translations; but the "deserted village" coincidence
above can be matched elsewhere. See "Crane and Zola," *English Language Notes*, I (September, 1963), pp. 46–48.

† In Thomas Hardy's "God-Forgotten," his Lord Most High, when
questioned, "dimly" remembers creating the earth:

> Some tiny sphere I built long back
> (Mid millions of such shapes of mine). . . .
> And it is strange—though sad enough—
> Earth's race should think that one whose call
> Frames, daily, shining spheres of flawless stuff
> Must heed their tainted ball!

The mathematics of a later century's astronomy would provide the
point of departure for even greater dismay: "As the frontiers of space
have widened, man's importance has shrunk, until Einstein's universe is
said to be 585,900,000,000,000,000,000 miles in circumference, and we
mammals have been reduced to the size of bacteria on the epidermis of
a huge apple." (Harry Hartwick, *The Foreground of American Fiction*,
p. 5.)

The conceit is, of course, man's ancient trust in the dignity of man, of the divine gift of reason, and in the sentience of his creator. Not many minutes afterwards the Swede does die, at the hands of a gambler whose knife shoots forward to the end that "a human body, this citadel of virtue, wisdom, power, was pierced as easily as if it had been a melon."

Now if, as Joseph Wood Krutch says, "Tragedy arises . . . when . . . a people fully aware of the calamities of life is nevertheless serenely confident of the greatness of man, whose mighty passions and supreme fortitude are revealed when one of these calamities overtakes him," and it is "an affirmation of faith in life, a declaration that even if God is not in his heaven, then at least Man is in his world," [28]— then that last savage taunt of Crane's is the true measure of the distance the naturalistic writer of the 1890's had travelled from the Renaissance concept of man; from the time when Macbeth, as much aghast at his act of murder as at the sight of the king's body, describes it in words that mix poetry and piety:

His silver skin laced with his golden blood.
And his gash'd stabs look'd like a breach in nature
For ruin's wasteful entrance. . . . (II, iii, 98–100.)

Where Crane and the nineteenth century left off such sentiments, Jack London carried them into our own. To the Scriptural question, "What is man . . . ?" he eventually found an answer as contemptuous as Crane's and Twain's. In commenting on his *Snark* voyage he wrote:

Here am I, a little animal called a man—a bit of vitalized matter, . . . all of it soft and tender, susceptible to hurt, fallible and frail. . . . Fallible and frail, a bit of pulsating, jelly-like life—it is all I am. About me are the great natural forces, colossal menaces . . . that have less concern for me than I have for [a] grain of sand. . . . [29]

For, like his hero in *Martin Eden*, he had read widely in the
naturalistic philosophers. Martin worships Herbert Spencer
for having provided an answer (evolution) to the question of
the meaning of existence. He quotes Nietzsche to the effect
that the world belongs to the strong, "the great blond
beasts." In one of his tirades he declares, "I believe the race
is to the swift, the battle to the strong. Such is the lesson I
have learned from biology. . . ." That is why the little So-
cialist speaker in Oakland fills him with disgust. He thinks
of "this withered wisp of a speaker" as "the figure that stood
forth representative of the whole miserable mass of weak-
lings and inefficients who perished according to biological
law on the ragged confines of life. They were the unfit." And
in "The White Silence" London demonstrated with a self-
conscious scientific detachment what happens when a man
finds himself on such confines and unfit to cope with them:
In that story what importance do the two men and Indian
woman have in his eyes as he watches them trudge along behind their savage dogs in the snow?

The afternoon wore on, and with the awe, born of the White
Silence, the voiceless travelers bent to their work. Nature has
many tricks wherewith she convinces man of his finity—the
ceaseless flow of the tides, the fury of the storm, the shock of
the earthquake, the long roll of heaven's artillery—but the
most tremendous, the most stupefying of all, is the passive
phase of the White Silence. All movement ceases, the sky
clears, the heavens are as brass; the slightest whisper seems
sacrilege, and man becomes timid, affrighted at the sound of
his own voice. Sole speck of life journeying across the ghostly
wastes of a dead world, he trembles at this audacity, realizes
that his is a maggot's life, nothing more. Strange thoughts
arise unsummoned, and the mystery of all things strives for
utterance.*

* ". . . alone with the White Logic, 'which, undefeated, has never
left me,' and which was 'the ardent messenger of truth beyond truth,

This is man as cipher, as member of the animal creation, and struggling for survival on the terms of Darwin's animal world:

Bursting into the camp, he saw the girl in the midst of the snarling pack, laying about her with an ax. The dogs had broken the iron rule of their masters and were rushing the grub. He joined issue with [the butt of his rifle], and the hoary game of natural selection was played out with all the ruthlessness of its primeval environment.

Thus does London restate the naturalism of *White Fang*, with its profusion of despairing attributives of life ("eating and being eaten," "blindness and confusion," "violence and disorder," "a chaos of gluttony and slaughter, ruled over by chance, merciless, planless, endless") that forsakes the long-range optimism of Spencerian teleology for the atheistic determinism so easy to read into Darwin's view of life's struggle for existence.* What more natural, then, for him to think of the Alaskan snows, where, as Maxwell Geismar puts it, "the ultimate drama of Darwinism was played out in the frozen abyss of night. Human survival was granted on terms that were absolutely inhuman. Death-ridden phantoms were the puppets of their own destruction in a landscape that reflected merely the sleep of death." [30]

To Henry Adams, the intellectual, Darwinism had also been an object of contemplation, and of a far more compre-

---

the antithesis of life, cruel and bleak as inter-stellar space, pulseless and frozen as absolute zero,' he watched the tragic play of life feeding on life. . . ." (Maxwell Geismar, *Rebels and Ancestors*, p. 206.)

* His Wolf Larsen, who has read Darwin, lectures the narrator in *The Sea-Wolf*: " '. . . life is the cheapest thing in the world. . . . Nature is a spendthrift. Look at the fish and their millions of eggs. For that matter, look at you and me. . . . Life? Bah! It has no value. Of cheap things it is the cheapest. . . . Nature spills it out with a lavish hand. Where there is room for one life, she sows a thousand lives and its life eats life. . . .' " (Ch. 6.)

hensive kind. In it he could find merely a scientific substitute
for religious faith, yet one even less satisfactory than religion.
Incapable of the faith of old, he was doomed to helpless
despair the first time deep personal loss overtook him, which
happened in the summer of 1870. Summoned from London to
the Italian bedside of his sister, who was dying an excruciat-
ingly painful death from lockjaw resulting from a cab accident, we read in a chapter of *The Education* fittingly entitled "Chaos," he perceives that of all the Italian summers
he has known, this is the most "winning" physically, and he
must redefine his understanding of nature's position regarding human mortality: "Nature enjoyed it, played with
it, . . . she liked the torture . . . ," he muses grimly with
"violent emotion." Although he had known death before, it
was all as nothing. Now he knows. "The first serious consciousness of nature's gesture—her attitude towards life—
took form then as a phantasm, a nightmare, an insanity of
force. For the first time, . . . the human mind felt itself
stripped naked, vibrating in a void of shapeless energies. . . .
Society became fantastic, a vision of pantomime with a mechanical motion. . . ." Gone then is his ability to believe
in "any personal deity," and travelling north from the terrible
scene, he makes a shocking discovery: "For the first time in
his life, Mont Blanc for a moment looked to him what it was
—a chaos of anarchic and purposeless forces *—and he
needed days of repose to see it clothe itself again with the
illusions of his senses, the white purity of its snows, the
splendor of its light, and the infinity of its heavenly peace."

In the company of these modern reflections we may place
Conrad Aiken. His artist Demarest tells us in *Blue Voyage*
(1927), that he has deliberately aimed at the effect of chaos,
"in the belief that the old unities and simplicities will no

* Eventually, order and anarchy are the same thing, but "the unity was
chaos." (Ch. 27.) And "the universe may be—as it has always been—
either a supersensuous chaos or a divine unity. . . ." (Ch. 33.)

longer serve . . . if one is trying to translate, in any form
of literary art, the consciousness of modern man." On the
map of Conrad Aiken's consciousness white is a signpost
pointing toward the extinction of death, whether of the body
in age or of the mind in childhood. In "Mr. Arcularis," on
the level of phantasy, a ship is moving more and more slowly
into a fog that is "thicker and whiter than ever"; on the
factual level, the hero's state is moving ever closer to death.
The same interpretation is intended for his frightening dream

> that I was walking alone, in a wide plain covered with snow.
> It was growing dark, I was very cold, my feet were frozen and
> numb, and I was lost. I came then to a signpost—at first it
> seemed to me there was nothing * on it. Nothing but ice. Just
> before it grew finally dark, however, I made out on it the one
> word 'Polaris.'
> "The Pole Star."
> "Yes. . . . And of course it rhymes with my name."

In "Silent Snow, Secret Snow" what gives Aiken's screw an
extra turn is that the horror befalls a child, a boy whose mind
finally breaks down, gradually but inexorably overpowered by
a silent and secret substance that is a continuous snowfall.
From nowhere it appears, muffling the ugly world of reality,
at first from a distance, then more closely and urgently, its
beauty "this extraordinary combination of ethereal loveliness
with a something else, unnameable, which was just faintly
and deliciously terrifying. What was this thing?" If we consider that this thing was the destruction of a human's mind,
then it was death. And even a personified death, as the
child's mind would imagine it with terrifying vividness, a
death that completely separates its victim from his school-
mates, his father and mother, and leaves him in its dubious
safety and security from reality—enveloped by its warmth

---

* For the ironic use of this word, see Chapter Four below.

but buried in its depths. Rightly the fairy-tale element is prominent, for that is the version of life and death whose terrible reality curdles children's blood. "No fairy story he had ever read could be compared with it," Paul Hasleman thinks of this silent, secret substance; and it whispers to him that, if he will forsake all others, it will reward him with "a better story than Little Kay of the Skates, or The Snow Ghost—I will surround your bed, I will close the windows, pile a deep drift against the door, so that none will ever again be able to enter." Bewitched by the insidious and hypnotic whiteness, he never struggles against it; and where the man in Frost's "Stopping By Woods" can shake off the inviting darkness by reminding himself of responsibilities, Aiken's boy sits by helplessly and is enveloped by the fatal whiteness. Placed beside this story, Hans Christian Andersen's horrors can seem subdued. If frivolous Karen loses her feet in her passion for the bewitched red shoes, eventually her repenting soul flies up to heaven; at length she is welcomed by the angel of God in white garments, by organ song and children's choir. Paul's death is the more painful for its freedom from physical pain; the afterlife that waits for him, the more appalling for its utter separation from human voices.

Partly because of its insistence and pervasiveness in his poetry and partly because of his prominence, the whiteness of Robert Frost's world is the most impressive exhibit in our chamber of spiritual horrors. "A terrifying poet," Lionel Trilling called him: "The universe that he conceives is a terrifying universe. Read the poem called 'Design' and see if you sleep the better for it." [31] The color of that universe is consistently symbolic, and usually is white. The "self-same Power" that once led Emerson to the Rhodora's soul-satisfying feast of color (the purple petals afloat on black water, the red of a bird possibly blending in) is now likely to lead him, if not simply in circles, then into a chamber of equally natural horrors. "Design" is merely the most frightening (and

for this reason, perhaps the least typical) of Frost's expressions of distaste, of disbelief in God—its heaped-up whiteness
of spider, moth, and clothlikeness, on a flower ordinarily
blue but here white, inviting the question of "Why?" and
evoking the shuddering question-answer of

What but design of darkness to appall?—
If design govern in a thing so small.

Is this not the piety of Gerard Manley Hopkins in reverse? As
that poet had praised Him for the Design of Daylight, for
Pied Beauty, so now the midnight poet denies Him for Blank
Horror, for the Design of Darkness with its absence of "All
things counter, original, spare, strange." Design did indeed
"govern in a thing so small" back in the devout seventeenth-
century world of Edward Taylor, whose spider had also been
the devil but one whose whipcord tangles a "mighty, gracious
Lord" could give man grace enough to break; and in the
eighteenth century world of Jonathan Edwards, who from
boyhood believed that "we shall find nothing, that is the continual effect of nature, but what is of the means by which it is
brought to pass," and so could observe the "wondrous way of
the working of the spider" with "wonderment and pleasure,"
confident that the spider's self-destruction was planned by the
same power that, he noted, left spider eggs behind for "a new
stock the next year."

Elsewhere again and again Frost answers his question in a
way that we would expect, for it is no question but, like
Melville's, an answer. And typically this determinism reveals
itself in his reflections on the whiteness, not of aesthetically
repulsive night-time objects at all, but of the traditional natural phenomena of God's world. The simple fact of the
formation of frost, for example, as Dickinson's "blond assassin," in the gentle, even droll "Two Tramps in Mud Time,"
with its casual warning: mind you, Frost tells us,

Be glad of water, but don't forget
The lurking frost in the earth beneath
That will steal forth after the sun is set
And show on the water its crystal teeth

—wherein, again like Melville, he interrupts a topgallant
meditation on the peacefulness of the ocean's surface, as it
were, by a recollection of the teeth of the shark just beneath
that surface.

And not only the phenomenon of frost, but the white stars.
The buoyantly confident Emerson, for whom, unlike Dickinson, "Nature never wears a mean appearance," had written
in *Nature* a description of the stars as "envoys of beauty" that
"light the universe with their admonishing smile." In the
next generation the sentimental Bret Harte had told, in the
poem "Cicely," how a desert dweller frantically searching at
midnight for his temporarily crazed pregnant wife was guided
to her (and their newly born baby) by a star in the eastern
sky that is deliberately suggestive of an earlier and more historic star ushering in the age of faith. Emerson had, to be
sure, gone on (the Coleridge fraction in him tempering his
Wordsworthian whole) to concede that the power to produce
this delight "does not reside in nature. . . . Nature always
wears the colors of the spirit"; that there may be a difference,
in regard to the effect on that spirit, between "breathless
noon" and "grimmest midnight." Just how grim twentieth-
century man might find those very stars we had had a fore-
shadowing of in the closing years of the preceding century: in
Stephen Crane's "Open Boat," with its despairing correspondent kneeling in supplication to the night-time heavens and
observing: "A high cold star on a winter's night is the word
he feels that she says to him. Thereafter he knows the pathos
of his situation." As does the humble questioner of Frost's
early, obscure "Stars" (in *A Boy's Will*, 1913). He too begins
with a wondering, a musing "How countlessly they congre-

gate/. . . As if with keenness for our fate" but ends with a
recognition of their inexorability (and his own helplessness):

And yet with neither love nor hate,
Those stars like some snow-white
Minerva's snow-white eyes
Without the gift of sight.*

But more than all else—snow. Now, that form of whiteness
is capable of inspiring thoughts other than dread in him
(wherein his difference from Poe); still, it is this aspect that
most frequently mirrors his loss of faith. Although we have
the evidence of "The Onset" that contemplation of a snow-
storm can inspire affirmation in Frost—

I know that winter death has never tried
The earth but it has failed. . . .
And I shall see the snow all go down hill
In water of a slender April rill. . . .
Nothing will be left white but here a birch
And there a clump of houses with a church †

* Maxwell Perkins felt that the narrative technique Fitzgerald used in
The Great Gatsby permitted him to portray just such a despairing
vision of man's lot on earth: "In no other way could . . . the reader
have been enabled so strongly to feel at times the strangeness of human
circumstance in a vast heedless universe. In the eyes of Dr. Eckleburg
[we find] a superb touch . . . : great unblinking eyes, expressionless,
looking down upon the human scene." (John Hall Wheelock [ed.],
Editor to Author: The Letters of Maxwell E. Perkins, New York, 1950,
p. 38.)

† In "On the Heart's Beginning to Cloud the Mind" he rises to an
affirmation quite similar to that in "The Onset." Here the single human
light on the desert is "flickering" and "pathetic" and "maintained
against the night . . ./With a God-forsaken brute despair" only to the
traveler whose heart is clouding his mind, which can as easily tell him
that there are other lights and that the desert night holds no terrors at
all for the brave people who actually live there.

    As I have indicated earlier, Frost can use both black and white as
symbols of despair.

—still, the brief if striking piety of that last phrase is effectively cancelled by the reflections of one of his most engrossing (and familiar) poems, "Desert Places." For *desert*, of course, we are asked to read *empty*, devoid of meaning. Nothing less than this is the modern man's Minerva, goddess of wisdom. Now Frost tells us that his is not fear such as might arise from contemplation of the vastness of the universe:

They cannot scare me with their empty spaces
Between stars—on stars where no human race is.

But if not, then by no means for the same reason that the first contemplators of the New Science, over two centuries before, were able to put behind them the metaphysical dread that it could inspire. Pascal, while confessing that "The eternal silence of these infinite spaces terrifies me" and that "Man is but a reed, the weakest in nature," yet proceeds to an affirmation of faith in man's importance notwithstanding: reed, yes,

but he is a thinking reed. . . . A breath of air, a drop of water, suffices to kill him. But were the universe to crush him, man would still be more noble than that which kills him, because he knows that he dies; and the universe knows nothing of the advantage it has over him.

Our whole dignity consists, then, in thought. Our elevation must be derived from this, not from space and duration, which we cannot fill.

And John Donne proclaimed: "I need not call in new philosophy . . . to prove . . . that nothing upon earth is permanent"; for him *these bones can live* by virtue of the spirit: "with this goodness of God, . . . for all this dissolution and putrefaction, he affords this body a resurrection." But if those infinite spaces do not terrify Frost, it is because they are unreal to him and because the creation closer up, the empirically real creation, is so much more spiritually annihilating.*

If it is true that only by seeing where we have come from do we know where we are, then nothing could give us a more reliable bearing on the modern poet than to compare Robert Frost's reflections as he looks out at the "snow falling and night falling fast, oh, fast" with those recorded by another New England poet of a century before. Just as Frost notes "the ground almost covered smooth in snow," so in "A Winter Walk" Henry Thoreau watched the snow falling "on every wood and field, and no crevice is forgotten." For Frost's

The woods around it have it—it is theirs,
All animals are smothered in their lairs,

we have Thoreau's "Quadrupeds are confined to their coverts . . . and silently [all objects] are concealed, and the tracks of men and beasts are lost." And as though anticipating the Frost implication in *smothered,* he comments "With so little effort does nature reassert her rule and blot out the traces of men." But he has no such point of view, of course. For, as he continues, we perceive that it is the might of nature to blot out that *impresses* him and even *endears* it to him. Indeed, he can easily superimpose on his winter scene its luxuriant summer counterpart: "The snow levels all things, and infolds them deeper in the bosom of nature, as, in the slow summer, vegetation creeps up to the entablature of the temple, and the turrets of the castle, and helps her to prevail

* Even to the extent of the color symbolism, this poem of Frost's seems a restatement of Emily Dickinson's "One Need Not Be a Chamber to be Haunted." We can haunt ourselves better than any house can, she writes:

> Far safer, of a midnight meeting
> External ghost,
> Than an interior confronting
> That whiter host.

over art." Not so, Frost. The whiteness of the snow falling
about him is frightening in its ability to cancel out all evidence of man's work and will, all contours and designs, all
relationships of objects to each other without which we have
no importance.* And we are at a time when night is merely
falling, when the ground is not quite effaced in whiteness.
When night takes over completely, alas, we shall see nature
at her worst. Then there will be nothing but an undifferentiated whiteness against a total darkness—a stark contrast of
pure white and pure black full of soundless fury ("no expression") and signifying nothing ("nothing to express"). *These*
are the truly frightening desert places, then—the ones "so
much nearer home": they mirror and reaffirm the modern
poet's prior intimations of doubt and despair at his helplessness,—he, so much concerned, as he tells the "Tree at My
Window," with "inner" weather.

These desert places can appear occasionally even in non-
philosophical contexts. The snow of Nelson Algren's "How
the Devil Came Down Division Street" (*The Neon Wilderness*) reminds us momentarily both of the simple opening
scene of Bret Harte's *Gabriel Conroy* and the conclusion of
James Joyce's "The Dead." † In Algren's seriocomic story
the presiding deity of death actually makes an appearance.
The slum apartment house which the Orlovs live in is
haunted for a while by a young man who had hanged himself
in their apartment. On the night he knocked on the clothes
closet door of the apartment, we learn at the end, it was the
devil knocking ("Mama O. now tells, after many years and
Papa O. in his grave . . . that the young man who knocked
was in truth the devil") and it was on this same night that the
whiteness came:

* "Into many a green valley/Drifts the appalling snow," writes W. H.
Auden in "As I Walked Out One Evening."

† See Appendix.

All that night a light snow fell, while Roman O. lay wakeful, fancying he saw it falling on darkened streets all over the mysterious earth, on the pointing roof tops of old-world cities, on mountain-high waves of the mid-Atlantic, and in the leaning eaves of Noble Street. He was just falling off to sleep when the knocking came again. Three times, like a measured warning.[32]

And the jesting manner of James Thurber's musing on the exactly opposing associations in the human mind with the color white does not conceal from us the fact that he is repeating and extending the speculations of Rabelais in the sixteenth century and of Herman Melville in the nineteenth:

One noon recently, I woke up, weak and weary, having spent the time between three o'clock and five o'clock in the morning trying to figure out all the possible reasons for what the psychiatrists call leucophobia, an irrational fear of white or whiteness. I couldn't find the word in any dictionary I own —I had picked it up in a conversation with a psychologist I know—and so I telephoned him and asked him to explain the origin of this peculiar phobia, for the normal mind, if any, finds it puzzling that the raiment of the bride, the color of the Cliffs of Dover, the symbol of snow and sleigh bells at Christmastime should be a source of terror. The explanation, insofar as anyone knows, is that the fear is rooted in that most ancient of superstitions, the notion that ghosts are always clad in white and that death itself is therefore white. "The Ku Klux Klan," said my psychologist friend, "unquestionably adopted robes and hoods of white to perpetuate in their victims the terror of the ghost." The next morning, at three o'clock, the waking hour, the ghostly hour, I began searching for other possible sources of fear in that innocent conjunction of all colors.*

* "Thurber's brain was restlessly at it all the time, making patterns against the great white vertiginous abyss of Nothing. . . . Toward the end of his life, in blindness . . . he built (sometimes desperately) in-

Like Rabelais, so long ago, he is confronted with the puzzle
of such starkly contrasting associations:

I thought of the white radiance of eternity, the white plague,
the White Lady, white heat, white cargo, white rage, white
water (the sign of the surfacing whale), and the White House
and the Great White Father, which and who, respectively,
have terrified, during one Presidential administration and another, not only the red man but also the paleface and, many
would like to believe, the yellow man. Then there are the
white corpuscles, whose increase can be fatal; the whited
sepulchre; and the Great White Way (a term often credited
to Albert Bigelow Paine, biographer of that great and far
from fearsome man who loved to dress all in white, Mark
Twain). We also have, in our culture or history, or folklore,
the whites of their eyes, white lies that can be dangerous, the
white feather of cowardice, the white flag of surrender—but
you can take it from there; if you are a three-o'clock waker it
will ensure your staying awake until the first white light of
dawn.[33]

"R.P.W." in Robert Penn Warren's *Brother to Dragons*
(1953) is such a waker.[34] "We have lain on the bed and de-
vised evil in the heart" he confesses; and the reason he dwells
so long on the spirit-piercing view of the whiteness of the
winter night ("in radius of more than a thousand miles the
continent/Glitters whitely in starlight like a great dead eye
of ice.") is that this whiteness is paradoxically both an image
of evil, of the force that drove Lilburn Adams on to murder
(that force being "but part of the unleashed and unhoused
force of Nature,/Mindless, irreconcilable, absolute") and of
good, of

---

tricately interlocking battlements of words against chaos and Nothing."
(Paul Jennings, "Eminent Contemporaries," *Punch*, CCXLVIII [March
10, 1965], pp. 345, 346.)

. . . . . . *lethal purity, the incessant*
And whirling dream of desperate innocence,
*The infatuate glitter of the land of Platonic ice.**

■

We have come full circle, then: though halfway through
the twentieth century, we are yet as puzzled by the conflicting associations our mind makes with whiteness as was
Rabelais. But we have reversed the sixteenth century's proportions: though not unaware of God's power and mercy, yet
we are increasingly besieged by the devil. For to us the
Eternal Antagonist is still as real as to Cotton Mather, even
if in his infinite resourcefulness he has put on a costume of
the color of the heaven he forfeited. When the next damp,
drizzly November smothers Ishmael's soul, when his hypos
get the upper hand of him, will he again quietly take to the
ship—he who has found coffin warehouses at sea far more
frightening than any in his confining insular city of the man-
hattoes? "The sea is his, and he made it. . . ."? Verily, His
infamous son, the prince of darkness, now insolently sails all
seven of the seas, resplendent in the white radiance once re-
served for eternity.

* Pp. 214, 95, 96.
  Alfred Kazin refers to "that unending insistence on man's guilt" in
Warren's work. (*On Native Grounds*, p. 409.)

Edward Eggleston

. . . I thought who is calling who a lost generation? . . . I
thought that all generations were lost by something and always
had been and always would be. . . .
Ernest Hemingway, A Moveable Feast

■

To read the story of the literary mind of western man during
the last half of the nineteenth century is to hear a clamorous
chorus of disenchantment, bitterness, and despair. Following
upon the generally unswerving affirmation of Browning, Carlyle, and Emerson, we find the dogged groping of Tennyson,
the crisp cynicism of Clough, and the cheerful stoicism of
Fitzgerald, the varying degrees of disgust of Rimbaud, Housman, and Baudelaire, and the bitter resignation of Hardy.
Why this mournful procession, we have already wondered
about. From change itself? In an era participating in such
revolutions as this one, such sentiments were to be expected.

There was the political: Chartism and the flowering of democracy, the Age of the Common Man. The sociological: factory and city were taking the place of farm and town as characteristic units of living. And the philosophical: as the great astronomical revolution of the seventeenth century was followed by a geological revolution in the eighteenth, so out of this, in part, came the third scientific revolution—namely, the promulgation and general acceptance of the doctrine of evolution. Was the mind of man wearying from revolution, from the successive shock waves of theory upon faith?

Matthew Arnold's teachers took his faith from him, he tells us in "Stanzas from the Grande Chartreuse," and left him "Wandering between two worlds, one dead/The other powerless to be born." He identified in "The Scholar-Gipsy" "this strange disease of modern life,/With its sick hurry, its divided aims" and saw his generation

. . . . as on a darkling plain
Swept by confused alarums of struggle and flight
Where ignorant armies clash by night.

Clough spoke in "The New Sinai" of "atheistic systems dark," and while Tennyson complained bitterly in *In Memoriam* of "the faithless coldness of the times," Herman Melville referred lightly in "The Piazza" to "these times of failing faith and feeble knees." In the 1840's Carlyle warned his generation not to "sink yourselves in boundless bottomless abysses of Doubt, of wretched God-forgetting Unbelief;—you were miserable then, powerless, mad"; [1] and by the 1880's William Butler Yeats, "deprived by Huxley and Tyndall, whom I detested, of the simple-minded religion of my childhood," had found it necessary to make his own religion, a new and "almost . . . infallible church of poetic tradition. . . ." [2] Finally, as the century wore on to its dismal close we find one Singleton, in Conrad's *Nigger of the Narcissus*, looking out upon the immortal sea with its "heartless

might" and finding it "unchanged, black and foaming under
the eternal scrutiny of the stars; he heard its impatient voice
calling for him out of a pitiless vastness full of unrest, of
turmoil and of terror. He looked afar upon it, and saw an immensity tormented and blind, moaning and furious. . . ."

No more than this? Yes, even in England, home of match-
lessly melodious cynicism and despair. Of one of its great
minds, John Stuart Mill (whose works appeared side by side
with those of the deterministic biologists), Malcolm Cowley
has observed that while not blind to the forces in society in
opposition to progress, all the same he

returns time and again to the idea of improvement, as if it
were a law of the social universe. Indeed, for a man born in
1806, who had seen the world transformed during his own
lifetime by an unparalleled series of inventions, who had
watched the slow triumph of political reforms and social pro-
prieties . . . , who[se] class and country grew more powerful
year by year . . . it was hard not to believe that the age of
Victoria was immeasurably superior to the past . . . and
. . . that the same process of improvement would not con-
tinue indefinitely. . . .[3]

Meanwhile, in this country the early optimism of Walt
Whitman's *Leaves* persisted: "Facing West from California's
Shores" in the 1860's he saw the Asian land from which man
had sprung, "very pleas'd and joyous" to find himself thus at
last come full circle; and he spoke later, in "A Backward
Glance," of a "clue and purpose in Nature," of "invisible
spiritual results."

But by the 1920's, in this country, when Robert Frost
would face westward "Once By the Pacific," he would see in
its "shattered water" and the eyelike gleam of the ugly clouds
above it only an omen of "a night of dark intent," and would
warn this democracy to be "prepared for rage," a warning that
Oswald Spengler had issued a little while before (propheti-

cally, as the latter-day Caesars would shortly demonstrate).
And the Englishman, E. M. Forster, would shatter Whitman's own exposition of nature's purpose with the "skeptical
blight" of his *Passage to India*, with its insinuation, in Austin
Warren's words, "that human values have no basis in the
nature of things; that our moral distinctions are factitious;
that the universe mocks sinner and saint alike; that both our
aspirations and our intellections are folly in the presence of
the blind if not malevolent destiny which begat us." [4] "Passage to more than India" indeed!

To this murmurous universal litany literary criticism has
added the voices of two nineteenth-century Americans, Mark
Twain and Henry Adams, whose literary testaments of despair acquire significance in view of the cultural importance
of the men's widely disparate selves.[5] My purpose here is to
add to theirs yet another American voice, Edward Eggleston's.
There is something surprising about this; for the one time
his voice was heard by the great American reading public, it
was an entertaining and uplifting voice. Also there is truth in
the generalization that "pessimism was so rare in the nineteenth century of America . . . that its expression in Mark
Twain has a kind of singularity,"—finding it as we do in a
land so "awestruck by the mirage of Progress." [6] Certainly it
is true if we simply contrast the alarmed pitchfork resistance
of George Eliot's rustics and the personal doubts of Tennyson
at the approach of that powerful embodiment of progress—
the railroad—with Walt Whitman's admiring and Emily
Dickinson's whimsical treatment and Thoreau's wry recom-
mendation. But the transatlantic contagion would spread
westward nonetheless to a band of American intellectual travellers through the second half of the century. They were,
many of them, members of an early Lost Generation: theirs
was the fate to be born to the true faith of another age, watch
the temple at which they had worshipped totter, feel the
ground beneath their feet quake, and then struggle on with

only the maimed rites of their century's close to be performed at their own.

Historians respect Edward Eggleston, and students of American literary history know that to him they owe Hamlin Garland (and to Garland, Sinclair Lewis); his own fictional production was, by equal consensus, ordinary. But to the student of the life of the spirit in America in the second half of the nineteenth century his limitations are his very importance: it is testaments like his that must be examined with care by one who would learn the extent of faith's decline during those years even in this progress-minded land of ours. For this man who, bred in a region and time dominated by the fervor of evangelical Methodism, embraced that creed, spread its doctrines in two states, then turned to nonsectarianism, and forsook that eventually for agnosticism—such a man comes much closer to our definition of the American intellectual than do his exact contemporaries, Mark Twain and Henry Adams, by whose spiritual pulses we customarily measure the health of those times. "He had been a teacher, a preacher, a bible agent, a traveling salesman, a soap maker, a showman, a journalist"; he had "vacillated between fiction and history," between historians' history and popularized history: "Thus even in his literary career his energies were dangerously divided. He tried for too many prizes and always fell short of winning the highest." [7] Let us therefore place him in the center of the stage between his famous fellows *

* Eggleston and Adams seem never to have met and, except for their membership in the American Historical Association, possibly never were in any common circle of activity.

Eggleston and Twain met on more than one occasion during 1888–1889, in connection with their efforts in Washington, D. C., on behalf of the international copyright legislation. (W. P. Randel, *Edward Eggleston*, pp. 184ff.)

Twain and Adams never met, yet shared many common friends; and Twain "was to learn enough about Adams . . . to write a broad travesty on his exclusiveness in 'The Million Pound Bank Note.'" (Ernest Samuels: *Henry Adams: The Middle Years*, p. 20.)

—the western commoner Twain and the New England aristocrat Adams—in order the better to see this decline full face.
With these two as background we can find in the progress
and turnings, the steps backward and forward, of Eggleston's
personal and professional life a motif of the troubled mind
of an entire age.

Born in southern Indiana in December, 1837, Eggleston
began his institutionalized affiliation with religion when he
was nineteen. In 1856–1857 he was a circuit-rider in his native
region for a period of several months, which ended with a
physical collapse precipitated, probably, by the malarial conditions of the region. In 1857 he left for Minnesota, where
earlier a short stay had improved his health. This time his
stay lasted nine years, during which he served first as Bible
agent, then as pastor of small congregations. His devotion
was so remarkable that by 1859, at the age of twenty-one,
Eggleston was already pastor of one of the largest Methodist
churches in Minnesota. In 1866, however, we note, he gave
up his pastorate to enter journalism, moving to Chicago,
where he became a contributor to leading juvenile periodicals. Nevertheless, his religious fervor seems not to have
suffered diminution, for during the five Chicago years he was
active in Sunday-school work, undoubtedly deriving much
pleasure from his association with children, who formed (and
still form) his greatest audience.

By 1871 Eggleston had moved eastward again and had published his first novel, *The Hoosier Schoolmaster*. In this his
great achievement was to populate a region unknown elsewhere with convincingly quaint sinners and saints in what
has been acclaimed one of the earliest and most influential
tributaries to that rapidly flooding river of regional humor
fiction that delighted readers on both sides of the Atlantic during the post-Civil War literary discovery of the
America that lay west of the Appalachians and east of the
Berkshires. Mark Twain, from whose celebrated betrayed

frog of only a few years before the movement officially dates,
was steeped in Artemus Ward and B. P. Shillaber, had gone
west and been roughing it and was telling or retelling tall
tales of the far west or Negro folklore of his southern background; away to the east in England, Henry Adams was as-
sociating with the intellectuals on both sides of the Channel
and noting in the skies the new stars of Auguste Comte and
Karl Marx. In New York, Edward Eggleston was looking in
both directions. He had been reading a fairly rare foreign
import, Hippolyte Taine; but what he wanted to do was to
put down in its true and warm colors what he had seen and
heard in southern Indiana not so many years before. This
was, moreover, the Taine of the recent *Art in the Nether-
lands,* not of the earlier *History of English Literature* with its
outrageously materialistic introduction—that corrosive sub-
limate of all piety whatever. And *The Hoosier Schoolmaster*
certainly indicates the vigorousness of his own early faith.
The subject of religion is given far greater prominence in his
later—and consistently inferior—novels, to be sure; but it is
nowhere discussed more honestly than in this first, a novel
whose continuing popularity through the years eventually
became a source of annoyance to him. True, it is the early
sulphur-and-brimstone preaching of Eggleston's earlier years
that causes the culprit of this simple little story to reveal the
innocence of the hero, Ralph Hartsook; but it is simple faith
in God that changes the bully, Bud Means, into a useful
citizen. The writer who had created him tells us that his
schoolmaster "had been all his life repressing the animal and
developing the finer nature"; and he describes the fight within
Ralph's breast as "the same fight that Paul described so
dramatically. . . . Paul . . . called this dreadful something
the Old Adam, and I suppose Darwin would call it the remains of the Wild Beast."

Perhaps the best expression of the frontier religious creed
that Eggleston embraced at this period in his life is evident

in Ralph's conversation with Bud as the two set up the spiritual foundations of the "Church of The Best Licks":

"Do you think he'd help a feller? Seems to me it would be number one to have God help you. Not to help you fight the other folks, but to help you when it comes to fighting the devil inside. But you see I don't belong to no church."
"Well, let's you and me have one right off. Two people that help one another serve to make a church."

For the materials of another novel, *The Mystery of Metropolisville* (1873), Eggleston went back to his Minnesota experiences. History had been made here, some of it unsavory; and the minister-turned-author wrote a fictional tract attacking the vicious land-grabbing of the speculators who had invaded the region when it was thrown open for settlement. Accordingly, we find him voicing his displeasure at this Mammon-worship and offering true faith as the only salvation for mankind. This he displays in his treatment of Albert Charlton, a young man unremarkable except that he introduces the note of skepticism to be observed in Eggleston's writing. Concerning ministers, Albert tells his shocked mother (in words that seem an echo of Melville's stricture) * that "not more than one in twenty of them is brave enough to tell the truth." Furthermore, there is his surprising assertion blending modern scientific theorizing with an *Ecclesiastes*-like naturalism: "I don't believe that God cares. Everything goes by the almanac and natural law. The sun sets when the time comes, no matter who is belated." †

* ". . . Solomon was the truest man who ever spoke, and yet . . . he a little managed the truth with a view to popular conservatism; or else there have been many corruptions and interpolations of the text." (Letter to Hawthorne, June 1[?], 1851.)

† In England Arthur Hugh Clough was lamenting that whereas in olden times He had told Moses that God was One, now from "The New Sinai"

This would seem to be a fictional projection of Eggleston's own first questioning of Biblical authority in that age of the New Criticism; for, as he recalled in middle age, while still a youth of nineteen living "the strenuous pioneer life of Minnesota in 1856" he had already "assumed such cosmical tasks" as "settling the six days of creation, . . . for in that time, when Darwin and evolution were yet below the horizon, our chief bother was to get the stratified rocks correctly created according to Moses." * But like his author, Albert Charlton eventually finds his way out of this dark forest by the aid of Holy Writ; for later, when Albert faces imprisonment, such pessimistically deterministic avowals afford him no solace, and he begins reading the Bible:

. . . he read the story of the trial and condemnation of Jesus. . . . Albert saw the profound essential unity of the narratives, he felt the inspiration of the sublimest character in human history. . . . Charlton, unbeliever that he was, wet the pages with tears, tears of sympathy with the high self-sacrifice of Jesus, and tears of penitence for his own moral weakness, which stood rebuked before the great Example.

By Science strict so speaks He now
To tell us, There is None!
Earth goes by chemic forces. . . .

In Europe, Dostoevsky's morbid "Underground Man" was rebelling against "the laws of nature, the deductions of natural science, mathematics": ". . . I dislike those laws and the fact that twice two makes four. . . . I am not going to be reconciled to it simply because it is a stone wall and I have not the strength."

* ". . . it would have been impossible to introduce, let alone to prove, a biological theory of gradual change, if geology had continued to teach that world-wide catastrophes had several times caused wholesale destruction in the world. . . . [Sir Charles Lyell's] uniformitarian principle . . . when applied to biology, implied both gradualness of evolution, and an attitude of mind which was unfavourable to the *ad hoc*, miraculous type of explanation, which, in the last resort, all Darwin's opponents relied on." (Alvar Ellegård, *Darwin and the General Reader*, Göteborg, 1958, p. 289.)

Finally, when he is put into prison, talks with the chaplain begin to weaken his skepticism, and his spiritual regeneration is apparent in his confession: "I . . . am coming to believe in a Providence! . . . I have been a high-church skeptic. . . . But I have learned some things. I am yet unsettled in my opinions about Christ. . . . But I believe *in* him with all my heart."

Was this fictional facing of the tempter in the wilderness in fact a projection of its author's own spiritual conflict? one wonders. Certainly Charlton's remarks above sound like those of the thinkers of the times, for by 1891 Thomas Hardy would be putting these remarks into the mouth of his young Tess Durbeyfield:

" 'I am forbidden to believe that the great Power who moves the world would alter His plans on my account. . . . I have been cured of the presumption of thinking otherwise . . . by my husband. . . . I have [religion] though I don't believe in anything supernatural.' " [8]

Actually the spiritual situation of *The Mystery of Metropolisville* had been faced before in Eggleston's novel *The End of the World* (1872), which concludes with a similar resolution of doubt and of despair of God's bounty. The action in this essentially humorous fiction concerns the Millerite end-of-the-world scare of 1843, but belief in the divinity of Jesus is the vitalizing element. Eggleston is amused at the strait-laced Cynthy Ann and Brother Goshorn, and attacks the petty basis of Millerism, which he considers a form of Mormonism. Throughout he advocates a truer faith, a putting into practice of the teachings of Jesus and an acceptance of God's love, as in *The Hoosier Schoolmaster*. Thus, when August Wehle is forced to run away, his mother and sister kneel with him and pray for his safety in a mid-Victorian tableau of piety and of devil of doubt shamed—a

Psalms-like victory over repeated promptings of despair. "Perhaps there is no God. Or perhaps He is so great that our praying has no effect. Perhaps this strong crying of our hearts to him in our extremity is no witness of his readiness to hear." So Eggleston begins. But he goes on:

Let him live in doubt who can. Let me believe that the tender mother-heart and the loving sister-heart in that little cabin *did* reach up to the great Heart that is over us all in Fatherly love, did find a real comfort for themselves, and did bring a strength-giving and sanctifying something upon the head of the young man, who straightway rose up refreshed and departed out into the night . . . carrying with him thoughts and memories and—who shall doubt?—a genuine heavenly inspiration.

Elsewhere in the book, with less pulpit rhetoric, Eggleston affirms the basic tenet of the Christian faith: "The sublimest self-sacrifice is only possible to a man by the aid of some strong moral tonic. God's love is the chief support of the strongest spirits." But the most eloquent of Eggleston's praise of the Bible is contained in Julia's reaction to the Gospel of Matthew:

"Come unto me all ye that labor and are heavy laden," she read and stopped. That means me, she thought with a heart ready to burst. And that saying is the gateway of life. . . . "And I will give you rest." And so she drank in the passage . . . and then God seemed to her so different. The old feeling was gone. She was no more a rebel nor an orphan. The presence of God was . . . a benediction. She had found rest for her soul, and He gave his beloved sleep.

". . . who shall doubt?" Yet perhaps "the old feeling" was never gone for long, and the rebel would not down. Actually it was a rebellion against doctrinal conformity that he had demonstrated a dozen years before this in Minnesota, when he had publicly denounced uniform Sunday school lessons for all different denominations, shoddy melodrama purveyed as temperance fiction, and the opposition of the Roman Catholic church to general distribution of the Bible; and even before this it was his decision to sell bibles that took him away from his study of New England unorthodoxy (Emerson, Channing, and Parker).[9] Concerning Eggleston's religious outlook now in the 1870's, a *Scribner's Monthly* writer had this reassuring report: "In some particulars his opinions have changed since he rode that first circuit in Indiana, but he has never unlearned his regard for the faithful men who hold forth the word of life to the dwellers of the border." [10] But in his brother's account, the emphasis was perceptibly different. George Cary Eggleston writes that Edward was still a member of the Minnesota Conference ("partly from a feeling of good fellowship and partly because he felt a keen sympathy with the preachers out there in the good work they were doing for morality and the amelioration of life"); but he adds that Edward "had become so unorthodox in his belief that one of them threatened him about this time with a heresy prosecution because he wrote in one of his novels [*The End of the World*] that it is only a theological quibble which denies to marriage an equal rank with baptism and the eucharist as a sacrament." [11]

Eggleston's religious views had evidently already begun to swing away from piety to critical inquiry. Yet no suggestion even of heterodoxy appears in *The Circuit Rider* (1874), a novel written as a tribute to the fervor of these itinerant clergymen and to the success of their labors—they to whom God was the "consuming fire" that Paul reminded the Hebrews of. It is they who convert the tormented Kike, the slipping Goodwin, and the haughty Patty, and who infuse into the meagre frontier existence a faith bordering at times on ecstasy. In short, *The Circuit Rider* is as enthusiastic a fictional rendition of the charm of Methodism as the church

itself could have wished. Eggleston's own estimation of the
nature of his attempt is revealing: "Up to this point I have
walked by faith; I could not see how the present generation
could be made to comprehend the earnestness of their grandfathers. But I have hoped that, none the less, they might
dimly perceive the possibility of a religious fervor that was as
a fire in the bones." Which in turn leads us to wonder: was
Eggleston giving public voice to the firmness of his devotion
to Methodism or actually writing a moving obituary of that
faith? Soon we know.

The financial returns from his books had by now made it
possible for Eggleston to devote himself entirely to writing,
but after the appearance of *The Circuit Rider* his interests
became more diversified. Of the years 1874–1878, George
Cary Eggleston writes that "he brought out no book except
a little volume of juvenile stories. He was writing a good deal
for the magazines, however. . . . He was also compiling and
editing two sumptuously published subscription books, the
one called 'Christ in Art,' and the other, 'Christ in Literature.' " His name had been dropped from the rolls of the
Methodist Conference of Minnesota, but it turns out that he
had by no means forsaken pastoral cares. Yet when, in the
autumn of 1874, he was asked to take charge of the Lee
Avenue Congregational Church in Brooklyn, he accepted on
terms that are indicative of the position we have seen him
approaching on religious matters. He insisted that he "could
not meet the requirements of any orthodox council, nor
would he on any account take charge of a church which im-
posed any creed upon its members or exacted any profession
of faith at their hands." The church's attendance grew rapidly. Eggleston waged no doctrinal wars, had no care for
creeds, and pleaded only for liberality. How far he had come
from the simple gospel of his frontier past!

During the five years of this new pastorate, Eggleston published only one book, but *Roxy* (1878) is all that we need for

an insight into the new Eggleston. Gone are the patient humor and gentle remonstrance with which he had looked upon the formalistic aspects of religion in the earlier novels. When Mark Bonamy, the erstwhile zealous minister, is called before the local church for having dared to attend a circus, Eggleston lashes out with a startling, unprecedented vindictiveness:

A man might in that time be a miser, he might be dishonest in a mild way, he might be censorious and a backbiter from a pious standpoint, he might put the biggest apples on the top of the barrel or the little potatoes in the bottom of the bag, and the church could not reach him. But let him once see a man ride on two bare-back horses and jump through a hoop: That was a tangible apostasy, sure to bring ecclesiastical penalties.

So far, this is a down-to-earth gloss of a familiar Biblical warning: "Shame upon you, Pharisees and Scribes, hypocrites—for you keep clean the outside of the cup, but the inside is full of extortion and excess!" Of such warnings the literature of his day contained many examples. (And he would find a modern scientific commentary for this in his final novel, *The Faith Doctor,* in which he quotes Charles Darwin as saying that "a man may be made more unhappy by committing a breach of etiquette than by falling into sin.") But as the outburst continues, it rises to the proportions of a violent censure that throws light upon the pursuit his mind was evidently already embarked upon:

Brave old ironside fathers: Blessings on you for chopping Charles Stuart's head off, and planting Plymouth Rock: You freed us from the Middle Ages; for which thanks. But you straightway bound upon us your own severe prejudices, and they have come down to us by all hands. The most dominant influence in this English-speaking world of ours today, is not that of Shakespeare, but of the brave cobblers and tinkers, whom the seventeenth century stuck in the stocks and prison-houses, and the fervent Wesleyan village blacksmiths and Yorkshire farmers of the eighteenth century are yet masters of the nineteenth. To this day we take our most innocent amusements in a guilty and apologetic fashion, bowing to the venerable prejudice, and saying "By your leave, sir!" *

It turns out, it should be added, that Eggleston was cavilling only at the letter of the religious law, not at the spirit; for at the end of the novel the once irreproachably pious Roxy Bonamy takes her place in church and for the first time hears the sermon's true message in a spirit befitting that of the cleansed souls of Eggleston's earlier work:

Every word dropped like a benediction into her heart. She bowed her head upon the back of the seat in front of her and wept. . . . And of all who knelt . . . in that old church that day to eat and drink the bread and wine, there were none who took the secret sacrament as did the woman who had dared to give her heart for others, after the pattern of the Master of self-sacrifice.

Still, the unprecedented loss of control cited above was not without meaning. A year later Eggleston gave up the ministry—this time, forever—and left immediately for Europe. His brother recalls that before the departure "he told me what I had already guessed, namely, that the strain which had done more than all else to bring on his collapse was not that of ceaseless work, but that of a mind ill at ease."

* In the South—where Wesley's proselytizing had had an immense harvest—in these years "Discourse had reigned over questions like diabolic pleasures and whether the use of a tuning-fork in church was not a violation of the word of God; and young people were expelled from congregations for dancing in circles instead of back and forth like bobbins in a shuttle." (Van Wyck Brooks, The Confident Years, London, 1953, p. 31.)

There, it was out,—if not to the world at large, to someone who would understand. George Eggleston's memoir continues in paraphrase of his brother's words:

"How can I go on preaching, . . . to profess what I no longer believe? For the last year I have had to study carefully every word I have spoken from the pulpit, lest I use terms that might imply a faith which I have not, and thus, while preaching morality, be guilty of an immorality on my own account. . . . I have wanted to go on with this work, because of the great good it is doing to others. . . . My only hope is that some one may be found who can carry it on . . . without having to compromise with his conscience, as I should have to do with mine." [12]

The break thus long postponed had inevitably come. Could the converse of the old article also be true—that works without faith were dead? In any event, he confided to *Forum* readers in 1887, his "struggle for emancipation from theological dogma" had been "long and painful" but irrevocable:

There came a time . . . when my intellectual conscience insisted that sentiment . . . be put aside in the search for truth. Doubtless there were numberless influences. . . . But I remember three words of Sainte-Beuve . . . that stung me like a goad when this change was approaching. . . . [T]here were certain doctrines which [an] ex-priest had *mis en reserve*. . . . I had also put many things in reserve. . . . From the time that I resolved that nothing should be any more "put in reserve" by me, but that all my opinions, even the most sacred and venerable, should go into the crucible, I date what I deem a truer and freer intellectual life than I had known before. . . .

There is a little copy of à Kempis that I used to carry on journeys with the purpose of quickening my spirit. . . . I am sure it did me good. But reading à Kempis is like saying one's prayers in a crypt . . . and it is hard for a real nineteenth

century man to go down stairs to pray. . . . Besides, . . .
the true way is to "look upward and not downward, outward
and not inward, forward and not backward." À Kempis may
rest where he is; I would rather walk in wide fields with
Charles Darwin. . . .[13]

Just how much comfort his restless mind would find in
those ampler confines, we shall see. It is, however, worth
mentioning that to his contemporaries Darwin's were fields
that could be thought of as wide. There was that famous
passage, with its mixture of inexorability and piety, that closes
The Origin of Species:

It is interesting to contemplate a tangled bank, clothed with
many plants of many kinds, with birds singing on the bushes,
with various insects flitting about, and with worms crawling
through the damp earth, and to reflect that these elaborately
constructed forms, so different from each other, and depend-
ent upon each other in so complex a manner, have all been
produced by laws acting around us. . . . Thus, from the
war of nature, from famine and death, the most exalted object which we are capable of conceiving, namely, the production of the higher animals, directly follows. There is
grandeur in this view of life, with its several powers, having
been originally breathed by the Creator into a few forms or
into one; and that, whilst this planet has gone cycling on
according to the fixed law of gravity, from so simple a beginning endless forms most beautiful and most wonderful have
been, and are being evolved.*

Surely this did what it could (even if then, as now, it would
have been impossible to say how much this was) to counter-
act such feelings as Darwin's older readers might have had
about certain remarks immediately preceding that passage

* "This was the new grand design that gave Victorians faith when the
old faith had eroded away." (Stanley Edgar Hyman, *The Tangled Bank*,
p. 39.)

(for example, that "species are produced and exterminated
. . . not by miraculous acts of creation" and that "no
cataclysm has desolated the whole world")* or such as
readers of any age might have had about his prediction there
that "it will be the common and widely-spread species, belonging to the larger and dominant groups within each class,
which will ultimately prevail and procreate new and dominant species." Also we need to be reminded of the consolation—for all the gloom—that might be derived from
Darwin's later book, *The Descent of Man*, particularly by
men who were believers; for, when read in the light of an
earlier optimism, Darwin could be seen to afford further
proof of progress: "The ascent of man was substituted for
the fall, and the duty to improve mankind was regarded as
an injunction of natural law certified by evolution." [14] But
Eggleston's position seems mere resignation when compared
with the glowing optimism of his contemporary intellectual
John Fiske (like Eggleston, a believer turned historian).
Fiske's retrospective glance at the Darwinian years is reminiscent of Wordsworth's *Prelude* passage about the rapture
he felt in the months following the fall of the Bastille:

To have lived when this prodigious truth was advanced, de-
bated, established, was a rare privilege in the centuries. The
inspiration of seeing the old isolated mists dissolve and reveal
the convergence of all branches of knowledge is something
that can hardly be known to the men of a later generation,
inheritors of what this age has won.[15]

Certainly Eggleston's last two novels betray more of a
deepening religious disillusionment. In *The Graysons* (1887),
a historical novel (he was tending more and more toward

---

* Or their children! Yeats as a schoolboy had read Darwin, Wallace,
Huxley, and Haeckel, and "was hot for argument in refutation of Adam
and Noah and the Seven Days." (W. B. Yeats, *Autobiographies*, pp.
73–74.)

fact and away from faith), the familiar religious digressions
are absent, understandably. Still, the devil would not down.
Once he sours a mere parenthesis. Speaking of social customs
in Illinois in the days before the Civil War, Eggleston recalls "athletic feats, practical jokes, and tales as rude as the
most unblushing of those told by pious pilgrims to Canter-
bury in the old religious time"—a caustic, Twain-like remark
which betrays the scientific mind of the historian displacing
the reverence of the former evangelist. But this is as nothing
beside a long passage in which cynicism gives way to unre-
deemed agnosticism. It begins with the sad and bitter reflection on the victimizing of youth by forces beyond its control,
or even its knowledge, that seems an interesting anticipation
of a certain reflection on a dairy-maids' dormitory by one of
the most pessimistic of Eggleston's English contemporaries:
"Is it not a rather poor fist of a world, after all, this in which
we live, where the most critical and irrevocable decisions
must be made while the unexperienced youth is tossed with
gusts of passion and blinded by traditional prejudices or cap-
tivated by specious theories?" * He continues, using as his
point of departure a famous painting by Retzsch which
allegorizes the ancient belief in the freedom and importance
of the human mind (and which, it happens, Darwin's spokesman, Huxley, had referred to in his "A Liberal Education
and Where to Find It"): "The old allegorists painted the
young man as playing chess with the devil; but chess is a
game of skill. What the young man plays is often a child's
game of pitch and toss, cross or pile, heads or tails, for stakes
of fearful magnitude."

This fatalistic despair continues into *The Faith Doctor*

* "The air of the sleeping-chamber seemed to palpitate with the hopeless passion of the girls. They writhed feverishly under the oppressiveness
of an emotion thrust on them by cruel Nature's law—an emotion which
they had neither expected nor desired." (Thomas Hardy, *Tess of the
D'Urbervilles*, Ch. 23.)

(1891). It is significant that here, in his last novel, Eggleston turns his attention to one of his century's various reactions to the grey melancholy brought on by its scientism and rationalism: now Eggleston adjusts his unsparing glance to the Christian Science movement. In opening, he disclaims any such purpose as "to depreciate anybody's valued delusions"; he has merely intended, he goes on, "to make a study of human nature under certain modern conditions." But the scientific approach implicit even in his disclaimer serves as a guide to his treatment of this recent fervor, which cannot have helped seeming to him his own earlier piety in another form: "There is nothing to it but to wait for the middle ages to pass," his preface states; "when modern times arrive, there will be more criticism and less credulity, let us hope." To give voice to his private brooding he returns to the fatalistic metaphor of *The Graysons* and exclaims: "What a haphazard world this is! Draw me no Fates with solemn faces, holding distaffs and deadly snipping shears. The Fates? Mere children pitching heads and tails upon the paving-stones!" These were the Fates of the famous Italian painting, whom Hawthorne had found chilling a generation before; whom Eggleston's contemporary, Thomas Hardy, was defining in the title of his poem "Hap," where they receive his execration in line after line ("Crass Casualty," "dicing Time," "purblind Doomsters"); and whom Eggleston's Lost Generation successors Faulkner and Hemingway would also berate.

Shortly afterwards, Eggleston set about writing yet another novel, again taking as its subject matter the religious movements of New York City of the day, but replacing *The Faith Doctor's* faith-healers and Christian Scientists with Salvation Army and temperance workers. But the new novel would not come to life, and Eggleston had to abandon it, his last book-length fictional undertaking. It was to have been entitled *Agnostic*.[16]

That would have fitted so much that his contemporaries

were writing. At this time in Eggleston's life, A. E. Housman
was advising: "Think no more lad, laugh, be jolly/Why
should men make haste to die?" And his Polish contemporary was creating in *Victory* a hero named Axel Heyst who,
as a young man, "had learned to reflect, which is a destructive
process," since "great achievements are accomplished in a
blessed, warm, mental fog, which the pitiless cold blasts
of . . . analysis [blow] away . . ."; who in the deepening
despondency of middle age tells the warm, unfathoming
sharer of his isolation that "Man on this earth is an unfore-
seen accident which does not stand close investigation": that
"every age is fed on illusions, lest men should renounce life
early and the human race come to an end." These are almost
the very words with which the lost man of our study was
taking leave of his own untenable role: "Let us not," Eggleston advises, "be of the class unbearable who are ever trying
to dissipate those lovely illusions that keep alive human complacency and make life endurable."

Half a century before, Eggleston's brother in spirit, Herman Melville, moved by who knows what Promethean anguish, had fired a round at tradition and dogma. One error
in a ship's log, Ishmael points out, could make seafarers for
years believe that what was only the expansive black back of
a momentarily resting whale was actually a reef to be avoided
at all costs; and so, sneeringly, "There's Orthodoxy for you!"
It was on this note that Eggleston now ended his long career
as a fictional accomplice of belief. He writes in *The Faith
Doctor*:

How many dogmas have lived for centuries, not by their rea-
sonableness but by the impressiveness of trappings! Creeds
recited under lofty arches, liturgies chanted by generation
following generation . . . —these all take considerable advantage from the power of accessories to impose upon the human imagination. The divinity that hedges kings is the result

of a set of stage-fixings which make the little great, and half
the horror inspired by the priest's curse is derived from the
bell and book and candle.

It was a determinist turned historian who derided those
anathemas. In truth, the spiritual Eggleston was dead; only
the scholar remained. But in no inactivity of doubt. Twenty
years of characteristically vigorous life remained to him, in
which he accumulated materials for a vast *History of Life in
the United States*. Two volumes made their appearance at
the turn of the century, their front matter demonstrating that
although it had not been possible for their author to write
fiction without writing history at the same time, there would
be no fiction mixed with history here: "The founders of the
little settlements," he tells us in the preface to *The Begin-
ners of a Nation*, "I have not been able to treat otherwise
than unreverently. . . . This walking backward to throw a
mantle over the nakedness of ancestors may be admirable
as . . . piety, but it is none the less reprehensible in the
writing of history." And, finally, in the preface to *The Transit
of Civilization*:

The little world of the seventeenth century man must be understood. . . . Right and wrong were thought of only as the
result of direct revelation; they had not yet found standing
room in the greater theater of natural knowledge. . . . It is
the last age which sought knowledge of physical things by
deduction. The next century brought philosophy and philosophy dawned into science.

With what penalties, at what price to individual peace of
mind, we have been witnessing. And yet, to have made his
transit from seventeenth-century piety and dogmatism to
nineteenth-century scientific enlightenment was, despite the
jars and shocks en route, to have transcended youth and

attained the spiritual comforts of the secular faith possible even to an incurably inquiring mind.

What had happened to those lamps of hope, of faith in man that the Renaissance had kindled, in whose bright light emperors had been humbled ever since? "An age of revolutions and constitutions," John Adams had termed the 1765–1815 period. "I have traveled in fair France," Thomas Jefferson tells Robert Penn Warren, "in that land/Of sunlight and the sunlit spirit that once/Itself shed light on all our faces. . . ." [17] "The morning is opening upon us," the great scientist and intellectual Joseph Priestley had written in 1782,* "and we cannot doubt but that the light will increase, and extend itself more and more unto the perfect day. Happy are they who contribute to diffuse the pure light of this everlasting gospel." [18] This, only seven years before the storming of the Bastille. Then, rulers across Europe had been threatened in the middle of the next century, this great Century of the Common Man: "It was not long after 1848; and, somehow, about that time, all around the world, these kings, they had the casting vote, and voted for themselves," the triumphantly democratic Herman Melville had facetiously written about royalty's predicament in "The Piazza." The revolutionary poets had celebrated Man. With him Wordsworth had peopled his early poetry and prose, announcing at the birth of the century his decision "to choose incidents and situations from common life. . . ." Wordsworth, Goldsmith, Burns, Cowper, Goethe, Carlyle—all the transatlantic idealists had earned Emerson's praise: they, he told the intellectual elite of Cambridge in 1837, had united "the lowest

---

* It was precisely to these years (and just possibly to Priestley himself) that Hawthorne refers in "The Birthmark," to their "faith in man's ultimate control over Nature." Those were the days, he tells us, "when the comparatively recent discovery of electricity and other kindred mysteries of Nature seemed to open paths into the region of miracle," when intellectual man could hope eventually to "lay his hand on the secret of creative force and perhaps make new worlds for himself."

trench" with the heights, had sung "the shop, the plough,
and the ledger. . . ." He too embraced the common, Emerson
had declared. Melville in 1851 had celebrated the "abound-
ing dignity" that he found "shining in the arm that wields a
pick or drives a spike. . . ." [19] In 1855 Whitman had spoken
of "the noble character of the young mechanics and of all
free American workmen," [20] (and said some years later "To a
Common Prostitute" that he did not exclude her). Just as in
the late years of the preceding century European liberals had
taken heart from American revolutionary action, so now during mid-century the leaders of the oppressed European masses
found enthusiastic crowds around them when they came to
these shores. "If there is any period one would desire to be
born in, is it not the age of Revolution?" Emerson had asked.
As a youth Howells heard Louis Kossuth in Columbus and
became a supporter of the Hungarian emancipator (even
adopting the Kossuth hat); [21] and Whitman had wished
courage "To a Foil'd European Revolutionaire." Was not
civilization thronging with devout daily worshippers at the
statue of Progress now in the place of the old one of the
Goddess of Reason that the equally optimistic Jacobins had
erected at the dawn of the century?

But that light was burning more and more fitfully in these
United States as the century waned. "That excitement about
Kossuth, consider how characteristic, but superficial, it was!
—only another kind of politics or dancing," Thoreau chided
his countrymen in "Life Without Principle" (1863). In
"Shooting Niagara" the aging and embittered Carlyle had
viewed the masses haughtily and, Walt Whitman thought,
"from the highest feudal point of view"; yet, he confessed in
Democratic Vistas (1871), he had to consider a "formidable"
point Carlyle's sneering question "whether we expect to
elevate and improve a nation's politics by absorbing" certain
"morbid collections and qualities therein." The Whitman of
the Gilded Age spoke differently from the Whitman of the

American Renaissance: "I myself see clearly enough the crude, defective streaks in all the strata of the common people; the specimens and vast collections of the ignorant, the credulous, the unfit and the uncouth, the incapable, and the very low and poor." Meanwhile, the Common Prostitute had never acknowledged his greeting.*

The price of progress was proving a high one. With industry had come more and larger cities, slums, and economic tensions and hostilities. As—or even before—the century began, the Romantic poets had intuitively rejected the city as sinister: the son in Wordsworth's "Michael" is corrupted there, where wealth accumulates, and men decay; Cowper speaks of cities as "a common and most noisome sewer" in "The Task"; and Blake's poem about "London" is a most mournful dirge. It was beginning to appear that Carlyle had been right in *Past and Present:* the medieval slave with a chain about his neck might have been more "free" than the worker of the 1840's.†

Eventually the United States would reach this position. From the beginning its idealists had resisted industry: Emerson tells us in "The American Scholar" that the best of American youth "are hindered from action by the disgust which the principles on which business is managed inspire," Thoreau scorned trade, and there was a proliferation of socialistic communities substituting for the disgusting principles some other—in Brook Farm, that of "association." Mel-

---

* By 1881 Sidney Lanier could say about the "democratic poetry" that the century thought it had brought into being: ". . . the two English poets who have most exclusively claimed to represent the people in poetry . . . , namely, Wordsworth and Whitman, are precisely the two whose audience has been most exclusively confined to the other extreme of culture." (Clarence Gohdes and Kemp Malone [eds.], *The Centennial Edition of the Works of Sidney Lanier*, Baltimore, 1945, IV, p. 44.)

† "After the French Revolution, naïveté about freedom should have disappeared." (Geoffrey Clive, *The Romantic Enlightenment*, New York, 1960, p. 174.)

ville was jibing at industry in *Mardi* and "The Tartarus of Maids"; and in "Calamus" Whitman confesses to posterity that he bequeaths it merely a few songs, not a "labor-saving machine." And now, almost half a century beyond the morning exuberance of "The American Scholar" the aged Emerson could see evidence that *plus ça change, plus c'est la même chose:*

In the law courts, crimes of fraud have taken the place of crimes of force. The stockholder has stepped into the place of the warlike baron. The nobles shall not any longer, as feudal lords, have power of life and death over the churls, but now, in another shape, as capitalists, shall in all love and peace eat them up as before.[22]

Albion Tourgée complained in 1890 that "During the last half-century, the segregation of capital in a few hands has been equaled only by the restriction of opportunity. . . . Already a new feudalism has been developed. . . . Those who serve and those who control are being separated by sharper lines and more inflexible barriers." And Sidney Lanier, in "The Symphony," "opposed chivalry to all-blighting trade in a fashion that merges chivalry with Christianity and makes trade the root of all evil." *

The aging Herman Melville who found in the pessimism of James Thomson's poetry "a counterpoise to the exorbitant hopefulness, juvenile and shallow, that makes such a bluster in these days," [23] is the same Melville whose own exorbitant hopefulness about the American experiment had led him

* Henry Nash Smith, *Mark Twain's Fable of Progress*, New Brunswick, New Jersey, 1964, pp. 9–10, 72–73.
  Van Wyck Brooks speaks of the "soulless forces" at work on the American scene and mind around the turn of the century: "forces that were changing the American scene, replacing the old world of the farm with an industrial world, undermining more and more, as the great monopolies grew in power, the old American sense of freedom and the will." (*The Confident Years*, p. 136.)

thirty-five years before to assert that "men not very much
inferior to Shakespeare are this day being born on the banks
of the Ohio." [24] Now, in his copy of *Julius Caesar*, beside
Casca's description of the inconstancy of the Roman public's
attitude toward Caesar, Melville wrote "TAMMANY HALL." [25]
And Emerson was now scorning, not embracing, the common, an 1867 book was pointing out (and Melville was
noting).*

From the disgruntled complaints of an aging poet-turned-
Inspector of Customs, a prosperous New York Stock Exchange broker-turned-poet could easily dissent. Certainly the
circumspective view of Edmund C. Stedman was done in
fresh, light pastels: "The general independence and comfort
have not bred those dramatic elements which imply conditions of splendor and squalor, glory and shame, triumph and
despair." In no other country, he was sure, "are there so
many happy little households," could a man's toil meet with
such certain rewards; "and the peerless exploits of our en-
gineers, capitalists, discoverers, speak louder than a minstrel's
words." All in all, it was an "amazing drama of triumphant
effort and organization. . . ." †

* "Even the kindly Emerson illustrates the temptation of the great
to scorn the commonalty, when he speaks of 'enormous populations,
like moving cheese,—the more the worse'; 'the guano-races of mankind';
'the worst of charity is, that the lives you are asked to preserve are not
worth preserving'; 'masses! the calamity is the masses.' " (William R.
Alger, *The Solitudes of Nature, etc.*, Boston, 1867.) For Melville's
bitter commentary, see Jay Leyda, *The Melville Log*, II, p. 720.

† *Poets of America*, Boston, 1885, p. 17. Published in September, this
book went through at least twenty printings before the end of the year.
    This kind of optimism appears in the fiction of the time as well.
Here are two random examples; both are satiric. A character fittingly
named Cockerel in Henry James's "The Point of View" (1882) "says
that Mamma is evidently not familiar with the march of improvement
in this country" after her long residence abroad; "she speaks of 1855 as
if it were a hundred years ago." (He is speaking in 1880.) And of course,
there is the brilliant future of Romper, Nebraska, as Old Scully pro-
claims it in Stephen Crane's "The Blue Hotel" (1898): " 'Why, man,

At the same time that Edwin Arlington Robinson was confessing to a friend that if not for occasional glimpses "of the
real light through the clouds of time" he would "be tempted,
as Tennyson used to be, to stick my nose into a rag soaked
with chloroform and be done with it," [26] he was admitting
that his own feelings were out of step with the times; that
"the whole trend of popular thought is in the wrong direction—not only that, but proud of the way it is taking. . . .
The age is all right, material progress is all right, Herbert
Spencer is all right, hell is all right." And the visiting T. H.
Huxley felt the need merely to call attention to the risks that
democracy and capitalism offered the peaceful and busy
land, along with the opportunities. He compliments us on
our "strings of great and well-ordered cities," on our "enormous actual, and almost infinite potential, wealth in all
commodities," saying that "in the energy and ability which
turn wealth to account, there is something sublime in the
vista of the future. . . ." Then, more soberly: "The great
issue, about which hangs a true sublimity, and the terror of
overhanging fate, is what are you going to do with all these
things? . . . You and your descendants have to ascertain
whether this great mass will hold together under the forms of
a republic, and the despotic reality of universal suffrage. . . ."
Probably mindful of the crises his own country was under-
going, he offers this warning and prayer:

as population thickens in your great cities, and the pressure of
want is felt, the gaunt spectre of pauperism will stalk among
you, and communism and socialism will claim to be heard.
Truly America has a great future before her; great in toil, in

we're goin' to have a line of ilictric street cars in this town next spring.
. . . And . . . there's a new railroad goin' to be built down from Broken
Arm to here. Not to mintion the four churches and the smashin' big
brick schoolhouse. Then there's the big factory, too. Why, in two
years Romper'll be a met-tro-*pol*-is.' "

care, and in responsibility; great in true glory if she be guided
in wisdom and righteousness; great in shame if she fail.[27]

Some years later William Dean Howells would more or less
restate these views in his celebrated *Criticism and Fiction*
(1886–1891). It is true—as we know from countless references
to the remark—that he counselled American novelists to
"concern themselves with the more smiling aspects of life,
which are the more American"; * but we should take note
that in the passage in which this famous participial appears,
there are at least three ominous concessions, warnings—
Howells' awareness that he is speaking more for the past
than the present and future. This very "march of mind," as
Tennyson had termed it, beginning with the Renaissance
—Howells is in effect saying—is precisely what had created
such situations as capital *vs.* labor that were so dismaying to
the very same mind. If, Howells wrote, the American's world
was different from the Englishman's (breathing, as he did,
"a rarified and nimble air full of shining possibilities and
radiant promises" unavailable to the "fog-and-soot-clogged
lungs" of the motherland),† still such conditions "are be-

---

* Among American writers, this position was not Howells's alone, nor
even first. In his review of Turgenev (*North American Review*, April,
1874), Henry James qualified the European point of view toward life
with his remark to American readers that "we hold to the good old
belief that the presumption in life is in favour of the brighter side."
    In 1893 Hamlin Garland complained that French writers "confine
themselves so largely to morbid sexuality and to criminal classes"; he
deems their books "diseased, not healthy"; and finds Paul Bourget's
Cosmopolis "a study of the abnormal pursued in the evident belief that
there is more human nature in crime and vice than in the commonplace, wholesome action of men and women. This is a mistake. . . ."
(Quoted in Åhnebrink, *Beginnings*, p. 90ff.)

† And yet never, it would seem in old age, actually free from Old World
fog and soot. Recalling in 1916 his newspaper occupation in the late
1850's, Howells writes that "if I had still been a compositor . . . I
could not have been received at any of the houses that welcomed me
as a journalist . . . something strange and sad; something that forever

coming always less so"; if "the wrong from class to class has been almost inappreciable," still "all of this is changing for the worse"; * and if conditions were not such as to "wrong anyone" or "cramp endeavor," at least this could be said about *former* times. And is he not grasping for certainties when he asserts that "in a land where journeymen carpenters and plumbers strike for four dollars a day the sum of hunger and cold is comparatively small. . . ."?

It depended on where (and possibly how hard) one looked. A few years before—and an entire generation after Carlyle's *Past and Present*—the leading American magazine had cited among "Certain Dangerous Tendencies in American Life" both the immobility of the upper classes and the increasing aggressiveness of labor.† Working conditions in the steel mills already were anticipating the shocking revelations about the meat-packing industry of Upton Sinclair in 1906:

" 'The lot of a skilled workman,' said Andrew Carnegie, 'is far better than that of the heir to an hereditary title, who is likely to lead an unhappy, wicked life.' But the Homestead workmen whom Hamlin Garland saw and talked to hardly bore

---

belies our democracy, but is so fast and deep-rooted in the conditions which our plutocracy has kept from our ancestral monarchies and oligarchies." *(Years of My Youth)*

* Twenty years after Howells's *A Hazard of New Fortunes* (1890), he had a retrospective comment about its conflict between capitalism and socialism as dispirited as the above prediction: "Certain hopes of truer and better conditions on which my heart was fixed twenty years ago are not less dear . . . though they have not yet found . . . fulfillment. . . . Events have not wholly played them false; events have not halted, though they have marched with a slowness that might affect a younger observer as marking time." (Preface to *A Hazard of New Fortunes*, New York, 1911, p. viii.)

† *Atlantic Monthly*, XLII (October, 1878), pp. 385–402. In the same year Francis Parkman was bitterly attacking our democracy. See "The Failure of Universal Suffrage," *North American Review*, CXXVII (July, 1878), pp. 1–20.

out this pious judgment. 'Everywhere in the enormous sheds
were pits gaping like the mouth of hell, and ovens emitting a
terrible degree of heat . . . one man jumps down, works desperately for a few minutes, and is then pulled up ex-
hausted.' " [28]

Yes, hell—such as Garland looked into—was "all right" to
Andrew Carnegie, who had created it; and Herbert Spencer
was all right, who had created Carnegie; for from the post-
Civil War years on American civilization was being reshaped
in his image. The only prophet (evolution and dissolution) of the new true god (change), Spencer may have dismayed the intellectuals of his day ("When Henry George
asked one of the leading American Spencerians what he proposed to do about poverty, the answer was a characteristically
unabashed, 'Nothing. You and I can do nothing at all. It is
all a matter of evolution.' "); but his theory it was, as applied
to industry, that designed those Homestead furnaces and
shaped the lives of the men who paid for their combustion
with their health. He it was who contributed so importantly
to this country's reconciliation to industrialism, particularly
with his *Study of Sociology:*

A nation asked to accustom itself rapidly to extremes of
wealth and squalor fumbled for a doctrine and a large seg-
ment of America found it in the iron words of the Englishman Herbert Spencer. Drawing an analogy from scientific
thinking of the day, Spencer maintained that successful busi-
nessmen, by virtue of their triumph in competition, had
proved superior fitness and that social legislation would dis-
rupt the "survival of the fittest" necessary for the "evolution"
of society to a better form.*

* Eric F. Goldman, "Books That Changed America," *Saturday Review*,
XXXVI (July 4, 1953), pp. 37–38.
   There is a valuable account of the influence of Herbert Spencer
(Hippolyte Taine, and others) on the formation of theory in literary

Here, then, was the welter of attitudes, of feelings about
the new age of America. How did Eggleston's famous literary
contemporaries fare in it? Were they borne aloft by its great
promise, overwhelmed by its threat?

Certainly disenchantment sounds loudly in Mark Twain's
reflections on common man from the 1870's on. In *Life on
the Mississippi* he recalled with a mixture of pity and contempt the victims of the river risings, the "jean-clad, chills-
racked, yellow-faced male miserables roosting on the top
rail, elbows on knees, jaws in hands, grinding tobacco, and
discharging the result at floating chips through crevices left
by lost teeth" and gaping in wonder at the high water: "Now
what *could* these banished creatures find to do to keep from
dying of the blues during the low-water season!" (Ch. XI.)
And in *Huckleberry Finn* the contemptibly degenerate and
vicious Arkansas villagers fit the insulting description that
Colonel Sherburn gives them to their faces.

Like Whitman, the patriotic Twain found himself re-
sponding to an Englishman's (Matthew Arnold's) aristocratic
disdain for the American "glorification of 'the average man.' "
Inspired by Andrew Carnegie's *Triumphant Democracy*, he
published in 1889 a satire about a New Englander at King
Arthur's court "as hotly anti-aristocratic"; and matching Carnegie's fervid salute to "the coming national hymn which is
to live and vibrate round the world when royal families are
extinct as dodos. God speed the day!" is Twain's 1888 notebook entry: "Royalty and nobility in *our* day. Those dodos
and pterodactyls." [29] And yet, unlike Whitman's, Twain's
fictional response to aristocracy was only unconsciously cor-
roborative. For when his *Connecticut Yankee* is not extolling

criticism in the 1870's–1890's in Donald Pizer, "Evolutionary Ideas in
Late Nineteenth-Century English and American Literary Criticism,"
Journal of Aesthetics and Art Criticism, XIX (Spring, 1961), pp.
305–310.

the theory of the democratic principle, he is compromising
his views "by his growing estrangement from the mass of the
people in whose behalf he has instigated his revolution" and
"finds it increasingly difficult to sustain this democratic
faith." *

And technology, of which Hank Morgan spoke so glowingly in the *Yankee?* Had it really made possible universal
suffrage and its attendant blessings and crowned the common
man king? It took the hostile British press to point out that
what Hank had praised was mere Yankee sharpery and Wall
Street chicanery, that the American masses had no more
freedom under Jay Gould than the Saxons did under King
Arthur.[30] And while it is true that in the late 1880's Twain
told American audiences that "there is today but one civilization in the world, and it is not yet thirty years old"; and he
could ask them to compare the "mighty miracles" of science
in the nineteenth century with the "trivial miracles" and
"humbug magicians" of the Middle Ages, to "conceive of the
blank and sterile ignorance of that day and contrast it with
the vast and many-sided knowledge of this"; [31] still, by the
time of his posthumous *Mysterious Stranger* he would permit
the title character this bitterest of the book's many bitter
ironies:

"You perceive," [Satan] said, "that you have made considerable progress. Cain did his murder with a club; . . . the

* Henry Nash Smith, *Mark Twain: The Development of a Writer,*
Cambridge, Mass., 1962, pp. 151–162.
  It should also be noted that Carnegie could speak in 1910 of his
Triumphant Democracy as having been "written at high noon [1886],
when the sun casts no shadow"; and that in 1906 Mark Twain could
observe about him (and himself as well): "He thinks he is a scorner of
kings and emperors and dukes, whereas he is like the rest of the human
race: a slight attention from one of these can make him drunk for a
week and keep his happy tongue wagging for seven years." (James D.
Williams, "The Use of History in Mark Twain's *A Connecticut Yankee,*" PMLA, LXXX, March, 1965, pp. 106–107.)

Christian has added guns and gunpowder. . . . It is a remarkable progress. In five or six thousand years five or six
high civilizations have arisen, flourished, commanded the
wonder of the world, then faded out and disappeared, and
not one of them except the latest ever invented any sweeping
and adequate way to kill people." (Ch. 8.)

Actually, the spiritual canker went deeper even than that.
The very spark that had ignited the Renaissance flame—reason itself, "that trumpery thing which the race regards as a
Mind"—must be demolished; for if ye learn the truth it will
make you not free but mad. Satan in fact makes Father Peter
mad in *The Mysterious Stranger* because "Only the mad can
be happy, and not many of those." In tracing the history of
modern philosophy, the transcendentalist Theodore Parker
had deplored the influence of English sensationalism, the
way Bishop Berkeley, "a thorough sensationalist, comes up
with the inductive method in his hand, and annihilates mankind, leaves me nothing but my own consciousness, and no
consciousness of any certainty there." [32] So now the embittered Mark Twain annihilates the world of Eseldorf (the
name itself a sneer) and leaves the grieving boy with this desperate counsel. " 'Nothing exists save empty space—and you!
. . . It is all a dream—a grotesque and foolish dream. Nothing exists but you. And you are but a *thought*—a vagrant
thought, a useless thought, a homeless thought, wandering
forlorn among the eternities!' "
    In Hank-Mark's reflections about "this plodding sad pil-
grimage, this pathetic drift between the eternities," is a desire, Professor Smith finds, to escape from the present, a
yearning for "a preindustrial Arcadia." Twain secretly missed
the simplicity of an agrarian way of life that his triumphant
fictional hero was destroying; dying, the Yankee pleads for
protection "against the hideous dream that he has been

brought back to the nineteenth century"—thirteen centuries removed from all that was dear to him, that could make life worth living.[33]

The Yankee even gives voice (out of character) to opinions that might have come from Hippolyte Taine—and not on art but on the material predominance of man's nature: ". . . what we call [human nature] is merely heredity and training. We have no thoughts of our own, no opinions of our own; they are transmitted to us, trained into us. . . . All the rest [is] atoms . . . inherited from a procession of ancestors" stretching back to the monkey "from whom our race has been so tediously and . . . unprofitably developed." Here is the germ of the bleak musings of *What Is Man?* with its identification of man and insect life, as we have seen. Like Eggleston, Twain found it hard for a real nineteenth-century man to pray. But he could not reach Eggleston's resolve to look upward and outward and forward; yearned in effect for the times of à Kempis; and found Charles Darwin's fields anything but wide.

And Adams? Unlike Twain and Eggleston, he had had no ties with the common man, and if his position with regard to the plight of the worker in the new industrial America sounds as detached and aloof as Carnegie's, it is because his distance from it was great. The attitude toward the domestic economic scene of the brooding and sardonic historian is, for a wonder, optimistic; but it is not an optimism of much account, for he has come by it too easily. An aristocrat, Adams understandably could consider the complaints of Henry George (in the much discussed *Progress and Poverty*) baseless. He believed that "the average man here is really twice as well off now [in 1882] as in 1800 in spite of Mr. George." The country's millionaires, he felt, didn't "affect the distribution more than five per cent." Indeed, from where he viewed it, American industry was healthy and beneficial.

So far as I can see, we are all right here. The country is at last
filled out; railways all round and through it, and everyone
satisfied." The building boom in Washington was ocular evidence. "There is a tremendous amount of activity in every
direction; and another generation will see the result. I consider ours to have already done its work, and on the whole it
is the biggest on record." *

For all that, Henry Adams had losses, and they were heavy
ones. When we separate his sanguine, aloof observations
about Americans as factors in an industrial equation from his
view about the great American experiment—its tarnished
image now bright again because, Lowell was saying, Americans had fought and died for a principle, not for dollars—we
are in for a surprise: it was, Adams felt, a vast disappointment. For all the respect his novel *Democracy* (1880) pays
to the essential dogma of the title, the institution receives
savage treatment. The civil service is merely another "Yankee notion"; representative government is merely as good as
the society it represents; George Washington shines more
and more as a symbol of a vanished civic integrity; Americans
are not inherently republicans, but snobs, toadies to aristocracy, and social climbers. It is enough to shake the heroine's
nerves to pieces and drive her off to Europe. Grim as this
picture of democracy was, it was only a "very modest forerun-
ner of *The Education*, a kind of interim report preceding by
a quarter of a century the definitive one." [34] *There* democracy is presented as both laughable and alarming, and all
reverence for the principle itself is now gone. Adams had
learned from experience that even the great senators were gro-

---

* Ernest Samuels, *Henry Adams: The Middle Years*, pp. 233-234.
Adams even brought about the writing of an article in 1882 with statistics to prove the rise of the standard of living, that "people no longer
brought up families on salt pork, having learned to prefer fresh meat."
(*Ibid.*)

tesque enough to invite ridicule and capable of "permanent and terrible mischief." As for the presiding deity of this great new concept's rites, General Ulysses Simpson Grant was all energy and no intellect: for *him* "the instinct of fight"; for him, action as "the highest stimulant." To think of Grant as the product of a process coming up from Alexander the Great and Caesar was to lampoon the idea of evolution: "The progress of evolution from President Washington to President Grant was alone evidence enough to upset Darwin." [35]

As it turned out, Adams himself had already upset Darwin back in his years in England, but he had been even more upset himself in the process. For not even here could he find comfort where so many of his contemporaries were finding it (when they were not losing it). Not for Adams, as for Eggleston, was science (biology) the bringer of a latter-day gospel, he tells us in Chapter Fifteen of *The Education*. Inquiring at the source (Lyell and Darwin in person), then pursuing their hints in nature itself, he came upon the *Terebratula*, which "appeared to be identical from the beginning to the end of geological time" and the *Pteraspis*, about which "geology offered no proof that [it] had been anything else." Darwin's great structure, then, was sheer inference: "Evolution . . . did not evolve . . . and Selection . . . did not select." As for real proof, "All he could prove was change." Not for Henry Adams to assent to the science-based argument for design that so many other doubters were substituting for the old, Scripture-based one:

"To other Darwinians—except Darwin—Natural Selection seemed a dogma to be put in the place of the Athanasian creed; it was a form of religious hope; a promise of ultimate perfection. Adams wished no better . . . , but when he came to ask himself what he truly thought, he felt that he had no Faith. . . ."

Edward Eggleston turned his back on the Middle Ages and preferred to follow his own century wherever it might lead; Mark Twain reviled and destroyed the Middle Ages while he yearned for them; Henry Adams confessed that "Like Catherine Olney in 'Northanger Abbey,' he yearned for nothing so keenly as to feel at home in a thirteenth-century Abbey" [36]: Gothic cathedrals exactly reflected Gothic faith. The unity of their art is so striking to us because we have lost that faith, and our art reflects it:

Neither his [Thomas's] Church nor the architect's church was a sketch, but a completely studied structure. . . . Science and art were one. . . . Both the 'Summa Theologiae' and Beauvais Cathedral were excessively modern, scientific, and technical. . . . The essence of [its art] was that of organic *unity* both in the thought and the building. From that time, the universe has steadily become more *complex* and less reducible to a central control. . . . [It] has insisted on expanding its parts; . . . it has *evaded* the attempt to impose on it a single will. Modern science, like modern art, tends . . . to *drop* the dogma of organic *unity.* . . . *Unity* [has] turned itself into *complexity, multiplicity,* variety, and even *contradiction.* All experience . . . assured man in the thirteenth century that the lines of the universe converged. How was he to know that these lines ran in every conceivable and inconceivable direction, and that at least half of them seemed to *diverge from* any imaginable centre of *unity*! . . . Naturally man [has] tended to lose his sense of scale and relation. . . .*

Adams recalls that fashionable and seductive vehicle of romantic cynicism of his day (and later days), Fitzgerald's

* *Mont-Saint-Michel and Chartres,* Ch. XVI. Yet only as recently as 1864 the hymn "Onward Christian Soldiers" had proclaimed that
    We are not divided,
    All in body whole,
    One in hope and doctrine. . . .

translation of the *Rubáiyát*, with its argument that there is
no design, there is only chance, mysterious, with man the
chance victim or beneficiary of cosmic force; that

The Ball no question makes of Ayes and Noes,
But Here or There as strikes the Player goes;
And He that tossed you down into the Field,
He knows about it all—HE knows—HE knows!

and he surmises:

[Suppose] that Omar's kinetic analogy of the ball and the
players turned out to be a scientific formula! . . . what wonder that art lost unity with philosophy and science! Art had
to be confused in order to express confusion; but perhaps it
was truest, so.[37]

Confusion and chaos . . . He had lost his faith in the power
of reason to influence man's destiny that all earlier ages had as-
cribed to the human race, which Adams saw stumbling from
one abyss of slaughter into another in a century that one
could not contemplate without a shudder.

Perhaps, by contrast with these two figures who overtow-
ered him, Eggleston had fared not so badly, then; his losses,
perhaps, were no greater than those any intelligent man
suffers during a lifetime without seriously impairing his per-
formance of his life's daily obligations or even of his underlying faith in daily living. Like his contemporaries Edward
Bellamy and William Dean Howells, he had "never unlearned his regard" for the people, whose faith he had nur-
tured for many years. In his first serious periodical publication
(1860), he had celebrated the late "Béranger, the Poet of the
People." During the 1860's, his pieces in the Chicago newspapers had spoken out against economic conditions (ex-
pensive rents and meals) victimizing the working man and

had exposed the appalling conditions in jails and poorhouses outside of Chicago. This faith continued after his arrival in New York in 1870 to join the staff of the *Independent*: soon he was its editor and crusading once more, his editorials neither extreme nor radical, neither stodgy nor pedantic, his biographer finds. We note next that during the five-year pastorate in Brooklyn (1874–1878) he had the largest Sunday-school in the city, built a library in the church, and organized a society of young men for discussing subjects of practical human interest: the tariff, trade unionism, and employer-employee relationship.* Later, in the 1880's, as chairman of the executive committee of the Copyright League he actively lobbied for a copyright law in Washington at a great expense of time and energy.[38]

The activity that Eggleston's secularized faith produced was his part in the reform movements of the day and was typical of the spokesmen of the moderate wing of the Social Gospel movement gathering strength as the century began to end. In their efforts to improve the common man's condition as capital and labor collided (and not, as in the case of the clergymen Herron and Rauschenbusch, to overthrow the capitalistic structure), they were following the same middle course as they did in preferring to modify their religious faith to accommodate science rather than simply to discard it.[39] Eggleston was one with the leaders of the Social Gospel, who burned to "bring the ethics of the church down into the factory, the street, and the market-place." [40] As Washington Gladden would recollect, they wanted "a religion that laid hold on life with both hands." [41] Surely we may look upon it as more than a coincidence that these words were written by a clergyman who had been added to the staff of the *Independent* by Edward Eggleston himself almost thirty years

---

* "Evolution views man as competing, not against the powers of darkness (as religion warned us), but against other men." (Harry Hartwick, *The Foreground of American Fiction*, p. 6.)

before, not long after the former Hoosier schoolmaster's arrival in the east.[42]

Disillusionment, increasing melancholy, and all, there were then in Eggleston's faith in Darwin and man abundant materials for a bulwark against despair: as the nihilistic compeer of them all, Friedrich Nietzsche, knew, so far from science and democracy being a renunciation of the illusions of Christian faith and order, "they were the same ascetic valuations in their most viable form. . . ."[43] Whereas we have seen what spiritual havoc was being wrought on Eggleston's two more prominent fellow-sojourners of that generation that sprawled over into the next century.

▩

" 'In principle,' " the shell-shocked Hemingway character Nick Adams of "A Way You'll Never Be" would tell Captain Paravicini on the Italian front, " 'I would have brought you a bottle of brandy.'

" 'In principle,' Para said and smiled, for the first time, showing yellowed teeth. 'Such a beautiful expression. Would you like some Grappa?' "

Nick's grandfathers had already suffered this awakening from the dream of idealism.* Twain and Adams, with Eggleston, were all members of an earlier Lost Generation; but only one of the three had been spared the fate of having considered man's destiny too curiously and found in it nothing sacred.

And yet perhaps the Egglestons were after all the more characteristic travellers in that pathless wood that was the Gilded Age. Perhaps in their progress from faith to doubt to

---

* Even, like him, as a result of war. Half a century after that most principled of wars, the American Civil War, William Dean Howells remembered a young Captain James A. Garfield telling "how the sense of the sacredness of other things of peace had gone out of some of the soldiers and never come back again." (*Years of My Youth.*)

acceptance they are our more reliable index to the average thinking man's spiritual transit during those disturbing years. While the intellectually non-violent lead less dramatic lives, perhaps after all it is they who carry it away. We remember Ishmael, who, while loving to sail forbidden seas and admitting himself quick to perceive a horror, could still be social with it; and the dark and brooding Robert Frost, who, for all his desire to be carried away from it never to return, would find only this earth to be the right place for love.

"Nothing at all"

" 'And what does it amount to?' said Satan,
with his evil chuckle. 'Nothing at all.' "

Mark Twain, *The Mysterious Stranger*

■

Mark Twain's tirade against Sir Walter Scott's medieval invasion of the south notwithstanding, no knights in armor ever did succeed in crossing the Atlantic to the New Eden —the confirmation of Goethe's blessings on the infant "America" in 1827 in fact eventually becoming the very grounds for Hawthorne's and James's complaints against it; but then, the new land had other ills that even the wide ocean could not keep away, whose germs were carried by the wind. This was the soul sickness of the times. The century, as it grew older, grew sicker. And as the new century turned, it

perpetuated the doubt and despair that the admirable goals
of the old century had bred in the mind of reflective man.
The impression that the creation was chaotic and directionless and man was not only a cipher but possibly only one in
an endless row of ciphers traced by an invisible and possibly
irresponsible hand, was reaffirmed and emphasized by the
new century's own contributions to despair. These were all
ultimately dismaying explanations of nature in one form or
another. "The War" . . . How—that phrase reminds us—
would it have been possible to think in terms of *another*
1914–1918 catastrophe?! That monstrous proof at last of the
proposition that man was not divine but simply another form
of nature red in tooth and claw: it killed men by the millions
("They mow the field of man in season" was Housman's pro-
phetic metaphor) and ushered in a generation of political upheaval on a world scale. Or the new applications of the old
precious bane, science: the uses to which man could put
invention, and to which it could then put him. Or new scientific theory: psychology, that first-born of philosophy, defining human personality as the captive of forces within (where
its parent had already made him the captive of forces without). Or the new astronomy, with its introduction of bewil-
dering concepts of time and space and its corresponding further reduction of man's sense of his importance to the
universe. So that by mid-century the American writer had no
need to consult Mark Twain's or Henry Adams's direful vale-
dictions: he had, as our most prominent poet put it in the
1930's, frightening desert places so much nearer home, in
terms of time as well as space. It was all a nothing and so
was he.

If the new phrase was new (but not completely), certainly the
sentiment went far back into the old century. We remember
that from the first appearance (1819) of *The World as Will
and Idea*, Schopenhauer set up his wail that wherever we
look in nature, from the forming hydra that begins to com-

pete for food with the parent organism of which it is still a
part, through man, on up to the stars, we see simply a "universal essential conflict of the manifestation of the will," of
restlessness and motion "without rest and without end." All
are expressions "of that nothingness, that failure of all aim
which . . . we shall be obliged to recognise in the striving of
will in all its phenomena." Thus will "appears as this blind
and unconscious striving in the whole of unorganised nature. . . ." [1] Montaigne had chided Renaissance man by
pointing to his vaunted reason as the source of his woes; now
Dostoevsky's sick man, writing his *Notes from Underground*
(1864), was finding in his age's cherished achievements the
root of its troubles. What those moans from toothache really
express, he tells us, is

all the aimlessness of your pain, which is so humiliating to
your consciousness; the whole legal system of nature on which
you spit disdainfully . . . but from which you suffer all the
same while she does not. They express the consciousness that
you have no enemy to punish, but that you have pain. . . .
[L]isten sometimes to the moans of an educated man of the
nineteenth century suffering from toothache, on the second
or third day of the attack, when he is beginning to moan . . .
not simply because he has toothache . . . but as a man affected by progress and European civilization. . . .

And even in this country, at a time when the land beyond
the Appalachians was largely unknown, three quarters of a
century before the closing of the frontier, the age—at least as
far as our seaboard civilization extended—was already an age
of introversion, if we credit Emerson's complaint in "The
American Scholar":

We . . . are embarrassed with second thoughts . . . ; the
time is infected with Hamlet's unhappiness,—"Sicklied o'er
with the pale cast of thought." . . . Do we fear lest we

should outsee nature and God, and drink truth dry? . . .
The mind of this country . . . eats upon itself. . . . Young
men of the fairest promise [find life too unspiritual], turn
drudges, or die of disgust, some of them suicides.

What kind of American darkness at midmorning he refers to,
we think we know where to find out: Poe will tell us, but,
wonderfully enough, so can his temporal neighbor and spiritual opposite, that Yankee reincarnation of the medieval
humour of sanguineness, Henry David Thoreau. So many of
his contemporaries were living lives of quiet desperation that
he had written a book of inspiration for them. For the moment let us tune out his reedy transcendental music and
listen to him play the minor keys that he knew so well too:
he was capable of attunement to the sickness under, as well
as to the Soul over, his civilization. "I rejoice that there are
owls," he writes in the "Sounds" of *Walden:*

Let them do the idiotic and maniacal hooting for me. It is a
sound admirably suited to swamps and twilight woods which
no day illustrates, suggesting a vast and undeveloped nature
which men have not recognized. They represent the stark
twilight and unsatisfied thoughts which all have. All day the
sun has shone on the surface of some usnea lichens, and small
hawks circulate above and the chickadee lisps amid the ever-
greens, and the partridge and rabbit skulk beneath; but now
a more dismal and fitting day dawns, and a different race of
creatures awakes to express the meaning of Nature there.

Into insects, too, he could read allegorical meanings. His
"Natural History of Massachusetts" presents a similar fasci-
nation by the alternation, the symmetrical arrangement, of
nature's great store:

Entomology extends the limits of being in a new direction. . . . In the autumn days, the creaking of crickets is

heard at noon over all the land, and as in summer they are heard chiefly at nightfall, so then by their incessant chirp they usher in the evening of the year. Nor can all the vanities that vex the world alter one whit the measure that night has chosen. Every pulsebeat is in exact time with the cricket's chant and the tickings of the death-watch in the wall.

He concludes the above observation on insect symbolism with this advice (to the mind of this country eating upon itself?): "Alternate with these if you can."

No one had greater need of such advice than Edgar Allan Poe, who seems never to have heard the chant or the chirp of an autumn noon. Daylight does not penetrate his inner sanctum; all is refracted, not reflected, by his gaze. As early as 1856 his soulmate Baudelaire had identified both Poe and his central fictional character as "the man with excessively acute faculties, . . . he whose gaze is fixed . . . on objects which increase in importance under his gaze"; and in "A Backward Glance" Walt Whitman could recall that as a young man, although he had not admired Poe's verses, yet he had seen that "beyond their limited range of melody . . . they were melodious expressions, and perhaps never excelled ones, of certain pronounced phases of human morbidity." Not for Poe the cricket, noon, and maturation; but *scarabaeus*, midnight, and death. For him, not even alternation of joy and gloom, but obsession with darkness. We turn to one of his most familiar stories, "The Tell-Tale Heart," for a special purpose: to place it in relationship with Thoreau's essay of one year earlier. Let us ignore, in "The Tell-Tale Heart," the effect of horror that the old man's eye evokes in X, or the unbearable suspense of the beating of his heart, and consider only the episode of the eighth night. The narrator X is not completely Montresor, the familiar fixated villain from a thousand ghoulish Gothic corridors, perversely, implausibly incited to murder by some innocent fact or feature: he is in flashes also the "normal" man who pities the object of his scrutiny as he recognizes in him a kindred grief. Which grief? The nameless dread of the night, with its eloquent yet unarticulated despair of the days—implicitly, despair of God's kindness and mercy in a dreadful universe. The old man, X observes that eighth night (when the devil begins *his* chronology?), has been lying awake during X's approach, and springs up in alarm at the noise X makes. But he does not return to sleep, X notices.

He was still sitting up in the bed listening; —*just as I have done, night after night, hearkening to the death watches in the wall.*

Presently I heard a slight groan, and I knew it was the groan of mortal terror. It was not a groan of pain or of grief— oh, no!—it was the low stifled sound that arises from the bottom of the soul when overcharged with awe. *I knew the sound well. Many a night,* just at midnight, when all the world slept, *it has welled up from my own bosom,* deepening, with its dreadful echo, the terrors that distracted me. I say *I knew it well. I knew what the old man felt,* and pitied him. . . . (italics mine)

This pity does not keep X from chuckling at the spectacle, to be sure; nor from going through with his scheme to murder the old man, in the best horror-story tradition. But those "death watches in the wall" to which old men hearken, those groans "welling up from the bottom of the soul"—X confesses that he shares them with the old man.* The old

---

* In the bitter *Mayor of Casterbridge*, Poe's despairing old man has become Hardy's despairing young woman, sitting up night after night nursing her mother (than which there is "no quicker way," Hardy comments, "to learn to take the universe seriously"). During the small hours of the night the silence in the town "was broken in Elizabeth's ear only by the time-piece in the bedroom ticking frantically against the clock on the stairs; ticking harder and harder till it seemed to clang like a gong; and all this while the subtle-souled girl asking herself why

man had been trying to fancy his fears "causeless," had been
telling himself it was "nothing"—Poe goes on to explain—but
"in vain," because the *nothing* that the old man had been
using to exorcise his fears was, ironically, the nothingness of
the death soon to overtake him.

That expression of Nothingness, whether of Schopenhauer's
or Dostoevsky's intellectual sick with the malaise of the century (thought), was infecting the intellect of America. Poe's
narrator knew it, for it had welled up from his own bosom.
Herman Melville knew it too. He told Hawthorne in 1856
that he had "pretty much made up his mind to be anni-
hilated," and we can find him turning to Nothingness in his
fiction. In *Pierre* he tells us that "By vast pains we mine into
the pyramid; by horrible gropings we come to the central
room; with joy we espy the sarcophagus; but we lift the lid
—and no body is there!—appallingly vacant as vast is the soul
of man." [2] As vacant as the soul of the universe he inhabits
—this is the corollary already propounded in *Moby-Dick,*
where he had asked whether, when we look at the white
depths of the Milky Way, "its indefiniteness . . . shadows
forth the heartless voids and immensities of the universe, and
thus stabs us from behind with the thought of annihilation"? *

To grasp the profundity of this despair, we might keep in

---

she was born, . . . why things around her had taken the shape they
wore . . . Why they stared at her so helplessly . . . ; what that chaos
called consciousness . . . tended to, and began in." (Ch. 18.)

* Chapter 42. In attempting to convey the sense of "the confluent
measureless force" of the whale as it achieved a concentration in its
tail, he muses that "Could annihilation occur to matter, this were the
thing to do it." (Ch. 86.)

Re-reading the *Mosses* a year after Hawthorne's death, when Melville
came, in "Monsieur du Miroir," to: "He will pass to the dark realm of
Nothingness, but will not find me there," he wrote in the margin: "This
trenches upon the uncertain and the terrible." (Jay Leyda, *The Melville
Log,* II, p. 674.)

mind the profundity of the Romantic piety of which it is an unwitting yet precise inversion. In the clear light of the Hartley-Wordsworth-Coleridge vision, God was the Biblical all in all; and man was the sensual mechanism through which natural piety was distilled by a "healthy state of association" —which is to say, by natural surroundings—until he could rise above all lower pleasures (the rocks, the cataracts) to the transcendent association with that Source of All Good.[3] But in the dismal twilight of Melville's despair, God was the creator of the frightful Nothing at All; and man was the poor creature who, if he was not saved by the visible creation of his fellow men (Queequeg's coffin), was doomed to sink through a contemplation of his natural surroundings to annihilation— which is to say, into the aboriginal Source of Nothingness.

But it was finally in the present century that Poe's Nothing came into its own. Of weakening or even loss of faith in the 1800's, we have seen abundant evidence in the preceding pages of this study; but it remained for the 1900's to reject God utterly, to find that the heavens, in Robert Frost's phrase, have "nothing to express." Allen Tate has repeatedly urged us to this recognition in recent years. He identifies Poe as "the transitional figure in modern literature because he discovered our great subject, the disintegration of the modern personality," * and finds in a sentence from *Eureka* the key to Poe's despair and longing for identification with the Nothingness of non-being: " '*In the original unity of the first thing lies the secondary cause of all things, with the germ of their inevitable annihilation.*' " Birth is the original Nothingness (unity), the state to which we return in the Nothingness of death. Poe, writing, in spite of classical and religious instruction, "as if the experience of these traditions had been

* His reference here is to Roderick Usher, who becomes "the prototype of the Joycean and Jamesian hero who cannot function in the ordinary world." ("Three Commentaries: Poe, James, and Joyce," *The Sewanee Review*, LVIII [Winter, 1950], p. 2.)

lost" was "well ahead of his time." He was "the conscious
artist of an intensity which lacked moral perspective," and
"if the trappings of Poe's nightmare strike us as tawdry, we
had better look to our own." Tate himself admits to membership in Poe's "melancholy troupe of the undead." [4]

The wording of that figure invites the inclusion into this
weird company of the speaker of T. S. Eliot's *The Waste
Land* (1922), who confesses that

> . . . . *I was neither
> Living nor dead, and I knew nothing,
> Looking into the heart of light, the silence,
> Oed' und leer das Meer,*

and whose nightmare of unfaith in "Preludes" is equally
tawdry:

> *Wipe your hand across your mouth, and laugh;
> The worlds revolve like ancient women
> Gathering fuel in vacant lots.**

Desolate and empty, too, is the undead mystic Mrs. Moore
in E. M. Forster's novel, after her experience with the
Marabar cave, with its all-negating echo that "robbed infinity
and eternity of their vastness, the only quality that accom-
modates them to mankind." Just what was it that it had said
to her, that had so weakened her hold on life?

> . . . it had managed to murmur, "Pathos, piety, courage—
> they exist, but are identical, and so is filth. Everything exists,
> nothing has value." If one had spoken vileness in that place,
> or quoted lofty poetry, the comment would have been the
> same—"ou-boom." [5]

* ". . . in the bleak, tortuous complexities of a T. S. Eliot . . . disgust
speaks with a robust voice. . . ." (Krutch, *The Modern Temper*, p. 17.)

This is also the Nothing that emerges in Aldous Huxley's
Antic Hay (1923). His Mrs. Viveash murmurs "nothing at
all" in answer to the question that the "Shakespeherean rag"
calls for as she dances, "as though she were worshipping
almighty and omnipresent Nil,"—"Nil, omnipresent nil,
world-soul, spiritual informer of all matter."

Mrs. Moore had been wrong, then, in ascribing her terror
to her physical depletion, in telling herself "that the despair
creeping over her was merely her despair, her personal weakness" [6]: the name of Mr. Tate's troupe is legion, and it includes Mrs. Viveash's and Mrs. Moore's contemporaries
across the Atlantic. It includes the expatriated Ernest Hemingway. This outdoorsman who was "always keeping the
thought of death in his work" and reminded a friend of "a
Medieval scholar who kept the skull on his desk to remind
him of his last end" [7]—Hemingway was reading Huxley en-
thusiastically in those postwar years because, he divulged after
his own death, "his books amused me and kept me from
thinking." * His waiter in "A Clean, Well-Lighted Place"
does not merely echo the cynicism of Mrs. Viveash's words
—he translates them into Spanish:

What did he fear? it was not fear or dread. It was a nothing
that he knew too well. It was all a nothing and a man was
nothing too. It was only that and light was all it needed and
a certain cleanness and order. . . . [H]e knew it all was nada
y pues nada y nada y pues nada. . . . Hail nothing full of
nothing, nothing is with thee. . . . Now, without thinking
further, he would go home to his room. He would lie in the
bed and finally, with daylight, he would go to sleep. After all,

* *A Moveable Feast,* p. 26.
Joseph Wood Krutch early perceived the essential kinship of these
two writers: ". . . one will discover in their tragic farces the picture of
a society which is at bottom in despair because . . . it has lost the
sense of any ultimate importance inherent in the experience [love]
which preoccupies it. . . ." (*The Modern Temper,* p. 67.)

he said to himself, it is probably only insomnia. Many must
have it.*

Ernest Hemingway, of course, had literally been blown up
on the Italian battlefront. His brother tells us that the shell
inflicted so great a psychic shock that Ernest could not sleep
without a light in his room. "The older bartender . . . knew
something of that feeling. Nick Adams says in 'Now I Lay
Me,' 'If I could have a light I was not afraid to sleep, because
I knew my soul would only go out of me if it were dark.'" [8]
There were the three Englishmen of a Thomas Wolfe novel
living in the 1920's in that Oxford house that seemed "a
magnetic centre for lost people," in whom Eugene sensed
"something ruined, lost, or broken—some precious and irre-
trievable quality which had gone out of them and which they
could never get back again." The fact that one of them, the
captain, had an explosion-ruined arm was even itself not related to the man's living-death quality:

No: the ruin that one felt in him was never of the flesh, but
of the spirit. Something seemed to have been torn away from
his life—it was not the nerve-centres of his arm, but of his
soul, that had been destroyed. There was in the man somewhere a terrible dead vacancy and emptiness.

All three of them, Eugene Gant tells us, "fought the emptiness in them" with a determined, almost desperate jazz-music
making, "with this deliberate, formidable, and mad intensity

---

* Professor Carlos Baker also interprets "Big Two-Hearted River" in
terms of this opposition of light (peace of mind) and darkness (Nada).
(*Hemingway: The Writer as Artist*, Princeton, 1963, pp. 125–127.)
    "This is Hemingway's world," Robert Penn Warren writes: "the
world with nothing at center. . . . And the sleepless man—the man
obsessed by death, by the meaninglessness of the world, by nothingness,
by nada—is one of the recurring symbols" in his work. (Introduction to
A Farewell to Arms, New York, 1949, pp. xiv, xvi.)

of a calculated gaiety, a terrifying mimicry of mirth; * a variation, possibly, of the somnambulism of Huxley's dancers.

But not all of the lost were battle casualties: Eric Maria Remarque dedicated his best-selling novel *All Quiet on the Western Front* (1929) to "a generation of men who, even though they may have escaped its shells, were destroyed by the war." These include E. E. Cummings, falsely detained by the French and interned for over four months in that Enormous Room; and Harry Crosby, a volunteer ambulance driver and spectator to the death of a boy next to him from a shell-burst—the experience haunting him henceforth. William Faulkner's first novel, *Soldier's Pay*, like Hemingway's, held up to the reader its "war-hardened" individuals, its "hurt romantics." The *New York Times* (April 11, 1926) found it a relentless "recital of irreconcilable factors of civilization meeting in an impasse of futility and irony," its characters "caught in this blind alley of life. . . . The old idealism . . . is gone forever."

The effects of course extended to people far from the spheres of military action. After the war Americans were "almost abnormally sensitive to a form of experience that may best be described by the term 'violation,' a term that indicates what happened to their sense of dignity and security as the result of events that had little or nothing to do with them." Regrettably, the perennial popularity of Ezra Pound's execration in "Hugh Selwyn Mauberley" of pre-World War culture ("an old bitch gone in the teeth, . . . a botched civilization") has obscured the fact of its unreliability as a register of the feelings of men of letters about the destruction of that culture. Indeed, the shock waves from Sarajevo reached not only the older generation (such as Henry James's)

---

* *Of Time and The River*, New York, 1935, pp. 623–627. Also see pp. 592–595 of this novel for Wolfe's discovery of the soullessness of post-World War America as seen in the "disturbing and sinister" quality of its mechanization.

but Ezra Pound's own. " 'Those whom the gods loved died in July, 1914,' [Max Beerbohm] wrote in his notebook. 'Those whom the gods hated lived to see the war's effects.' " And when the next war was already visible in the distance, Elmer Davis wrote that "Spiritually and morally, civilization collapsed on August 1, 1914—the civilization in which people now middle-aged grew up, a culture which with all its shortcomings did give more satisfaction to more people than any other yet evolved." [9] Finally, was it The War, as André Gide proposed,* that resulted in the Riot of Nothingness in 1916–1924 that was "dada"? This "thoroughgoing attempt to dismiss the civilization then being fought over on the battlefields of Europe," this "violent attempt to kill off Western civilization by ridicule and laughter . . . was against all systems, defied all logic and reason; full of sound and fury, it stressed the absolute significance of nothing." If not from the pronouncement of its founder, Tristan Tzara, that "*DADA ne signie rien*," then the movement proclaimed the death of meaning in its actions, which defied comprehension.†

■

And of all the Hollow Men of our age, who suffered more than F. Scott Fitzgerald, he who never got to the War? When he closed *This Side of Paradise* (1920) with the crashing discord, "Here was a new generation . . . grown up to find all Gods dead . . . all faiths in man shaken," he was speaking for an entire generation of intellectual humans and shaking its fist at a number of the forms of Nothingness. At the international turmoil leading up to and away from the

*Writing in the *Nouvelle Revue Francaise* for April, 1920, Gide "spoke of the physical ruin wrought by the war and suggested that 'the mind has a right to some ruins too.' " (Hoffman, *The Twenties*, p. 209.)

† Hoffman, *The Twenties*, pp. 207–209; Malcolm Cowley, *Exile's Return*, New York [1951], 1956, pp. 135–141; Edmund Wilson, *Axel's Castle*, New York, 1931, pp. 304–312.

war, as had the writer of the periodical article appearing in the same year:

They give us this Thing, knocked to pieces, leaky, red-hot, threatening to blow up; and they are surprised that we don't accept it with the same attitude of pretty, decorous enthusiasm with which they received it, way back in the '80's. . . .[10]

Schopenhauer had viewed "that nothingness" of nature's blind and directionless will, eventually, with equanimity: man could, he insisted, thwart that Nothingness, even if only with yet another form of it—namely, by *refusal* to will, to be a party to meaninglessness, and thereby could attain a kind of meaningfulness. It was this quality of his thinking that Friedrich Nietzsche paid tribute to at the close of his *Genealogy of Morals*. Ascetic ideals, he said, at least did this for mankind: they gave an explanation of the wherefore of human suffering; and thus, in the ascetic Will to Nothingness "the door to all suicidal Nihilism was closed"; for "man will wish *Nothingness* rather than not wish at all." ("Ascetic Ideals") But modern men achieve no such purgation, no victory over Nada by refusing to do battle with it, and in this lies their particular doom.

Kant had faith in the moral law within and the starry heavens above. . . . The Romantics believe in nature, history, and art. . . . Other ecstasies modern man has experienced include the Party, Science, Nation, Race, and Money. Little wonder that by the twentieth century there emerged a growing number of believers in nothing.[11]

An aged priest of Ignazio Silone's is talking to his former pupils midway between twentieth-century wars: alas, he complains,

"the study of Greek tragedy and my comments did not help you, could not help you, to face and understand the obscure

tragedy that was about to overwhelm you.* . . . Certainly
we are no longer victims of the ancient Fate of the Greeks,
Anangke, Nemesis, but what is this new Fate that prevented
you from being what you wanted to be? What is this obscure
and pitiless destiny that has played havoc with your generation in the last fifteen years . . . —this destiny that caused
many of you, who were Catholics, to become, first, Nation-
alists, then Socialists, then Fascists, then advocates of the
corporate state, and now . . . Socialists again? † What is
this new and inexorable demon, this new and ferocious destiny, that has taken the place of the Fate of the ancients and
plays with your lives like a drunkard playing with dice?" ‡

But least of all had Sören Kierkegaard wondered at the reason
for it a century before—he who like his contemporary Poe
had to wait for his age: it was our contempt for the individual

* Alfred Kazin speaks of "the lean tragic strain in our modern American writing, that sense of tragedy which is not Aristotle's, not even
Nathaniel Hawthorne's, but a clutching violence, and from Dreiser to
Faulkner, an often great depth of suffering." (*On Native Grounds*,
p. ix.)

† In 1931, W. B. Yeats was recording these observations of the same
ferment: "Forty years ago intellectual young men, dissatisfied with the
political poetry of Young Ireland, once the foundation of Irish politics,
substituted an interest in old stories and modern peasants, and now the
young men are dissatisfied again." (Collected in *Essays and Introductions*, New York, 1961, p. 411.)

‡ *Bread and Wine*, New York, 1937, pp. 15–16.
    When, in today's sophisticated society, "its heroes (sad mis-
nomer . . .) are struck down it is not, like Oedipus, by the gods that
they are struck but only, like Oswald Alving, by syphilis, for they know
that the gods, even if they existed, would not trouble with them, and
they cannot attribute to themselves an importance in which they do
not believe." (Joseph Wood Krutch, *The Modern Temper*, p. 88.)
    "Tragedy arises when you are in the presence of a man who has
missed accomplishing his joy. But the joy must be there, the promise
of the right way of life must be there. Otherwise pathos reigns, and an
endless, meaningless, and essentially untrue picture of man is created
—man wholly lost in a universe which by its very nature is too hostile
to be mastered." (Arthur Miller, "On the Nature of Tragedy," 1950.)

life, our belief that the mere individual counts for nothing.* Science, too, now no longer marching from point to point, but running (even flying), was contributing its share to the spiritual disintegration of the new century. Allen Tate remembers that in one of his poems Edgar Allan Poe confided that he had a demon in his view; for the inheritors of the great thinkers of the nineteenth century, that demon was science in one form or another, whether of theory or of application. In 1837 Emerson could challenge science with the lofty declaration that "Not he is great who can alter matter, but he who can alter my state of mind"; [12] in the twentieth century it was not possible to take for granted so discrete a division between the two. On September 17, 1919, the British scientist

Sir Oliver Lodge, in a summary of what science had learned about the atom delivered before the James Watt Centenary celebration in London, made the statement, widely quoted at the time and for years after, that if the atomic energy of an ounce of matter could be utilized it would be sufficient to raise the German ships sunk at Scapa Flow and pile them on top of the mountains of Scotland.[13]

Twenty-six years later, scientists succeeded in accomplishing this atomic feat in New Mexico, and what cataclysmic alteration in the state of men's minds this alteration of matter could bring to pass! No Place to Hide was appropriately the title of a best-seller that followed, and in 1950 William Faulkner summed up the effect of Hiroshima and Nagasaki

* ". . . in the midst of the self-importance of the contemporary generation there is revealed a sense of despair over being human. Everything must attach itself so as to be a part of some movement; men are determined to lose themselves in the totality of things, in world history, fascinated and deceived by a magic witchery; no one wants to be an individual human being." (Concluding Unscientific Postscript, quoted in H. J. Blackham, Six Existentialist Thinkers, p. 13.)

on the human mind with his remarks at Stockholm: "There
are no longer problems of the spirit. There is only the question: When will I be blown up?" Yet not even Emerson was
held more in disrepute by the twentieth century than the
new god he had spurned. Hear Henry Adams's reaction to the
findings of the textbooks of the latest New Science:

Chapter after chapter closed with phrases such as one never
met in older literature: "The cause of this phenomenon is
not understood"; "science no longer ventures to explain
causes"; ". . . science gets on only by adopting different
theories, sometimes contradictory." Evidently the new American would need to think in contradictions. . . .[14]

In any investigation of the spiritual climate of this society
of new Americans, the historian V. L. Parrington should be
given extended hearing:

"The conclusions of the physical sciences were ravaging the
orderly preserves of biological evolution, with its cardinal doctrine of organic growth and historical continuity and were
leaving far behind the benevolent universe conceived of by
Victorian thinkers. . . . The universe that unfolded itself
. . . was vaster and colder than biological evolution, with its
doctrine of the conservation of energy, had imagined—a
vibrating mechanism shot through with energy, that revealed
itself in action and reaction, impersonal, amoral, . . . a universe in which the generations of men have shrunk to a
pinpoint in limitless space and all teleological hopes and
fears become the emptiest of futilities. It was the conception
of determinism that after long denial was at last coming to
wide acceptance—a conception that underlay the thinking
of . . . Comte and Spencer and Marx . . . and now disen-
cumbered of its teleological wrappings, disillusioned with the
doctrine of progress, it was to shape the new intellectual attitude towards life.

Out with the old metaphysics and ethics and in with the new—physics, chemistry, and psychology; from these

must come an endeavor after a fresh evaluation of man's duty and destiny in a universe of immeasurable energy . . . a de-personalized universe, wherein man is but a single form of imprisoned energy, localized for a brief instant and rising to momentary consciousness in the eternal flux, about and through whom flows the energy of an unprobed universe. . . . [E]verywhere change, disintegration and reintegration, a ceaseless and purposeless flux to what final end the human mind could not forecast. . . . Spencer's "ultimate of ulti-mates," the Permanence of Force, that follows the law of evolution and dissolution, had given way to Faraday's elec-tro-energy that is indifferent to purpose.[15]

Had Parrington lived, he would have found it necessary to add to Faraday the name of Max Planck, author of the theory that has caused so much consternation in the mind of the modern intellectual: the quantum theory, which carries with it the possibility that our universe is made up of tiny particles known as *quanta* that are governed not by orderly causality but by chance.*

* If not consternation, then at least confusion; for there is the irony that Albert Einstein, who helped to develop this theory, has also said "I cannot believe that God plays dice with the cosmos,"—a remark that does not differ in any way with Ralph Waldo Emerson's, a century before, that "God never jests with us, and will not compromise the end of nature by permitting any inconsequence in its procession." (*Nature*, Sec. VI.)

Planck's theory invites misinterpretation, says Charles C. Walcutt: "According to the physicists it is impossible really to understand the quantum theory in any language but mathematics. But . . . certain very eminent physicists [Eddington and Jeans] seize upon Planck's con-cept . . . and build upon it whole volumes devoted to re-introducing an element of 'freedom' or 'will' or 'uncaused effects' into the realms of material causation. . . . Planck himself published a volume (*Where Is Science Going?*, 1932) in which he sought to combat . . . Eddington and Jeans by reaffirming that man's inability to measure certain phe-

In Krutch's book, *The Modern Temper,* which Malcolm
Cowley singles out for its systematic expression of "a tendency toward a type of pessimism that claimed to be founded
on modern science," * we read that whereas T. H. Huxley had
"faith in the power of the light of knowledge" to banish
man's fears and a faith that that light would help us to see
better than before, Huxley's confidence has oozed away
because

the abyss of Nature is darker and deeper than he supposed,
and . . . because the light which illuminates it does not reveal as clearly as he had anticipated what our bearings are as
we wing our way, like Milton's Satan, through a vast emptiness. Science, though it fulfills the details of its promises,
does not in any ultimate sense solve our problems.†

---

nomena did not prove that they were . . . evidence of 'freedom.' In a
colloquium appended to this volume Albert Einstein explained that
Eddington and Jeans were moved by the British literary tradition, a tra
dition that is rich indeed in its affirmation of the human spirit, to write
volumes that went counter to what they as scientists must have known
about the proper application of Planck's theory." (*American Literary
Naturalism, A Divided Stream,* pp. 16–17.)

* *Books That Changed Our Minds,* p. 255. See also Frederick J. Hoffman: "Of the hundreds of books and essays published in the 1920's on
the matter of science and its gifts to man, two stand out as especially
pertinent: Bertrand Russell's 'A Free Man's Worship' (1918) and
Joseph Wood Krutch's *The Modern Temper* (1929)." (*The Twenties,*
p. 240.)

† *The Modern Temper,* pp. 43–44. ". . . if any modern temper . . .
does actually exist it is very different from that scientific optimism
which, though it is being widely popularized at the present moment,
really belongs to nineteenth-century thought." Unlike our "spiritual
fathers, the philosophers and scientists of the nineteenth century,"
Krutch tells us, we "have begun to doubt that rationality and knowledge
have any promised land into which they may be led." (*Ibid.,* xviii.)

That scientific optimism had, for example, cancelled out the dismal
Malthus; and to his prediction at the beginning of the nineteenth century that population would exceed the capacity of the earth to support
it and that the ever-fiercer struggle for existence would leave the

Darwin, Marx, Frazer, Freud—all these influential thinkers

seem characteristically nineteenth-century . . . because of their assumption of teleology. Even Freud . . . assumed without question an ontogenetic teleology. . . . It is precisely this secure faith in progress toward an appointed goal that our century has lost. . . . Where the nineteenth century characteristically saw evolution, we characteristically see only change.*

Tennyson's remarkable 1844 vision of "airy navies" "grappling in the central blue," of the heavens filled with shouting, of "a ghastly dew" raining down was confirmed in Zeppelin raids after 1914; and if his vision of the heavens filling with commerce, as well, was also confirmed, one of its cargoes, alas, would eventually be a derivative of uranium ore that

---

weakest to perish, the ecologist at the end of the century had shouted, Not at all! For chemistry and physiology by then had told mankind that "the capacity of the earth for yielding food for man is almost unlimited. In this view of the possibilities of plant-production, which the whole tenor of scientific research and practical experience makes more and more certain, the prospect for the future of the race is not one of Malthusian dreadfulness, but full of inspiring hope." Justifiably the author of this article could conclude that "Faith has always had its reply to Malthusian pessimism, though that reply has been vague. The Science of today makes it clear. So Faith and Science rightly joined ever lead us to the light." (W. O. Atwater, "The Food-Supply of the Future," *The Century Magazine*, XLIII [November, 1891], pp. 101, 112.)

* Yet by 1920 (*Beyond the Pleasure Principle*) even Freud would break with the other three in the assumption of teleology. (Stanley Edgar Hyman, *The Tangled Bank*, pp. 428, 389.)

"The age of Victorian complacency has closed everywhere; those who are whistling to keep up their courage and deceive their neighbors merely succeed in hoodwinking themselves." (Charles A. Beard, *Whither Mankind?*, New York, 1928, p. 3.)

"To those who study her, this Nature reveals herself as extraordinarily fertile and ingenious in devising *means*, but she has no *ends* which the human mind has been able to discover or comprehend." (Joseph Wood Krutch, *The Modern Temper*, p. 27.)

could end all commerce forever. No wonder, then, that by 1927 an artist in Conrad Aiken's *Blue Voyage* can speak of creating "not so much a unitary work of art as . . . a phantasmagoric world of disordered colours and sounds, a world without design or purpose; and perceptible only in terms of the prolix and fragmentary." Or that in 1928 Theodore Dreiser would define life as a "play of inscrutable forces," among which "the utterly infinitesimal individual weaves a floss-like and wholly meaningless course. . . . I catch no meaning from all I have seen, and pass quite as I came, confused and dismayed." *

Science, "The False Messiah," Clarence E. Ayres was calling it. And explaining his play *Dynamo*, produced in 1929, Eugene O'Neill identified it as a

symbolical and factual biography of what is happening in a large section of the American (and not only American) soul right now. It is really the first play of a trilogy that will dig at the roots of the sickness of today as I feel it—the death of an old God and the failure of science and materialism to give any satisfying new one for the surviving primitive religious instinct to find a meaning for life in, and to comfort its fears of death with.[16]

This is precisely the trouble with the heroine in Flannery O'Connor's story, "Good Country People." She scorns the human race, denouncing women ("Women! do you ever look inside and see what you are *not?* God!") and looking "at nice young men as if she could smell their stupidity." Among her books she has underlined this passage:

* "Statements of Belief," *The Bookman*, LXVIII (September, 1928), p. 25.

In 1939, in *The Wild Palms*, William Faulkner would characterize Fate as "the force and power of blind and risible motion," and in the "Peasants" section of *The Hamlet* (1940) he would speak time and again of the *purposeless violence* of the Texas horses that explode in the midst of the listless Mississippi village.

"Science, on the other hand, has to assert its soberness and seriousness afresh and declare that it is concerned solely with what-is. Nothing—how can it be for science anything but a horror and a phantasm? If science is right, then one thing stands firm: science wishes to know nothing of Nothing. Such is after all the strictly scientific approach to Nothing. We know it by wishing to know nothing of Nothing."

These words work on Joy's mother (named, note, Mrs. Hope-well) "like some evil incantation in gibberish" and she drops the book "as if she were having a chill." And if Joy (self re-named the ugly-sounding "Hulga") herself relates sentiments such as these to the young man cautiously, it is in part for fear of discouraging him: love, she tells him, is " 'not a word I use. I don't have illusions. I'm one of those people who see *through* to nothing. . . . We are all damned . . . but some of us have taken off our blindfolds and see that there's nothing to see. It's a kind of salvation.' " But the irony the author has planned works out so that Joy's auditor and intended victim—the naïve, callow-looking, "good country people" kind of itinerant salesman—is "one of those people" too. Symbolically, his huge heavy suitcase turns out to be full not of faith (Bibles) but of cynicism and despair (a flask of whiskey, a deck of playing cards, and a package of contraceptives); and he departs with the taunt, " 'I been believing in nothing ever since I was born!' "

With science, as the other of the "two invincible facts" of modern society, Charles A. Beard learned from his symposium, *Whither Mankind? A Panorama of Modern Civilization* (1928), is its product, the machine.* But the poets knew this. As Archibald MacLeish tells The Social Muse in his "Invocation," it is true

* In addition to such factors as the breaking down of faith in the democratic theory and the feeling of being not so much at peace as between two wars. (*Ibid.*, pp. v, 1–3.)

That we use the machines: that a sight of the god is unusual:
That more people have more thoughts; that there are
Progress and science and tractors and revolutions. . . .

As a boy, Sherwood Anderson had seen the machine triumph-
ing in America in the form of the railroad, that "terrible new
thing." The machine's essence, standardization, was equally
repellent, a "sterile land." Anderson comes to the conclusion
that "modern man cannot escape the machine," and thus
arrives at last at a state of impotence.*

And the Southern Agrarians knew it too, to their dismay.
In their introductory "Statement of Principles" in *I'll Take
My Stand* (1930), they complain that "Religion can hardly
expect to flourish in an industrial society" and that the
"amenities of life" also suffer under its "curse"; they wonder
how "a majority of men anywhere could ever as with one
mind become enamored of industrialism: a system that has
so little regard for individual wants"; finally, they exhort any
community or age "groaning under industrialism" to "find
the way to throw it off."

If, as this group maintained, the machine was replacing
man, then perhaps the machine was also replacing God? In
a "distorted thought" of Sherwood Anderson's that he recalls
in *A Story Teller's Story*:

Many men and women are going along a street. They all have
long hair and bear vessels of precious ointment. They are
going to wash the feet of a Rockefeller, of . . . Gates, of a
Henry Ford or the son of a Henry Ford, the gods of the
new day.

* Quoted from *Poor White* (1920), *A Story Teller's Story* (1924), and
Perhaps Women (1931), in Harry Hartwick, *The Foreground of American Fiction*, pp. 125–126.
  The second of these books, it should be noted, is dedicated to Alfred
Stieglitz, that influential practitioner and theoretician of photography,
which brought to art the very mechanization that Anderson's book itself
deplored.

While in England Aldous Huxley's *Brave New World* would
replace this metaphor with fact: now the expression "For
God's Sake" has become "For Ford's Sake." And Progress
and Science have replaced Woman? Huxley's people of the
future, created from ova fertilized outside the human body,
sing hymns at hell's gate now to That Dear Old [Decanting]
Bottle of Mine.*

This is scientific phantasy serving as metaphor for spiritual
recoil and outrage; and Edmund Wilson's censure of Huxley's negative reaction to the harvest of his own grandfather's
sowing, of his espousal of Vedanta,† reminds us of the reactions of New Humanist and Agrarian in the post-World
War I years. Both, the historian of that period observes,
"opposed the progress of industrialism, together with its liberal humanitarian gospels and its glorification of science practically realized and applied." [17] This may serve as a map to
the territory of Robert Penn Warren's literary creation, he
who contributed to the Agrarian symposium *I'll Take My
Stand.* Warren's is a land sown with all the explosive technological and scientific realities of today and the horrors they
are capable of kindling: and in his eventual safe return we
have a re-telling of the Edward Eggleston story in the new
age. When, in *All the King's Men* (1946), Jack Burden thinks

* The technological superseding of woman had been projected at least
as early as the 1880's in Paris, where Villiers de l'Isle-Adam "was
planning *L'Éve future*, with Edison as a hero, about an artificial woman
who was made of steel springs." (Van Wyck Brooks, *The Confident
Years*, p. 2.)

† ". . . like the Humanists, he has been frightened back into one of
those synthetic cults which do duty for our evaporated religions. . . ."
("The Boys in the Back Room," in *A Literary Chronicle: 1920–1950*,
p. 238.)

   In "The Critic and American Life" (1928), the prominent New Humanist Irving Babbitt found André Siegfried's assertion that "Europe,
appalled at the American excess of standardization, is inclined to turn
from Henry Ford to Gandhi" to be "more picturesque than convincing."

about the frontal lobotomy Adam Stanton is to perform, it occurs to him that "this operation was going to be more radical even than what happened to Saul on the road to Damascus"; and after it has been performed he proposes that the patient be re-baptized, for his re-birth has been mechanical ("not of woman")—" 'in the name of the Big Twitch, the Little Twitch, and the Holy Ghost. Who no doubt, is a Twitch, too.' " The term he uses is part of his west-coast nightmare, "the dream that all life is but the dark heave of the blood and the twitch of the nerve"—and this nightmare is not private, for his dream is "the dream of our age." * All is a Nothing; the entire human race is an undifferentiated mass

with only the illusory difference of name, which meant nothing, for names meant nothing and all the words we speak meant nothing and there was only the pulse in the blood and the twitch of the nerve, like a dead frog's leg in the experiment when the electric current goes through.

At this point Burden is the modern intellectual, victim of a generation of scientific theorizing all contributing to the demolition of the concept of human spirituality. Of Ernst Haeckel, who in 1900 had declared that the conception of the soul as "an immortal, immaterial being, a spiritual agent, whose mysterious activity is entirely incomprehensible to us" was a "trivial" notion, was "a product of poetic imagination": "the same must be said of the parallel belief in the 'immortality of the soul,' " whose "scientific impossibility" he promised to prove in a later chapter. Of Jacques Loeb and his

---

* "Realists of the current type are in point of fact intimately allied with the psychologists,—glandular, behavioristic, and psychoanalytical,—who, whatever their divergences among themselves, unite in their deterministic trend and therefore clash fundamentally with both religious and humanistic realists." (Irving Babbitt, "The Critic and American Life.")

"tropisms" and his *Mechanistic Conception of Life* (1912), whose influence on Dreiser was noted earlier. Of John B. Watson and *Behaviorism* (1925); he along with Morgan, Thorndike, and others, offered a conception of man as "a pure animal, a reaction-mass, operating like a clock and capable of being measured by scientific instruments," and of thought as a "muscular phenomenon":

Substituting Pavlov's "conditioned reflexes" for the older . . . "instincts," he looks upon the human being as an organism with a body but no soul, and with no mind, or at best a mind snared in an unbroken circuit of "stimulus and response," and helpless to interfere.[18]

But Warren's modern man cannot rest until this nightmare of Nada is exorcised. He begins to wonder, like Pascal centuries before him: ". . . if the twitch was all, what was it that could know that the twitch was all?" Eventually he wakes up from the dream and sees that in destroying each other Stark and Stanton were confessing their incompleteness "with the terrible division of their age" (into fact and idea); but that "though doomed they had nothing to do with any doom under the godhead of the Great Twitch. They were doomed, but they lived in the agony of will." * In

* *All the King's Men*, New York, the Modern Library, pp. 336, 338, 329, 328, 333, 462.
    "Since the rise of Einstein, Rutherford, and Heisenberg, the notion that Science (and Science only) would be able to reduce all nature to the definitely knowable and fully predictable has been abandoned. The new school admits that there are limits to what can be ascertained through scientific methods. . . . Nineteenth-century materialism drew man's attention to his base origin; twentieth-century science and philosophy point to the advances that all living creatures have made. . . . The account which modern science gives of evolution is not so preoccupied as it was in the nineteenth century with the *descent* of man from the ape. It gives at least equal importance to man's occasional *ascent* into the genius, the hero, or the saint." (Ernest Bernbaum, *Guide Through the Romantic Movement*, New York, 1949, pp. 306–307.)

Brother to Dragons (1953) Jack reappears as "R.P.W." himself. This time the evil is dateless, is simply evil itself. From
crippling "naturalistic considerations," from the chill of the
Great Whiteness without and of the Great Blackness within,
he rises to Hope; for, he says of his generation,

. . . we . . . *feel a need to leave that house*
On the dark headland, and lift up our eyes;

we must, he tells us, "we must argue the necessity of
virtue." [19]

Similarly, although the characteristic despair of the refrain
in Edwin Arlington Robinson's "The House on the Hill"
(1894)—

They are all gone away,
The house is shut and still:
There is nothing more to say—

literally exemplifies the usual description of modern man's
plight,* Robinson's "Credo" is proof of the doggedness of his
faith in Christianity. In keeping with these testaments,
Beard's epilogue to his symposium states that "nowhere in
these pages is there a signal for surrender or retreat," that
through understanding the terms of his society man "may
subject the scattered and perplexing things of this world to a
more ordered dominion of the spirit." [20] This, William

---

* "Enlightenment was militantly Pelagian. The Romantics, though suffering . . . , continued to sing of liberty and tear-stained joy. Contemporary man often has nothing left to say." (Geoffrey Clive, *The
Romantic Enlightenment*, p. 181.)

"The romantic movement with its turbulent heroism, its self-
assertion, is over, superseded by a new naturalism that leaves man
helpless before the contents of his own mind," W. B. Yeats wrote in
1931. (*Essays and Introductions*, p. 405.)

Faulkner would restate a generation later at Stockholm, when he gave his assurance that "man will not merely endure: he will prevail." *

Was man, in creating bigger and bigger things, ironically reducing himself to insignificance in the process? In 1890 the Hamlin Garland character had suggested this as he contrasted the Brooklyn Bridge with the manswarm beneath it.²¹ Yet forty years later, an American poet returned to this scene and added to Beard's evidence. To assert the mastery of the American spirit over the powerful voices of defeat and despair was also the hope of Hart Crane in *The Bridge*. Taking his inspiration from Walt Whitman's suggestion in the preface to *Leaves of Grass* (1855) that the United States "are essentially the greatest poem," he attempted, he said, "the Myth of America" in this poem, which was the greater part of the 1920's in the writing. During those years he had to find his way along the dark path, and confront its strange and menacing beasts. In general, the "maladie moderne," his phrase for the sickness of the times: maybe, he would wonder in moments of doubt, the technological feat (the great

---

* It is remarkable that these words were spoken by the same novelist of whom it had been written: "What he has to say is that there is nothing to say. A windy melancholy tosses in his pages. . . . Nihilism, the only philosophy apparent in Faulkner, is as much an implication of his style as his treatment of character." (Harry Hartwick, *The Foreground of American Fiction*, p. 165.)

Writing many years later, however, Leslie Fiedler could qualify this; the "nothing" in Faulkner, he believes, is merely Faulkner's next-to-last word: "In the end the negativist is no nihilist, for he affirms the void. Having endured a vision of the meaninglessness of existence, he [refuses to retreat]. He chooses, rather, to render the absurdity which he perceives. . . . To know and to render, however, mean to give form; and to give form is to provide the possibility of delight—a delight which does not deny horror but lives at its intolerable heart." ("No in Thunder," 1960.) Earlier Alfred Kazin found in Faulkner's "passion for form . . . a register of too many points of view, and . . . a substitute for one. . . . [I]t has been possible to read every point of view into his work and to prove them all." (*On Native Grounds*, p. 354.)

bridge) that was his inspiration "has no more significance beyond an economical approach to shorter hours, quicker lunches, behaviorism and toothpicks." In particular, the gloomy writing of Oswald Spengler * and the "Eliotic pessimists": for it seemed to Crane "that Eliot ignores certain spiritual events and possibilities as real and powerful now as, say, in the time of Blake. Certainly the man has dug the ground and buried hope as deep and direfully as it can ever be done." [22] Toward the end Crane might confide that "The spiritual disintegration of our period becomes more painful to me every day, so much so that I now find myself baulked by doubt at the validity of practically every metaphor that I coin"; and even the final prayer of the completed poem expresses doubt, *The Bridge* thus ending without the completeness that he hoped his "great affirmation" would have. Yet it was a heroic passage to Cathay, after all, with the yea-saying Whitman as the *anima cortese Mantovana*, the guide. Thus in reviving Walt Whitman's celebration of technology as the mastery of mind over matter, *The Bridge* is one of the remarkable achievements of the Between-Wars literature of this country.[23] As is, in its murky, barely articulate way, the close of the Wilbourne-Charlotte half of *The Wild Palms*. Here Faulkner's condemned hero chooses *not* to consign himself to death's dateless night but to live on in order to remember joy, even in a state of unbearable grief (" '*Yes, . . . between grief and nothing I will take grief* '"). One could, after all, do something more to the meat than bury it: one could live and remember it, and in so doing elevate it beyond the level of meat: was it not in its fleshly garb that the living man's mind was doing the remembering?

* *The Decline of the West* was a complex book that "disconcerted the theorists of progress by rejecting their linear view of history and substituting for it a concept of cyclical change. . . . If Spengler was correct, the enormous advances of science and the less impressive development of social utilitarianism were aspects of the last stage of Western culture." (Hoffman, *The Twenties*, pp. 345–346.)

Yet these last examples are the exceptions, for the characteristic literary experience of the 1920's and later in the
United States *was* of surrender and of defeat. In fact, Faulkner himself, a generation before Stockholm, had written *The
Sound and the Fury*, in which Quentin is asked to believe
"that a love or a sorrow is a bond purchased without design
and which matures willynilly and is recalled without warning
to be replaced by whatever issue the gods happen to be floating at the time. . . ." In Shakespeare, from whom Faulkner
took the phrase that is his title, the sound and the fury signify, of course, Nothing. And if Hemingway's faithless waiter
was right in thinking that "many must have it," he was wrong
in thinking "it" to be "only insomnia." Not that his bravely
suffering soul does not know that "it" is Nada, Nil, Nothing.
The first part of Edna St. Vincent Millay's "Spring" (*Second
April*, 1921) is redolent enough of fervor for nature's abundance to suggest Thoreau or Dickinson; but the poem shifts
suddenly to the theme of death which pervades the slender
volume in which the poem appears and we read that

*Not only under ground are the brains of men
Eaten by maggots,
Life in itself
Is nothing,
An empty cup, a flight of uncarpeted stairs,*

and the very abundance of spring is a riot of sheer life without meaning; for April "Comes like an idiot, babbling and
strewing flowers." In part her sense of Nothing (Shakespeare's
tale told by an idiot, again) results, one supposes, from yet
another great tyranny over the mind of modern man—sex. In
her lament elsewhere that "Whether or not we find what we
are seeking/Is idle, biologically speaking" she is voicing
F. Scott Fitzgerald's generation's feeling of victimization of

the spirit by its own body.* In *This Side of Paradise* Eleanor tells Amory: " 'I'm hipped on Freud and all that, but it's rotten that every bit of *real* love in the world is ninety-nine per cent passion and one little soupçon of jealousy. . . .' " Amory agrees: " '[T]he truth is that sex is right in the middle of our purest abstractions. . . .' " [24] To his ingredients for modern man's despair cited above, Parrington had added a "complexity" resulting in part from "mechanistic psychology. Behaviorism; stimulus and response; ducts and glands. The individual conceived as a mechanism driven by instincts and habits." † Here Parrington joins with Krutch, who singles out, not J. B. Watson, but "Freudianism, certainly the most far-reaching of any attempts to rob man of such shreds of dignity as had been left to him," and says of man that "in the world of metabolism and hormones, repressions and complexes, he finds no answer for his needs." ‡

---

* Hamlin Garland, whose own *Rose of Dutcher's Coolly* (1895) had treated sex too frankly for its generation, by the 1930's was offended by its importance in literature, complaining as an evolutionist against the implied "return to the life of the animals who are supposed to be lower on the scale of life" (Åhnebrink, *Beginnings of Naturalism*, pp. 204–207.)

† *Main Currents*, III, p. 327. Stanley Edgar Hyman has noted that "The principal emphasis in [Freud's] *The Psychopathology of Everyday Life* [1904] is on vastly increasing the area of the determined. 'Certain performances which are apparently unintentional prove to be well-motivated,' Freud writes. 'Determinism reaches farther than we suppose,' he adds, concluding boldly: 'There is nothing arbitrary or undetermined in the psychic life.' " (*The Tangled Bank*, p. 341.)

‡ *The Modern Temper*, pp. 132, 11.
"As a delver into . . . the psychology of instinct, Freud unquestionably belongs with those writers of the nineteenth century who . . . stand opposed to rationalism, intellectualism . . . —in a word, to the belief in mind held by the eighteenth and somewhat also by the nineteenth century. . . ." (Thomas Mann, "Freud's Position in the History of Modern Thought"; quoted by Stanley Edgar Hyman, *The Tangled Bank*, p. 7.)

Certainly the record of imaginative literature in the years
after Freud's theories became widely known bears this out.
Add to Fitzgerald's Eleanor, Sherwood Anderson's Rosalind
in "Out of Nowhere into Nothing." She contemplates finding an answer to her wonder in the new theory: "All the
books that dealt with life at all dealt with it through the lips
of the crowd that had newly come into the sacred place. The
writer had hold of the key. It was his time to be heard. 'Sex,'
he cried." But she rejects this: "If the sex impulse within
[my body] had been gratified in what way would my problem
be solved? I am lonely now. It is evident that after that had
happened I would still be lonely." ²⁵ And Percy Marks's Hugh
Carver "had heard plenty of fellows argue that love was
nothing but sexual attraction anyway. . . . Freud said something like that, he thought, and Freud knew a damn sight
more about it than the poets. Yet . . . he wanted something
more than that. . . ." * Arthur Miller would repeat this in

---

* *The Plastic Age*, New York, 1924, p. 314.
Here, as he recalled them much later, are the reflections of a young
Englishman in the year 1923:
"*The great revelation which was Freud!* . . . his own generation really
was a new creation, a new kind of human being, *because of Freud!* For
theirs was the first generation in the whole cave-to-cathedral history
of the human race completely to disbelieve in sin. Actions nowadays
weren't thought of as 'right' or 'wrong' any more: they were merely
judged social or anti-social, personal fulfilment or frustration . . . :
theirs was a generation relieved of the necessity even of active evan-
gelistic atheism because the whole 'god' idea had now subsided below
the level of belief or disbelief. 'God' and 'Sin' had ceased to be problems because Freudian analysis had explained how such notions arise
historically: i.e., that they are merely a primitive psychological blemish
which, once explained, mankind can outgrow. . . ." (Richard Hughes,
The Fox in the Attic, p. 73.)
"We studied Freud, argued Jung, checked our dreams by Havelock
Ellis and toyed lightly with Adler. And all these authorities warned us
of the danger in repressing our normal instincts and desires . . ." (From
a 1927 *Vanity Fair* essay by a thirteen-year-old girl. Quoted in Hoffman,
The Twenties, pp. 89–90.)
"Convention has not made, and cannot make, any headway against

essence in 1950: "Our modern literature has filled itself with an attitude which implies that, despite suffering, nothing important can really be learned by man that might raise him to a happier condition. The probing of the soul has taken the path of behaviorism." * Thus had they all at last recognized the Nothingness of Schopenhauer, who had spoken of the will at it objectifies itself in sex: ". . . we see it every moment seat itself, as the true and hereditary lord of the world, out of the fulness of its own strength, upon the ancestral throne, and looking down from thence with scornful glances, laugh at the preparations which have been made to . . . master it. . . ." †

By 1936 F. Scott Fitzgerald found himself (as Tate says Poe had done a century before) an unwilling witness of the weirdest of all executions—"the disintegration of one's own personality." He derides those "to whom all self-revelation is contemptible, unless it ends with a noble thanks to the gods for the Unconquerable Soul," adding that "I had been thanking the gods too long, and thanking them for nothing." He

---

a chemical scheme of life which puts sex desires first," Theodore Dreiser wrote in 1920 (*Hey Rub-a-Dub-Dub*).

If the final proof of the vitality of a theory is its assimilation into the humor of a culture, then one should not overlook Anita Loos's *Gentlemen Prefer Blondes* (1925).

The statistics, meanwhile, are impressive: two hundred books on Freudianism by 1920 and appearance of the word in Webster by 1927. (Harry Hartwick, *The Foreground of American Fiction*, p. 129.)

* "On the Nature of Tragedy."

† *The World as Will and Idea*, III, p. 314.

Yet possibly, as Professor Hoffman has written, self-consciousness in modern art stems not from Watson's Behaviorism (which did not venture into the province of moral significance), nor yet from "the rational destruction of illusion, which seemed to be one of the tasks of Freudian psychoanalysis": it was characterized by "a fundamental pessimism" which was "a pessimism *faute de mieux*: there seemed no justification for optimism, an attitude apparently founded upon an evasion of psychological truth." (*The Twenties*, p. 203.)

turns down the conventional inspirational panacea (altruism) as merely "an all-weather beatitude for gloom in general" but of use only in the daytime: for another hour, it will not serve, no more than the rationalization of the old man in "The Tell-Tale Heart" will serve, for

at three o'clock in the morning, a forgotten package has the same tragic importance as a death sentence, and the cure doesn't work—and in a real dark night of the soul it is always three o'clock in the morning, day after day.

And closing his books as a bankrupt he parts with the analysis that, whoever it was "who could have helped me to keep my shop open, [i]t wasn't Lenin, and it wasn't God." [26] But to eliminate faith in man and faith in God is to leave Nothing!

Another mid-century creation, by Robert Penn Warren, has had to close his shop for the same reason. Dr. Charles Lewis tells his modern creator why he left Kentucky and his family after the death of his wife. He went back to Virginia, in effect forsaking his obligations, to be sure, but

> Not that it mattered.
> Can it matter where wanders the emptiness of air?
> Wind, force without body, word without
> Meaning, accident without essence. . . .
> We buried her
> Alone in the wild earth, and my heart said: "Oh, Lucy,
> My Lucy, rot to nothingness, enter
> The dark and depth of nothingness, rot,
> And rot quickly, into the absolute oblivion,
> That in nothingness we may at long last love
> In the appropriate mutuality, nothing
> To nothing.[27]

In truth, never had that air been emptier than since the 1920's began to yield metaphysical speculation from the relativity theories of Albert Einstein. No matter—except to furnish an irony—that Einstein was himself a man of great faith who believed "in a universe of order and harmony," that "questing man may yet attain a knowledge of ultimate reality," that "to this end [Einstein] has looked . . . outward to the stars, and beyond them to the vast drowned depths of empty space and time." [28] Nor that T. S. Eliot's vision of the worlds revolving haphazardly had no basis in astronomy. For the poet's thoughts would range where they wished. As early as 1903 Bertrand Russell had declared that

. . . Man is the product of causes which had no prevision of the end they were achieving; . . . his origin, his growth . . . are but the outcome of accidental collocations of atoms; . . . all the . . . inspiration, all the noonday brightness of human genius, are destined to extinction in the vast death of the solar system. . . . [29]

The historian of that age's descendants, Joseph Wood Krutch, says of modern man's plight that "For the cozy bowl of the sky arched in a protecting curve above him he must exchange the cold immensities of space and, for the spiritual order which he has designed, the chaos of nature." [30]

Yet the greatest physicist of all the ages before Einstein, the man from whose findings Einstein himself took his beginning, had been worshipped as the discoverer of a cosmological perfection impressive to the mind and invigorating to the spirit. It had been announced in 1713 that because of Sir Isaac Newton

The gates are now set open, and . . . we may freely enter into the knowledge of the hidden secrets and wonders of natural things. . . . Therefore we may now more clearly behold the beauties of Nature . . . and be thence incited the more profoundly to reverence and adore the great Maker and Lord of all. . . .

And in 1775, that "Our views of Nature, however imperfect, serve to represent us, in the most sensible manner, that mighty power which prevails throughout, acting with a force and efficacy that appears to suffer no diminution from the greatest distances of space or intervals of time. . . ." Had not Newton himself, for that matter, predicted not only that the principles he had discovered were a key to unlock other mysteries, but that "such further discoveries would lead us back towards heaven"? [31]

Alas, how better could we illustrate modern man's altered attitude toward the heaven of the *Principia* than to set the piety of Joseph Addison's "Ode"—its "spacious firmament on high" still (almost two hundred years after Copernicus) moving "in solemn silence" around the earth and all its stars and all its planets, if no longer literally making music, yet "in Reason's ear" rejoicing, publishing "the work of an Almighty Hand," and singing, " 'The hand that made us is divine' "— than to set this beside the reflections of "R.P.W." in 1953 that "The stars are arctic and/Their gleam comes earthward down uncounted light-years of disdain . . ."? [32]

What had astronomy done to the O'Connors, the Warrens, the Krutches of our day? Consider, from the numberless expositions of time-space, of the fourth dimension, merely this passage from Sir Arthur Eddington. Here he is, centuries upon centuries after Ptolemy's comforting cosmology, demonstrating that not only the stars but "universes stretch one behind the other beyond sight"; that "the modern view is that space is finite—finite though unbounded," that

the radius of space is of the order twenty times the average distance of the nebulae observed, or say 100 million light years. That leaves room for a few million spiral [nebulae]; but there is nothing beyond. There is no beyond—in spherical space "beyond" brings us back towards the earth from the opposite direction.[33]

Now Melville's Captain Ahab had reached an intuitive understanding of that great celestial emptiness that is quite close to the modern writer's:

". . . in each event . . . some unknown but still reasoning thing puts forth the mouldings of its features from behind the unreasoning mask. . . . How can the prisoner reach outside except by thrusting through the wall? . . . Sometimes I think there's naught beyond." *

But Ishmael, while intermittently an unbeliever, characteristically stops short of nothingness, of those appalling desert places of the stars; he can still stretch out hands of faith, however lame, and speculate that "some certain significance lurks in all things, else all things are little worth, and the round world itself but an empty cipher, except . . . to fill up some morass in the Milky Way." (Ch. 99.)

Even this little hope is beyond Conrad Aiken. A modern nothingness is his; for the horror of his fiction "lies not in the possibility that other worlds exist but in the certainty that they do not. The cosmic vacuity, the central *nihil* haunts him. . . . The horror is . . . Einsteinian; . . . the interstellar gulfs . . . and the atomic near-void are translated into sensual acrophobia." [34] His "Mr. Arcularis" could justifiably

---

* Ch. 36. Thomas Hardy, forty years later, agrees. In a scene that may strike the modern reader as just possibly revenge on Gainsborough for the idyllic pastorality of his "The Market Cart," Abraham Durbeyfield, travelling at night in the "rickety little waggon" with his sister Tess, "leaned back . . . and with upturned face made observations of the stars, whose cold pulses were beating amid the black hollows above in serene dissociation from these two wisps of human life. He asked how far away those twinklers were, and whether God was on the other side of them." (*Tess of the D'Urbervilles*, Ch. 4.)

But Eddington's own contemporary, E. M. Forster, it is who displays the unwitting horror of his matter-of-fact cosmology. The more she pronounces God's name in India, the less satisfaction it affords the mystic Mrs. Moore: "Outside the arch there seemed always an arch, beyond the remotest echo a silence." (*Passage to India*, p. 52.)

be renamed for the word which is used exactly twenty times in its brief span—*Nothing*. Here the terror is at the Absolute, at Infinity. Sometimes this is completely implicitly stated: at one point Harry and Mr. Arcularis indicate its tyranny by a phrase from a popular song ("We're here because we're here because we're here because we're here," etc.); at another, by a musing from *Macbeth* ("Tomorrow and tomorrow and tomorrow"). In one place Aiken uses a sly metaphor to indicate his revulsion from the concept of infinity with its absence of divine personality. When Harry jestingly tells Mr. Arcularis (who, we think, is recuperating from surgery but is actually dying under it) to send him "a picture postcard from the Absolute" and Mr. Arcularis asks him whether he wants it "finite or infinite," Harry replies, "Oh, infinite. But with your signature on it." But that awful dream ("of going round a star, the same terrible coldness and helplessness. That awful curve. . . .") is a nightmare from which Mr. Arcularis only desperately hopes he can awaken. In his last revery he frantically attempts to avoid the association of death with mere emptiness: "the coffers of the poor—not coffers, not coffers, not coffers. Oh, God, not coffers, but light, delight, supreme white and brightness, whirling lightness above all. . . ." And yet, coffers it is, "the terrifying fixed curve of the infinite, the creeping curve of logic which at last must become the final signpost at the edge of nothing. After that —the deluge. The great white light of annihilation."

Indeed, the anguish of Poe's old man and of Herman Melville reaches out across the years to the continuingly lost intellectuals of the present; and they, in turn, find themselves like that Hawthorne Everyman named Brown, suddenly and unaccountably present at a black mass in the forest of unfaith and hearing the congregation told that only by recognizing the universality of—in this instance—Nothingness, of *Nada*, of *Nil*, can they truly tell the terms of their membership in the community of man. Conrad Aiken's narrator in "Ge-

henna" speaks for his neighbors when he tells us that "the
void whistles beneath me; I am absolutely alone in a world of
which the only tenable principle is horror." Off blows the top
of the circus tent in Archibald MacLeish's "End of the
World" and over the thousand faces with their dazed eyes
hangs in the starless dark

There with vast wings across the cancelled skies,
There in the sudden blackness the black pall
Of nothing, nothing, nothing—nothing at all.

Some Other Whitenesses

[SEE PAGES 101, 112, ABOVE]

In transatlantic literature of the past century, a similar process of change in the symbolic use of whiteness may also have been occurring, to judge from the random notes I have been able to take. In Charlotte Brontë's *Jane Eyre*, we find the girl Jane sitting absorbed in Bewick's History of British Birds, with its "suggestion of the bleak shores of Lapland, Siberia, Spitzbergen, Nova Zembla, Iceland, Greenland, with 'the vast sweep of the Arctic Zone, and those forlorn regions of dreary space,—that reservoir of frost and snow, where firm fields of ice, the accumulation of centuries of winters, glazed in Alpine heights above heights, surround the pole, and concentre the multiplied rigors of extreme cold.' Of these death-white realms," she confides, "I formed an idea of my own: shadowy . . . but strangely impressive."

In Hardy's "The Darkling Thrush" the frost is "spectre-gray." In his *Tess of the D'Urbervilles*, as the winter air "afflicted to pallor with the hoary multitudes [of snow] that infested it" twists and spins the girls working on the hillside, it suggests "an achromatic chaos of things." Here the heralds of winter are the "strange birds from behind the North Pole": "gaunt spectral creatures with tragical eyes—eyes which had witnessed scenes of cataclysmal horror in inaccessible polar regions of a magnitude such as no human being had ever conceived, in curdling tem-peratures that no man could endure; which had beheld the crash of icebergs and the slide of snow-hills by the shooting light of the Aurora; been half blinded by the whirl of colossal storms and terraqueous distortions; and retained the expression of feature that such scenes had engendered." (Ch. 43.)

This curious passage looks both forward and backward. It seems to invert the piety of Melville's encounter with his first albatross: "Through its inexpressible, strange eyes, methought I peeped to secrets which took hold of God. As Abraham before the angels, I bowed myself. . . ." (*Moby-Dick*, Ch. 42.) Yet it also introduces the disturbing quality of the seagulls in Stephen Crane's "Open Boat." (See Chapter One, above.)

Another rewarding glance backwards and forwards is at a snowy landscape etched by Bret Harte in 1876 and then at a British copy of it a generation later. It is a journey from Currier and Ives into the present, from the awe-ful to the appalling. Whiteness is the color that envelopes and obliterates the entire world of Harte's *Gabriel Conroy*:

SNOW. Everywhere. As far as the eye could reach . . . filling ravines and gulches, and dropping from the walls of canyons in white shroud-like drifts; fashioning the dividing ridge into the likeness of a monstrous grave, hiding the bases of giant pines, and completely covering young trees . . . ; rimming with por-celain the bowl-like edges of still, cold lakes, and undulating in motionless white billows to the edge of the distant horizon. Snow lying everywhere over the California Sierras . . . and still falling.

It had been snowing for ten days: snowing in finely granu-lated powder, in damp, spongy flakes, in thin, feathery plumes;

snowing from a leaden sky steadily; snowing fiercely, shaken out
of purple-black clouds in white flocculent masses, or dropping in
long level lines, like white lances from the tumbled and broken
heavens. But always silently! The woods were so choked with
it . . . that all sound was deadened. The strongest gust, the
fiercest blast, awoke no sigh or complaint from the snow-packed,
rigid files of forest. There was no cracking of bough nor crackle
of underbrush; the overladen branches of pine and fir yielded
and gave way without a sound. The silence was vast, measureless,
complete! Nor could it be said that any outward sign of life or
motion changed the fixed outlines of this stricken landscape. . . .

There was no track or imprint; whatever foot might have left
its mark upon this waste, each succeeding snowfall obliterated all
trace or record. Every morning the solitude was virgin and unbroken; a million tiny feet had stepped into the track and
filled it up.

It is this snow that has marooned the Conroy party of emigrants.
It has caused the death of some and will cause that of yet others
of the party. It humbles men to the level of animals crawling on
all fours and even eating each other (we learn by indirection), in
imitation of the actions of the members of the Donner party of
the same year (1848). But the whiteness is simply a nightmare
from which Harte's story awakens into life. The passage quoted
above is the first in Harte's long novel. Immediately we realize
that it is meant to be merely a menacing shadow passing over the
stage as the curtain goes up; for all that follows is human bustle
—romance, buried treasure, etc. We find ourselves back on familiar ground, in the smiling-eyes-shining-through-tears of Harte's
successfully sentimental world of the 1870's.*

Now in his most widely acclaimed short story James Joyce not
only borrowed the names of his hero Gabriel Conroy from
Harte's novel, and of Gabriel's wife Gretta (changed slightly
from Harte's Grace): he also chose to take over a good part of
Harte's snowfall for his own use at the close of "The Dead."

A few light taps upon the pane made him turn to the window. It

---

* "His long novel, *Gabriel Conroy*, is as much like Dickens as if Dickens
had written it himself." (Mark Twain, *Mark Twain in Eruption*, p. 267.)

had begun to snow again. He watched sleepily the flakes, silver and dark, falling obliquely against the lamplight. The time had come for him to set out on his journey westward. Yes, the newspapers were right, snow was general all over Ireland. It was falling upon every part of the dark central plain, on the treeless hills, falling softly upon the Bog of Allen and, farther westward, softly falling into the dark mutinous Shannon waves. It was falling, too, upon every part of the lonely churchyard on the hill where Michael Furey lay buried. It lay thickly drifted on the crooked crosses and headstones, on the spears of the little gate, on the barren thorns. His soul swooned slowly as he heard the snow falling faintly through the universe and faintly falling, like the descent of their last end, upon all the living and the dead.*

But note that there has been a considerable change in the intervening years. Whereas Harte had begun his novel with snow as the Great Obliterator, Joyce chose to end his *Dubliners* with it. And whereas Harte's whiteness is the shadow from which the sunshine of the entire story emerges (Gabriel escapes the whiteness into life), Joyce's is the shadow into which whatever there is of sunshine in the Dublin world disappears forever, the shadow unto which his Gabriel yields himself: "His soul had approached that region where dwell the vast hosts of the dead. . . . His own identity was fading out into a grey impalpable world. . . ." Joyce's snow "falls indifferently upon all things, covering them with a neutral whiteness and erasing all their differentiating details. . . ." The man whom Joyce has been describing, "good husband though he may be, can never mean to his wife what the dead boy who once stood shivering beneath her window means —till he too has been buried under the snow which is Death's symbol." †

A century after Emerson's "Snow-Storm," Thomas Mann would take a much closer look at the work of the same fierce

* These correspondences were noted in Gerhard Friedrich, "Bret Harte as a Source for James Joyce's 'The Dead,'" *Philological Quarterly*, XXXIII (October, 1954), pp. 442–444.

† David Daiches, *The Novel and the Modern World*, Chicago, 1939, pp. 98–99; Frank O'Connor, "And It's a Lonely, Personal Art," *Highlights of Modern Literature*, New York, 1954, p. 78.

artificer and he would shudder. Although Hans Castorp views the snowflakes on his sleeve "with the knowing eye of the nature-lover," we read that he has also seen them under the "good lens" of a microscope, and that that is why he can balance his admiration for the "endless inventiveness" of their variety with a spiritual revulsion at the deathliness of their individual perfection. (*The Magic Mountain*)

Professor Sydney J. Krause of Kent State University has called to my attention the use of whiteness as a death motif in Ibsen's *Rosmersholm*. " 'They say the dead come back to Rosmersholm in the shape of rushing white horses,' " Rebecca West tells us; and at the close of the play the suicide pact of Rebecca and Rosmer coincides with the reappearance of the White Horse of Rosmersholm. Like Albert Ryder's white horse in the painting, this horse appalls as does the vision or thought of a ghost: they recall the passage in the "Whiteness" chapter of *Moby-Dick*: ". . . all ghosts [rise] in a milk-white fog—Yea, while these terrors seize us, let us add, that even the king of terrors, when personified by the evangelist, rides on his pallid horse." (Yet the familiar white horse of the Diego Rivera paintings symbolizes the aristocracy and cruelty of the Spanish *gachupines*, so hated by the Mexican peasants.)

This leads to a final note on whiteness and the modern American painter Andrew Wyeth. We have his own admission that he views nature in terms that we associate with Robert Frost: "Some horrible thing—violence—always hits you in nature. . . . Nature is not lyrical and nice." Yet this attitude takes the form, in "River Cove," of the suggestion of the inevitability of the tide that is slowly covering the shells on the bank; and, in "Ground Hog Day," of the winter light and the bare lunch dishes ("that is peace, yes, but to me behind it is violence suppressed"), and of the reddish tint of the jagged edge of the log outside the window. Conversely, Wyeth is *excited* by whiteness: "I love white things. . . . Oh, I love white. Marvellous. It excites my imagination." * Thus, "Lime Bank," a labor of love that began in Wyeth's view of the bank in the moonlight, reflects the *warmth* that its whiteness conveyed to the painter—if in truth it is pos-

* *Life* Magazine, LVIII (May 14, 1965), 93ff.

sible to define the exact quality of the light in the painting. As for snow itself, in confessing that his "wild side" comes out in his water-colors, Wyeth says that this is true "especially of snow, which is absolutely intoxicating to me. I'm electrified by it—the hush—unbelievable." * This from a man who greatly admires Robert Frost's poetry!

NOTES

■ CHAPTER ONE

1 Perry Miller (ed.), *The Transcendentalists: An Anthology*, Cambridge, Mass., 1950, pp. 486–489.
2 Henry James, *Hawthorne*, 1879, Ch. IV.
3 Perry Miller, *The Transcendentalists*, pp. 47–48, 29–31.
4 George F. Whicher (ed.), *The Transcendentalist Revolt Against Materialism*, Boston, 1949, pp. 80–81.
5 Perry Miller, *The Transcendentalists*, p. 324.
6 Laurence Stapleton (ed.), *H. D. Thoreau: A Writer's Journal*, New York, 1960, p. 7.

7   "Literary Materials in Thoreau's A Week," PMLA, LXXX (March, 1965), 77–78.

8   Perry Miller, The Transcendentalists, p. 492.

9   George Boas, Essays on Primitivism, etc., Baltimore, 1948, p. 100.

10 "Of the Dignity of Man," E. L. Forbes translation.

11 Arthur Schopenhauer, The World as Will and Idea, I, pp. 191–193.

12 Ibid., III, pp. 315–317.

13 "The American Pessimist," The Atlantic Monthly, LXIX (March, 1892), 366, 363.

14 "The American Idealist," The Atlantic Monthly, LXX (July, 1892), 90–91.

15 Ibid., 85.

16 Joseph Wood Krutch, The Modern Temper [1929], New York, 1956, pp. 130–131.

17 "The Influence of Darwin on Philosophy," in The Influence of Darwin, etc., New York, 1910, pp. 9–11.

18 Paxton Hibben, Henry Ward Beecher, New York [1927], 1942, pp. 302, 185.

19 John Dewey, "The Influence of Darwin on Philosophy," op. cit., p. 16.

20 John Fiske, The Destiny of Man, Boston [1884], 1899, pp. 22–23, 23–25, 28–32.

21 Book One, ll. 339–350.

22 John Dewey, "The Influence of Darwin on Philosophy," op. cit., p. 11.

23 Ibid., p. 12.

24 B. J. Loewenberg, "Darwinism Comes to America," op. cit., 362.

25 Malcolm Cowley and Bernard Smith (eds.), Books That Changed Our Minds, New York, 1939, p. 254.

26 "The Village" chapter in Walden.

27 Quoted from The Descent of Man by Stanley Edgar Hyman, The Tangled Bank, pp. 46–47.

28 The American Mind, New Haven, 1950, p. 108.

29 Malcolm Cowley, "A Natural History of American Naturalism," in J. W. Aldridge (ed.), Critiques and Essays on Modern Fiction, New York, 1952, p. 385.

30 Confessions of a Young Man, Ch. 8.

31 Rebels and Ancestors, 1890–1915, Boston, 1953, p. 157.

32 General Notes on the Rougon-Macquart series, c. 1870. In Matthew Josephson, Zola and His Time, New York, 1928, p. 151.

33 Nature, VI, 5; IV, 2.

34 The Excursion, I, 203 ff.

35 The Nation, LXIII (July 2, 1896), 15.

36 V. L. Parrington, Main Currents, III, p. 333.

37 Lars Åhnebrink, *The Beginnings of Naturalism in American Fiction*, Uppsala and Cambridge, Mass., 1950, pp. 300–301.
38 *First Principles*, 4th edition, Summary and Conclusion.
39 *Ibid.*
40 Sherwood Cummings, "What Is Man?: The Scientific Sources," in Sydney J. Krause (ed.), *Essays on Determinism in American Literature*, Kent, Ohio, 1964.
41 *The Modern Temper*, p. 71.
42 Quoted in Charles A. Beard (ed.), *Whither Mankind*, New York, 1928, p. 276.
43 "Life Without Principle" (1863).

■ CHAPTER TWO

1 See Dante's *Purgatory*, Canto Eight.
2 D. W. Robertson, Jr., "Why the Devil Wears Green," *Modern Language Notes*, LXIX (November, 1954), 470–472.
3 *Farbenlehre (Theory of Colors)*, Charles Eastlake translation, London, 1840.
4 David Levin (ed.), *What Happened in Salem*, New York, 1952.
5 "Hawthorne and His Mosses" (1850).
6 I owe both reference and translation to Professor Neville Rogers, of Ohio University.
7 *The Power of Blackness*, New York, 1958, p. 32.
8 *Sartor Resartus*, Book Two, Chs. 9, 7.
9 Charles Anderson, *Emily Dickinson's Poetry*, New York, 1962, p. 227.
10 *Poe: A Critical Study*, Cambridge, Mass., 1957, Ch. 6, *passim*.
11 "From Earth to Ether: Poe's Flight into Space," *PMLA*, LXXVII (March, 1962), 87.
12 "Hawthorne and His Mosses."
13 See James R. Baird, *Ishmael*, for an interpretation of this basic incongruity in *Billy Budd*. (Pp. 272, 273.)
14 George Boas, *Essays on Primitivism*, pp. 97–100.
15 *Mont-Saint-Michel and Chartres*, Ch. XVI.
16 William Braswell, "Melville as a Critic of Emerson," *American Literature*, IX (November, 1937), 327–334.
17 "The American Pessimist," *op. cit.*, 365–366.
18 *The Power of Blackness*, p. 28.
19 *Main Currents*, III, p. 317.
20 A. D. McKillop, *The Background of Thomson's "Seasons,"* Minneapolis, 1942, pp. 33–34. Also see E. A. Burtt, *The Metaphysical Foundations of Modern Physical Science*, Ch. VII.

21 *Time*, August 17, 1953; "Education."

22 *Mark Twain in Eruption*, p. 265.

23 *A Son of the Middle Border*, New York, 1919, pp. 323–324.

24 *Century Magazine*, XLIII (March, 1892), 747–751. When issued as a book, re-titled *A Little Norsk* (1892).

25 George Boas, *Essays on Primitivism*, pp. 90–91.

26 Lars Åhnebrink, *The Beginnings of Naturalism in American Fiction*, pp. 96, 105.

27 Atwood H. Townsend translation, New American Library, p. 466.

28 *The Modern Temper*, pp. 84, 86.

29 Quoted in Maxwell Geismar, *Rebels and Ancestors*, pp. 193–194.

30 *Loc. cit.*, pp. 195–196.

31 "A Speech on Robert Frost," *Partisan Review*, XXVI (Summer, 1959), 451.

32 Professor William J. Holmes, Jr., of Ohio University, called this passage to my attention.

33 "The Watchers of the Night," in *Lanterns and Lances*, New York, 1961, pp. 171–172.

34 See Victor H. Strandberg, "Theme and Metaphor in *Brother to Dragons*," PMLA, LXXIX (September, 1964), 498–508.

■ CHAPTER THREE

1 *On Heroes, Hero-Worship*; Lecture V ("The Hero as Man of Letters").

2 *Autobiographies*, p. 142.

3 *Books That Changed Our Minds*, pp. 247–248. But for a differing view, see Curtis Dahl, "The Victorian Wasteland," *College English*, XVI (March, 1955), 341–347.

4 *Rage for Order* [1948], Ann Arbor, 1959, p. 137.

5 See Harry Hartwick, *The Foreground of American Fiction*, p. 173; Tony Tanner, "The Lost America—The Despair of Adams and Twain," *Modern Age*, V (Summer, 1961); reprinted in Henry Nash Smith (ed.), *Mark Twain: A Collection of Critical Essays*, 1963; and Henry Nash Smith, *Mark Twain: The Development of a Writer*, 1962; Henry Nash Smith, *Mark Twain's Fable of Progress*, New Brunswick, 1964.

6 Bernard DeVoto, *Mark Twain's America*, Boston, 1932. Also see: John Chamberlain, *Farewell to Reform*, 1932, pp. 17 ff; Robert G. McCloskey, *American Conservatism in the Age of Enterprise*, 1865–1910, New York [1951], 1964, p. 134.

7 William P. Randel, *Edward Eggleston* [1946], Gloucester, Mass., 1962. When not from Randel or other acknowledged sources, bio-

graphical data about Eggleston is from the *Dictionary of American Biography* entry.

8　*Tess of the D'Urbervilles*, Ch. 46.

9　W. P. Randel, *Edward Eggleston*, pp. 64, 31.

10　Washington Gladden, "Edward Eggleston," *Scribner's Monthly*, VI (September, 1873), 562.

11　George C. Eggleston, *The First of the Hoosiers*, Philadelphia, 1903, pp. 338–339.

12　*Ibid.*, pp. 356–357.

13　Edward Eggleston, "Books That Have Influenced Me," *Forum*, III (August, 1887), 585–586.

14　B. J. Loewenberg, "Darwinism Comes to America, 1859–1900," *loc. cit.*, 352.

15　Quoted in Richard Hofstadter, *Social Darwinism in American Thought*, p. 1.

16　W. P. Randel, *Edward Eggleston*, pp. 199–203.

17　*Brother to Dragons*, New York, 1953, p. 37.

18　*History of the Corruptions of Christianity*. Quoted in Basil Willey, *The Eighteenth Century Background*, pp. 170–171.

19　*Moby-Dick*, Ch. 26.

20　Preface to *Leaves of Grass* (1855).

21　*Years of My Youth* (1916).

22　"Historic Notes on Life and Letters in New England," in Perry Miller, *The Transcendentalists*, p. 495.

23　Letter to James Billson, January 22, 1885. Quoted in William Braswell, "Melville as a Critic of Emerson," *op. cit.*, 333.

24　"Hawthorne and His Mosses."

25　Charles Olson, *Call Me Ishmael*, New York [1947], 1958, p. 70.

26　Letter to Harry De Forest Smith, March 15, 1897.

27　*American Addresses*, New York, 1877.

28　Robert G. McCloskey, *American Conservatism, etc.*, p. 145.

29　James D. Williams, "The Use of History in Mark Twain's *A Connecticut Yankee*," *PMLA*, LXXX (March, 1965), 106–107.

30　Henry Nash Smith, *Mark Twain*, pp. 157–159.

31　James D. Williams, "The Use of History in Mark Twain's *A Connecticut Yankee*," *op. cit.*, 102.

32　George Whicher, *The Transcendentalist Revolt Against Materialism*, p. 68.

33　Henry Nash Smith, *Mark Twain*, pp. 150–157.

34　Ernest Samuels, *Henry Adams: The Middle Years*, pp. 74–84, 70.

35　*The Education of Henry Adams*, Ch. XVII.

36　*Ibid.*, Ch. XV.

37　*Mont-Saint-Michel and Chartres*, Ch. XVI.

38 W. P. Randel, *Edward Eggleston,* pp. 62, 102–103, 111–114, 182–183.
39 George E. Mowry, *The Era of Theodore Roosevelt and the Birth of Modern America,* 1900–1912 [1958], New York, 1962, pp. 26–30.
40 *Ibid.,* p. 29.
41 *Ibid.;* quoted from *Recollections* (1909).
42 W. P. Randel, *Edward Eggleston,* p. 114.
43 Quoted in H. J. Blackham, *Six Existentialist Thinkers,* New York [1952], 1959, p. 34.

■ CHAPTER FOUR

1   *The World as Will and Idea,* I, pp. 192–195.
2   Charles Olson, *Call Me Ishmael,* pp. 99–100.
3   Basil Willey, *The Eighteenth Century Background,* pp. 144–145.
4   "Our Cousin, Mr. Poe," in *The Man of Letters in the Modern World,* New York and London, 1957, pp. 140, 144.
5   *Passage to India,* New York, 1924, pp. 150, 149.
6   *Ibid.*
7   Morley Callaghan, *That Summer in Paris,* New York [1963], 1964, p. 14.
8   Leicester Hemingway, *My Brother, Ernest Hemingway,* Cleveland, 1962, p. 56.
9   Frederick J. Hoffman, *The Twenties,* New York, 1955, pp. 53, 57; *Newsweek,* April 19, 1965, p. 106; "We Lose the Next War," *Harper's Monthly Magazine,* CLXXVI (March, 1938), 342.
10 John F. Carter, Jr., "These Wild Young People," *The Atlantic Monthly,* CXXVI (September, 1920), 302.
11 Geoffrey Clive, *The Romantic Enlightenment,* p. 180.
12 "The American Scholar."
13 Quoted in Mark Sullivan, *The Twenties,* New York, 1935, p. 521.
14 *The Education of Henry Adams,* Ch. 34.
15 *Main Currents,* III, pp. 317–318.
16 Quoted in Barrett H. Clark, *Eugene O'Neill,* New York, 1929, pp. 188–189.
17 Frederick J. Hoffman, *The Twenties,* p. 146.
18 Ernst Haeckel, *The Riddle of the Universe,* New York, 1900, pp. 90–91; Harry Hartwick, *The Foreground of American Fiction,* p. 102.
19 *Brother to Dragons,* pp. 29, 95, 214.
20 Charles Beard, *Whither Mankind,* p. 404.
21 See Chapter One, above.

22   See the "Spirits Grown Eliotic" section of Frederick J. Hoffman, *The Twenties*, pp. 380–388.

23   *Ibid.*, pp. 223–239.

24   "Young Irony" chapter.

25   *The Triumph of the Egg*, New York, 1921, pp. 203, 205.

26   *The Crack-Up*, New York [1945], 1956, pp. 76, 75, 80.

27   *Brother to Dragons*, pp. 97–98.

28   Lincoln Barnett, *The Universe and Dr. Einstein*, New York, 1948, p. 29.

29   "A Free Man's Worship."

30   *The Modern Temper*, p. 6.

31   Basil Willey, *The Eighteenth Century Background*, pp. 138–140.

32   Robert Penn Warren, *Brother to Dragons*, p. 95.

33   *The Nature of the Physical World* [1928], Ann Arbor, 1958, pp. 166, 176.

34   John Updike, "Snow from a Dead Sky," *The New Republic* CXLIII (November 28, 1960), 26.

Faulkner, William (*cont.*)
   The Wild Palms, 69–72, 199, 207
Feidelson, Charles, vii, 96
Fenollosa, Ernest, 104
Fiedler, Leslie, 206
Fiske, John, 42–43, 154, 226
Fitelson, David, 55
Fitz Gerald, Edward, 137, 175
Fitzgerald, F. Scott, 84, 85, 130, 191, 208–212, 231
Fletcher, Giles, 15
Ford, Henry, 201, 202
Forster, E. M., 139, 187–188, 215, 230
Francis, Convers, 37
Frazer, James G., 198
Freud, Sigmund, 33, 46, 60, 198, 209–211
Friedrich, Gerhard, 222
Frost, Robert, 127–133, 223–224, 228
   "Acquainted With the Night," 54
   "Birches," 178
   "Departmental," 25
   "Desert Places," 131–133, 180, 186
   "Design," 83, 127–128
   "For Once . . . ," 79
   "Mending Wall," 83
   "Once By the Pacific," 139
   "The Onset," 130
   "On the Heart's . . . ," 130
   "Range-Finding," 74
   "Stars," 54, 129–130
   "Stopping By Woods . . . ," 83
   "Tree At My Window," 133
   "Two Tramps . . . ," 128–129
   "The White-Tailed Hornet," 45–46

Galaxy, The, 45
Gandhi, M. K., 202
Garfield, James A., 177
Garland, Hamlin, 102, 103, 114–118, 141, 165, 167, 206, 209
   Ol' Pap's Flaxen, 114–116, 228
   "Under the Wheel," 62

Geismar, Maxwell, 49–50, 123–124, 226, 228
George, Henry, 36, 167, 171
Gide, André, 191
Gladden, Washington, 176, 229
Godwin, William, 100
Goethe, 80, 159, 179, 227
Gohdes, Clarence, 161
Goldman, Eric F., 167
Goldsmith, Oliver, 159
Gould, Jay, 169
Grant, U. S., 173
Gray, Asa, 41, 43

Haeckel, Ernst, 46, 77, 154, 203, 230
Haight, Gordon, 108
Hardy, Thomas, 33, 137
   Far From the Madding Crowd, 109
   The Mayor of Casterbridge, 184–185
   Poetry, 121, 156, 220
   Tess of the D'Urbervilles, 105, 146, 155, 215, 220, 229
Harte, Bret, 67, 109–112, 129
   Gabriel Conroy, 133, 220–222
   "The Outcasts of Poker Flat," 89, 110–112
Hartley, David, 186
Hartmann, Eduard von, 33, 34
Hartwick, Harry, vii, ix, 41, 77, 121, 176, 204, 206, 211, 228, 230
Hawthorne, Julian, 50
Hawthorne, Nathaniel, 50, 75, 82, 87–88, 95, 99, 144, 156, 159, 179, 185, 216
Hearn, Lafcadio, 104
Heisenberg, Werner, 204
Hemingway, Ernest, ix, 84, 156, 188–189
   "A Clean . . . Place," 84, 188–189, 208
   A Farewell to Arms, 15, 72–75, 84–85
   A Moveable Feast, 85, 137, 188
   "My Old Man," 72
   "Now I Lay Me," 189
   "The Snows of Kilimanjaro," 85